international education in practice

**dimensions for national &
international schools**

edited by
**Mary Hayden
Jeff Thompson
George Walker**

Routledge
Taylor & Francis Group

LONDON AND NEW YORK

First published 2002 by Routledge
2 Park Square, Milton Park, Abingdon, Oxon OX14 4RN
605 Third Avenue, New York, NY 10017

Routledge is an imprint of the Taylor & Francis Group, an informa business

British Library Cataloguing in Publication Data

A CIP record for this book is available from the British Library.

Typeset by Saxon Graphics Ltd, Derby

Publisher's Note
The publisher has gone to great lengths to ensure the quality of this
reprint but points out that some imperfections in the original may be apparent

ISBN 13: 978-0-7494-3835-7 (pbk)

Contents

PART B: CURRICULUM

PART C: PROFESSIONAL DEVELOPMENT

Notes on contributors

Keith Allen

Keith Allen is Vice-Principal at St Clare's, Oxford. His involvement in international education started in British comprehensive schools and led to his appointment to teach biology at the United World College of South-East Asia in Singapore. Subsequently, he has frequently found himself involved in the development of new IB (International Baccalaureate) schools. This includes working as Area Manager for Curriculum Development at the first City Technology College in the United Kingdom, managing the development of a bilingual school in Argentina and acting as Chief Executive Officer for the New International School of Thailand.

Roger Brown

Roger Brown is Research Manager for the International Baccalaureate Research Unit, located within the Department of Education at the University of Bath. He began his teaching career in Melbourne, Australia, where he taught in both government schools and independent schools. He became involved in international education through attending international conferences, which resulted in his participation in a worldwide professional development network. Roger then joined the International Baccalaureate Organization, firstly taking up the role of Subject Area Manager for mathematics in the Cardiff Curriculum and Assessment Unit before moving to the Research Unit in Bath. His interest in assessment from a socio-cultural perspective results from a recognition of the influence of culture on the forms of assessment used in different countries.

James Cambridge

James Cambridge has been a biology educator in the United Kingdom, North Yemen, Lesotho and South Africa in both national and international schools. He is currently a Research Officer with the Centre for the study of Education in an International Context (CEIC) at the University of Bath, and his research interests focus on schools in an international context and, in particular, on the organizational and national cultures associated with them.

Helen Drennen

Dr Helen Drennen has been Director for Academic Affairs of the International Baccalaureate Organization (IBO) since 1997 and, from October 2002, will be an IBO Regional Director, based in Singapore. Her involvement in international education began with her first teaching appointment at Altona North High School in Melbourne, Australia, at a time when significant numbers of refugee children from the Vietnam conflict arrived at the school. While there, Helen was awarded an international teaching fellowship to Wisconsin in the USA and on her return to Australia lectured at the Faculty of Education at the University of Melbourne. Subsequently, she was appointed to Wesley College in Melbourne and was responsible for introducing the IB Diploma Programme there. As a head at Wesley, she was instrumental in developing international partnerships with schools in France, China, Thailand, Japan and Indonesia.

Brian Garton

Brian Garton is Project Manager for Fieldwork Education in Abu Dhabi, where they are establishing a world-class school with a clearly international orientation for students from the United Arab Emirates. He was previously Director of the Anglo-American School of Sofia in Bulgaria, and has served as the Head of international schools in Moshi (Tanzania), Lusaka (Zambia) and Baguio (the Philippines). He was also the Head of an all-Nepalese boarding school in Kathmandu, for which services he was awarded the Prabhal Gorkha Dakshin Bahu by His Late Majesty King Birendra. From 1986 to 1988 he was a member of the Management Committee of the Headmasters Standing Conference of the International Baccalaureate Organization. His wife has taught in seven different international schools, and both of their sons graduated with IB Diplomas from IS Moshi.

Charles A Gellar

Charles A Gellar is Director of the Brussels English Primary Schools (BEPS) and founder of the recently established World International School, all located in Belgium. He served as Head of the Copenhagen International School for many years, and under his leadership the school was one of the first to introduce the IB programme (in 1968). He served on the Board of the European Council of International Schools (ECIS) for several years, and played a seminal role in the development of the ECIS Accreditation Programme. For 12 years he has co-edited the *International Schools Journal* (*ISJ*) with Edna Murphy, its founding Editor. He has been a teacher of IB chemistry, physics and mathematics and, for some years, the Theory of Knowledge course. After almost 40 years in education, his interest both in the development of international education and in the history and teaching of the physical sciences continues unabated.

Mary Hayden

Dr Mary Hayden is a senior lecturer in the Department of Education at the University of Bath, and is Head of the International Education Research Group, as well as being Deputy Director of the Centre for the study of Education in an International Context (CEIC). She has particular responsibility for directing the campus-based Summer School and overseas Study Centre dimensions of the modular Masters programme in Education offered to teachers and administrators based around the world. Mary Hayden's involvement in international education began when she took up a post in 1982 with the International Baccalaureate Organization: her research interests are based in the field of international schools and international education, an area in which she has published widely.

Terry Haywood

Terry Haywood has been involved in international education for 28 years. He taught physics and history before going into counselling and administration. As Headmaster of the International School of Milan since 1985, he has been closely involved with ECIS, having served on the Professional Development Committee, the Accreditation Committee and the Strategic Planning Committee as well as being a member of the Board of Directors, which he chaired from 1999 to 2001. His special interests lie in the development of tools for school improvement (especially using the accreditation model) and in the promotion of international education as a unique form of curriculum and life experience.

Ian Hill

Dr Ian Hill started his career in Tasmania as a teacher and administrator in government schools, and a university lecturer in teaching methodology. As senior private secretary/advisor to the Minister for Education (1986–90) in that state, he represented the Australian Education Council (of ministers of education) on the IBO Council of Foundation and was a member of the national Australian United World College committee. In 1990 he became director of the International School of Sophia Antipolis (France), a bilingual IB Diploma school, and moved to Geneva in 1993 as regional director for Africa/Europe/Middle East in the IBO where he has been Deputy Director General since 2000. His PhD thesis focused on policy processes related to the origins and development of the IBO and its Diploma Programme.

Jackie Holderness

Jackie Holderness is course leader of the MA in Education (International Schools) at Westminster Institute of Education at Oxford Brookes University. She has spent the last 10 years in Continuing Professional Development, working with international school colleagues, offering school-based INSET, lecturing on the Brookes' MA in Education summer school programme and providing online tutorial support. Having grown up as a 'global nomad' herself, working within a multicultural and multilingual environment seemed logical. Jackie spent several years as a class teacher and language coordinator at the British School in the Netherlands before returning to the United Kingdom, where she was a Deputy Head before joining Oxford Brookes. As a language specialist, she has a particular interest in EAL and EFL and in extending able children in English. She has published widely in those areas, and her current research interest is the evaluation of the long-term impact of CPD on school effectiveness.

Richard McDonald

Richard McDonald began his international career in education as a student teacher in both France and Austria. He subsequently taught French and German at Charterhouse and later at Christ's Hospital in the United Kingdom. From 1994 to 2000 he held the post of Headmaster at Aiglon College, Switzerland. During this time he served as a Director of Round Square, a worldwide association of schools sharing a commitment to service, challenge and international understanding as core educational pillars. Since 2000 he has continued to live in Switzerland and has dedicated himself to a diversity of independent writing projects including fiction, musical libretti and social commentary.

Neil Richards

Neil Richards obtained his first teaching post in Kathmandu, Nepal, and has since worked in the Canary Islands, Egypt, Chile, Lesotho and Japan; for the last 17 years he has held senior administrative posts in international schools. His headship of Machabeng High School in Lesotho led to a particular interest in the composition of staff and staff morale in international schools, and became the basis of a postgraduate research degree completed through the University of Bath. His present appointment is as Headmaster of Yokohama International School in Japan.

Martin Skelton

Martin Skelton was a teacher and headteacher for 20 years. He is a co-founder of Fieldwork Education, which manages a number of international schools around the world and provides staff development and a range of consultancy services to many more. In the past 10 years Martin has worked with more than 40 international schools. He is also director of The International Primary Curriculum, a new curriculum for internationally-minded primary and elementary schools.

Bob Sylvester

Dr Bob Sylvester is currently serving as an international consultant to the Sri Lankan government in support of a secondary school modernization project in Colombo. He previously served as Principal of Westwood International School in Gaborone, Botswana for a period of

10 years. Since 1976 his work in international education in Africa also included research, teacher training and curriculum development for the United Nations, and responsibility for the K–12 reading programme at the International School of Lusaka in Zambia. He is a member of the Research Committee of the IBO and his current post-doctoral research, which centres around the history of international education in the 20th century, is being undertaken in collaboration with the Centre for the study of Education in an International Context at the University of Bath.

Jeff Thompson

Professor Jeff Thompson CBE is Director of the Centre for the study of Education in an International Context (CEIC) and Professor of Education at the University of Bath. With effect from September 2002 he is also Academic Director for the International Baccalaureate Organization. Jeff Thompson first became active in international education in the 1960s when working with Alec Peterson at the University of Oxford Department of Educational Studies, and has continued his involvement since that time in a number of different capacities. He was Chair of the IB Examining Board and member of the IB Curriculum Board, Executive Committee and Council of Foundation; his current roles with the IBO also include being Director of the IB Research Unit based at the University of Bath. His major research interests are linked to the field of international education, in both national and international contexts.

George Walker

Professor George Walker OBE is Director General of the International Baccalaureate Organization and Visiting Professor at the University of Bath, through the Centre for the study of Education in an International Context. George Walker's earlier career was in science education, and included a spell as an educational consultant for Imperial Chemical Industries (ICI); he subsequently took a central role in the development of comprehensive education in England. He was Deputy Head and Head in a number of schools in Britain before taking on the role of Director General of the International School of Geneva, a position he left to join the IBO in 1999. George has also participated in a number of ECIS accreditation teams and, in his capacity as Visiting Professor, teaches and supervises Master's and Doctoral students at the University of Bath.

David Wilkinson

Dr David Wilkinson is the founding head of the Mahindra United World College of India. David has worked in international education for over 20 years as a teacher and school administrator, in countries including Italy, Lesotho, Thailand and Hong Kong, and has conducted research in international education – particularly within the context of the International Baccalaureate. He has also served on the Council of the IBO.

Preface

At no time has interest in the field of international education been so high as it is at present, not only among those in international schools, but also for those in schools and universities within national systems. And at no time has such interest assumed such a high level of importance as events on the world stage in recent times have demanded.

One indication of the growth of interest has been the welcome increase in publications relating explicitly to this developing field of international education. In addition to output in research journals, the debate on issues relating to international education has surfaced much more explicitly through the media and the popular press, and the use of the Internet by practitioners to exchange experiences is becoming increasingly common.

As interest in the field has strengthened, so has the confidence of practitioners and researchers in sharing their experiences not only among their immediate peer group, but also with a wide range of other stakeholders in education. This willingness of teachers, administrators and researchers to reflect on their experience and activities and to share them with others through a range of professional and academic avenues has been a powerful influence on the development of the field. Nowhere has this been more evident than in the collections of contributions from colleagues working in the field published in our two previous volumes: *International Education: principles and practice* (1998 and 2001) and *International Schools and International Education* (2000).

A feature of the heightened contribution by practitioners writing in the area of international education has been the stimulus provided for such activity by the development of an increasingly wide range of courses and programmes focused within the international sphere and delivered in institutions of higher education around the world, leading to formal qualifications. It is also true to say that the level of debate on issues relating to international education has been raised by the willingness of editors to encourage such discussion in publications including the *International Schools Journal* and *IS* magazine, from the European Council of International Schools (ECIS), and *IB World* and *Research Notes* from the International Baccalaureate Organization (IBO). A further indication of the growing importance of this area is the launch in 2002 of a new academic journal, the *Journal of Research in International Education* (*JRIE*), devoted entirely to the definition and exploration of the field of international education at the highest academic levels.

Out of what has been essentially an expression of individual views and opinions arising from practice and research has arisen a clear perception that future development of our understanding of the nature of international education will depend upon the extent to which the wide range of interests comprising the international education constituency can work together towards a deeper understanding of the subject.

In order to test out the possibility for a model of collaboration between interested parties, a group of international educators from a range of institutional and professional affiliations came together in June 2001 to participate in a seminar organized jointly by the International Baccalaureate Research Unit (IBRU) and the Centre for the study of Education in an International Context (CEIC) at the University of Bath. The seminar consisted of a variety of stimulating presentations and discussions focused around a series of questions of the form 'Where is the international in… ?' relating to a range of dimensions of international education. At the conclusion of the seminar the group agreed that an enhanced awareness of the nature and application in practice of international education had been gained through the exchange of views arising directly from the willingness of those present to share their diverse experiences freely with one another.

The group went on to discuss ways in which such debate might be extended to a much wider number of participants, and it resolved to explore the possibility of mounting a major conference as a means of making this possible. In addition, it was suggested that an important contribution might also be a publication further developing the issues that arose during the seminar. This volume is the direct response to that latter intention.

The status accorded any field of enquiry in an academic or professional sense is related not only to the range of activities undertaken by the practitioners in that field, but also to the theoretical underpinnings of the subject arising from rigorous and systematic research. The status is also related to the history of ideas that have contributed to the models and conceptual frameworks that define current orthodoxy.

Whilst the field of international education is a relatively new one in terms of explicit acknowledgement in academic study, it nevertheless possesses a rich history of philosophies, values, ideals and practice as antecedents. Perspectives on the history and nature of international education therefore form Part A of the collection of contributions to this volume. Bob Sylvester, writing from his personal research on the history of ideas contributing to international education, identifies a number of important milestones in the origins of both the ideas and the practice of international education. Ian Hill's contribution focuses on the history of what is widely acknowledged to be the most significant development of a curriculum for international education over the past 30 years, the International Baccalaureate Diploma Programme. An additional dimension to the discussion on the evolution of the nature of international education is provided by Charles A Gellar's reflection on the values underpinning the range of interpretations given to international education over a considerable time.

The translation of ideas on the nature of international education into formal curriculum frameworks constitutes the main theme of Part B of the book. Starting from a consideration of established definitions of international schools and curricula, Martin Skelton takes forward a range of issues raised by contemporary writers about integral theory and explores the ways in which they can be used as an integrating relationship in the generation of curricula aimed at promoting international education. In doing so, he draws upon his experience in the development of the International Primary Curriculum (IPC). Helen Drennen describes the way in which the process of curriculum development across the three International Baccalaureate programmes has led to the identification of a framework for curriculum continuity, which she offers to others for debate. The assessment dimension of an international curriculum is explored by Roger Brown from the perspective of culture and values. In doing so, he identifies possibilities for the ways in which internationalism may be incorporated into assessment regimes appropriate to different cultural and ethnic student groups.

The ways in which teachers, administrators and others, charged with the responsibility of translating international ideals into practice within schools, national or international, are most appropriately supported through professional development form the overall theme of Part C. Mary Hayden and Jackie Holderness, both with experience in the creation and implementation of programmes of professional development offered by universities for practitioners throughout the world, debate issues arising directly from that experience. The contribution from Neil Richards complements the university perspective in offering a model arising directly from the school context.

Whilst the formal curriculum and the preparation of teachers for their role in programmes that promote international education have attracted much of the interest of those writing in the field of international education to date, relatively little has appeared in the literature based upon the organization and management of schools specifically in an international context. This may be thought to be surprising, given the enormous general interest throughout the world in institutional analysis arising from the school effectiveness and school improvement movements in recent decades. Those contributing to Part D, on the organization and management of schools and their communities, have attempted to sketch out the major issues that would need to be placed on the agenda in any attempt to redress this state of affairs.

Keith Allen opens this part with a consideration of internationalism in the context of the relationship that exists between schools and their local, regional and global communities. Brian Garton follows this with a specific consideration of the context in which the international status of schools can be identified in relation to their links with the wider community within the host country. James Cambridge widens the context still further and draws on some of the points arising in Part C in discussing the distinction between international and global aspects of the organization of schools in the particular dimension of the recruitment and deployment of staff. From his perspective both as the head of an international school and as a former chair of the Board of Directors of ECIS, Terry Haywood explores the distinction between management and leadership skills in school organization and draws a useful distinction between pragmatic and visionary aspects. In bringing together issues arising from other contributors, David Wilkinson points to the importance of the role of governance for international education – at school or network levels – in formulating policies consistent with best practice and espoused philosophies, and the context is widened still further by Richard McDonald, who offers a further reflection on the role of the school board in contributing to the dynamic process of vision creation for successful international education.

In the closing chapter, George Walker, writing from his experience as teacher and administrator in both national and international schools, and from the perspective of his leadership of the IBO, reflects on the contributions made within this volume. He suggests that the experience represented amongst the writers should be used to construct a language of international education with which to engage schools in national systems around the world.

The editors wish to express their gratitude to Jonathan Simpson and his colleagues at Kogan Page for their encouragement and support in publishing this further volume of contributed chapters. They also wish to acknowledge assistance given in a number of different ways by colleagues within IBO and CEIC, and particularly by James Cambridge in constructing the index. Above all, we wish to express our gratitude to each of the contributors to this book, who have exercised both patience and skill in the generation and revision of materials submitted to us, and who have demonstrated generosity in the extent to which they have been prepared to share their ideas within the group. We also wish to acknowledge contributions made by countless colleagues in schools, colleges and universities throughout the world who, by their endeavours over the years, have contributed to the development of a deepened understanding of the field of international education, which we believe, in turn, offers the best foundation for the provision of an international education appropriate to the needs and aspirations of young people in the future.

Part A

HISTORY AND NATURE OF INTERNATIONAL EDUCATION

Chapter 1

The 'first' international school

Bob Sylvester

Introduction

Thomas Friedman (2000), in his book *The Lexus and the Olive Tree,* argues that the present age of globalization is, in fact, the second era of globalization, especially when one considers the volume of trade and cross-border capital flow relative to GNP as well as the flow of labour across borders. The first period of globalization, he posits, occurred from the mid-1800s to the late 1920s. That era witnessed a period when, in Friedman's words, the world shrank from a 'large' size to a 'medium' size. He further points out that the first era of globalization was broken apart by the successive impacts of the Russian Revolution, World War I and the Great Depression. This present era of globalization is distinguished, in his view, by the speed and the power of the global changes in communications and travel, and the concurrent rise of multinational corporations. In this latter period of globalization the world shrank again, from a size 'medium' to a size 'small'.

The focus of this chapter is an investigation into the rise of efforts to establish international schools during this first Victorian period of globalization of the late 19th century. These efforts have, for the past 45 years (Bibby, 1956), been lost to any serious consideration by researchers in international education. This historical investigation may well be of assistance in forming a more complete understanding of the present rise of international schools in the second era of globalization, which has become even more evident during the last decade of the 20th century. The story of the early international schools and, especially, the first international school in the West, needs to be told in the historical context of a tension between the parallel growth of national systems of education and a popular awareness of international relations and sentiments. As Scanlon (1960) noted in his text *International Education: A Documentary History*:

> The nineteenth century also marked the beginning of great national systems of mass education. The motives behind these systems varied, from the despotism of the Frederick Williams to the warm humanitarianism of a Pestalozzi; but all were committed in one way or another to the advancement of national interests. It is against this background of vigorous nationalism that the efforts of early pioneers in international education should be examined. For fundamentally all were out of step with the nineteenth century. In an era of provincial loyalties, they argued for loyalty to mankind. And in an era of mass education for patriotism, they contended that the school was the only agency capable of advancing education across national boundaries. Little wonder that their proposals were viewed as radical, visionary, and utopian.

Butts (in Deighton, 1971) viewed the historic rise of international education and the tension that existed with the rise of nationalism in the following manner:

> In the eighteenth and nineteenth centuries the appeal for greater cooperation among the scholars and educational institutions of nations began to grow more insistent. French *philosophes*, German cosmopolitans, and English internationalists of the Enlightenment began to speak of the necessity for transcending national barriers through educational understanding. In general, however, their voices were drowned during the nineteenth century by growing claims that education should become an instrument of national policy rather than of international understanding.

Stomfay-Stitz (1993) observed more recently, in a history of peace education in North America, that the hidden strands of the history of international education may have yet to be discovered and treated in a serious fashion by researchers and historians. What is considered a progressive attitude toward a global approach to educational planning today has its roots in international educational and peace education efforts that emerged, in her view, during the Victorian Age.

The Spring Grove School

The story of the 'first' international school is British in presence and European in scope. Brickman (1962) notes that the International

College at Spring Grove, London, just a few kilometres east of the present Heathrow International Airport, was established in 1866 and operated until 1889 when the premises were sold to the Borough Road Training College. The college was established under the inspiration of Richard Cobden, the chairman and founder of the International Education Society, as well as under the leadership of the scientists Thomas H Huxley and John Tyndall. Brickman indicates that 'the idea for an international school originally came from a committee set up by the commissioners of the Paris Universal Exposition [1855] to conduct an essay contest on the advantages of a school for pupils of various national origins'.

Richard Cobden, one of the leading supporters of the Spring Grove School, detested both war and imperialism and was a fierce opponent of the hawkish policies of Prime Minister Palmerston. He advocated free trade, international arbitration and disarmament. He showed an enthusiasm for phrenology, the pseudo-science whose advocates believed that the nature of human character could be divined from minute examination of the shape of a skull. But he was also a true cosmopolitan. At his death, the *Daily Telegraph* wrote that 'he taught political economy to the gentlemen of England, and he brought untaxed bread into the poor man's home. Of no other politician can so much be said' (in Hobson, 2001).

Stewart (1972), in giving the background to the establishment of the Spring Grove School and the influence of the Radical politician Richard Cobden in the venture, noted: 'Many leading advocates of free trade hoped to realize their vision of international harmony by the creation of a new type of education which would enable the citizens of different countries to become international ambassadors'. Stewart also reports that the first contingent of students in 1867 numbered 12 day scholars between the ages of 10 and 14, who enjoyed the advantage of 8 acres of ground. There was one master to each 10 students and, in the absence of corporal punishment, the school incorporated isolation and deprivation of privileges as the primary forms of discipline. The student body of the Spring Grove School of that time included French, German, Spanish, Portuguese, Indian, North American, Brazilian, Chilean, Nicaraguan and Bermudan boys (Brickman, 1962).

Bibby (1959) notes that a scheme to establish a series of international schools in Europe was first proposed at the Paris 1855 exhibition through an essay contest under the theme of 'the advantages of educating together children of different nationalities'. Bibby, like Brickman (1950) seems to have assumed that the Paris Exhibition of 1855 witnessed the first time that an essay contest on international education was launched. Stewart (1972), however, using several distinct primary sources, credits the first substantive essay contest on the establishment of international schools to have taken place (interestingly, under the auspices of the French Committee) at the London International Exhibition of 1862, a date that may therefore be considered as the dawning of the first organized attempt to establish international schools in the West.

Importantly, Stewart also characterized the Spring Grove School as the 'one genuine and successful attempt at international education in the nineteenth century'. He notes that there were three proposals made between 1855 and 1862 towards the establishment of a form of international school in Europe. The proposal by the French Inspector General of Public Instruction, Eugene Rendu, was first made in 1855, probably as a result of discussions at the Paris Exposition of that year, but was delayed in publication until 1862. James Lorimer, a lawyer in Scotland, published two articles in the summer of 1861 with a proposal similar to Rendu's (in Stewart, 1972). Lorimer called for a 'rational study of languages' and the application of travel in the service of 'international understanding'.

The French business magnate, Aristide Barbier, made the third proposal for an international school in 1862 on the occasion of the International Exhibition in London. It was he who donated 5,000 francs to the French Committee of the Exhibition as a prize for the best essay on the 'means of establishing international education in Europe'. The 1862 essay contest was ultimately won by Edmond Barbier (only a namesake – not a relative – of the business magnate) who also happened to be the translator of the 'definitive' French edition of Darwin's *Origin of Species*. The successful essay resulted in the creation of the European Association for International Education based in Paris, with Eugene Rendu as its secretary. There is, as yet, no historical evidence of any connection between this Paris-based European Association of International Education and Cobden's International Education Society that owned and operated the Spring Grove School.

In the same work, Stewart reports that the governors of the Spring Grove School in England were not initially organized until 1863 when a provisional committee was formed that included Richard Cobden (who died before the school would open), Dr W B Hodgson, Thomas Twining and the scientists John Tyndall and T H Huxley. Stewart notes that Edmond Barbier acted as secretary to this committee. The committee sent out a circular in 1863, which tried to answer various criticisms of the school project, especially the fear (apparently in the popular mind) that the pupils would, as a result of their time at the school, 'lose all sense of national feeling'. When Richard Cobden died in 1865, his place as

Chairman of the International Education Society was taken by A W Paulton, a fellow activist in the Anti–Corn Law League (Bibby, 1959).

An article in the *Journal of the Society of Arts* (Bell, 1863) published in London, noted that 'The recent International Exhibition [in London] seems naturally to have led to the discussion, amongst the many distinguished men of different nations then in this country, of various plans for removing national prejudices'. A published report resulted from the essay contest sponsored by M Barbier and the French Committee of the London Exhibition. The report proposed that 'a European Company' be formed 'for the purpose of establishing a college, or rather school, in each of the four great countries in Europe'. The colleges would receive children of equal numbers from the four countries and it was envisioned in the report from the essay contest that students would be instrumental in teaching each other languages in a sort of peer-tutoring system. The students would migrate to another college at the end of a year and would find that the 'rules would be exactly alike; so that a boy going from one college to another would be certain to find there the continuation of the studies he had begun'. The *Journal* article optimistically observed that a great deal of time needed to learn the European languages would be saved and 'national prejudices and antipathies would be modified, a new generation endowed with more liberal and enlightened views would be formed, the whole tending to the promotion of peace and social progress in the various nations' (Bell, 1863).

The biographer of T H Huxley (Bibby, 1959) in outlining Huxley's role as an educator, relates the rise of the Spring Grove School to the widespread discontent with the public schools in England that led to the establishment of the Clarendon Commission in 1864 (Bibby, 1956). By his account: 'forward-looking citizens set about the establishment of educational institutions with fewer cultural and domestic deficiencies'. As Bibby further observed: 'If today it were proposed to found boarding schools in different countries, with similar curricula and methods of teaching so that their pupils might migrate from one to another and thus acquire linguistic fluency and an international outlook without disrupting their studies, what charges of Utopianism might not be made!' (1959).

Brickman (1962) indicates that international secondary schools were, in fact, established in the 1860s at Chatou, near Paris and at Bad Godesberg near Bonn, but were discontinued soon after in response to the Franco-Prussian War. However, Charles Dickens (1864) in his weekly publication called *All the Year Round*, outlined in significant detail, in an article entitled 'International Education', the planning for the founding of a series of international schools in Europe, first in

France. He detailed the establishment of a school in St Germain-en-Laye (just outside Paris – about 'five leagues distant'), which would take a 'bold theoretical swing', undertaken under the auspices of the European Association for International Education through the leadership of M Eugene Rendu, the Inspector General of Public Instruction:

> The plan is to establish in the different countries of Europe a series of international and corresponding schools for the middle and upper classes, which will enable a boy during the course of a liberal general education, to acquire thoroughly several modern languages, each being learned with the others, among school fellows of all nations, in the land where it is spoken. The arrangement of classes and method of study being precisely the same in each international school.

Dickens later noted that this arrangement would be established in such a way 'so that the pupils in passing from one nation and language to another, would find no notable change in the course of study to retard the progress of their education'. Dickens further noted that the 'international school' would contain pupils of different countries and different creeds in such a way that 'the school receives all creeds on equal terms, the growth of cosmopolitan indefferentism [sic] is said to be guarded against by the careful maintenance of a high moral and religious feeling in the school'. He then notes that 'it would be well if boys could thus learn that there is but one common religion, whatever the number of theologies'.

Dickens compared this effort to form international schools to the establishment in the 14th–16th centuries of the European universities into a 'republic of letters' in which a sense of individual nationality would not be diminished. 'It certainly would not denationalise the young English mind. English boys, sure to be numerous in any school of the sort thus proposed, would be a community ready to fight in play-hours with the boys of any other nation if the honour of their country were brought into question'. Dickens further observed that

> Every boy would uphold and magnify his own, and the result in each case would be, with the tolerance that comes of near acquaintance with different ways of thought, anything but the undesirable state of mind in which a man don't care to think himself a Frenchman, or a German, or an Italian, or an Englishman, but prides himself on being a citizen of the world at large.

Dickens apparently did not view the education available in England at the time with much appreciation, as he noted in the *Journal* article that the educational choices of the time were 'a choice of evils variously mixed with good' and then added the strikingly modern sensibility that 'the spur of some added international competition may quicken the pace of school reform at home'.

In the following year, 1865, an extensive article in a weekly London magazine, *The Reader* (Bohn, 1865) detailed the progress of the planning for a series of international schools in Europe. The justification for such a development, it was noted, lies in the observation that 'our public schools are insufficient to secure the thorough acquaintance with modern continental languages which the needs of the present day demand'. The article noted also that the student 'must have that living acquaintance with modern languages which will enable him to communicate on terms of equality with his compeers in other countries'. The *Reader* article cited impediments in commerce, literature and science as a result of the failure of the public school systems to provide effective language instruction. The plan was then outlined in a manner clearly prescient of the type of efforts undertaken almost exactly 100 years later by the International Baccalaureate Organization (see Ian Hill's chapter in this book on the history of the IB Diploma Programme) to create a practical system of international education:

> It is proposed to establish, in two or more countries, schools or colleges for the instruction of pupils in the language of the country in which each school is situated, as well as of those in which sister establishments may be founded... The combined operation of sister institutions implies uniformity, not only in the subjects taught, but also in the method of teaching. Thus the pupil would continue the study of his native tongue in the same method as at home, and the irreparable injury at present inflicted by change of system on those children who are sent abroad to private schools would be avoided. In passing from one school to another, even from one form to another in the same school, the chances are very small that a boy finds himself on an equality with his new class-fellows. The parallel arrangement of the courses in different countries proposed by this scheme would enable the *émigré* pupil to enter a class of the same degree of proficiency as that which he had just left, and with less risk of inequality than in the supposed case at home.

The article then assured the reader that the scheme had been entrusted to the competent hands of 'an accomplished scholar' who was able to 'direct a system of international education'. However, this proposed system of international education was still rooted in national interests as it was also noted that 'the scheme deserves the support of all who have an interest in the cause of education, and who feel it a duty to provide a future generation with the means of maintaining our and their country on a footing of equality with other States'.

A grand Victorian opening of an international school

Bibby (1972), in his extensive biography of T H Huxley, notes that the most remarkable event for 1866 was the 'opening at Isleworth of the International College, which, with Huxley and Tyndall among its governors, provided a fascinating and successful experiment in the common schooling of a wide range of nationalities'. Stewart (1972) notes that the main benefactor for the school was William Ellis, who provided a large part of the money that was required for the purchase of the site in Isleworth (Middlesex) as well as for the erection of buildings. Ellis (1800–81) amassed a fortune in marine underwriting and himself founded five schools named after George Birkbeck (Bibby, 1959). The completion of the construction of the first buildings, and the unofficial opening, took place on 1 May 1866, with the official opening of 'The London College of the International Education Society' at Spring Grove near Hounslow, south-west of the centre of London, taking place on 10 July 1867.

The Illustrated London News in its issue of 20 July 1867 reported on the official opening, with the formalities conducted by a former pupil of Ellis, the Prince of Wales, and a striking half-page illustration is included in the newspaper. The illustration reflected the international nature of the school, with flags of many nations seen in the background of the scene. It is worthwhile to quote, in large part, this historically important contemporary account from the *News* of 20 July:

> *The Prince Of Wales And The International Education Society* – The new building for the London College of the International Education Society, at Spring Grove, near Hounslow, was opened by the Prince of Wales on Wednesday week. This society, of which the late Mr Cobden and M Michel Chevalier were two of the earliest promoters, aims at providing the means of going through a continuous and systematic course of education – English, French and German, or vice versa – at several different establishments in succession, conducted on the same plan and under the same general superintendence. It will prevent the interruption of studies and the distraction of which parents frequently complain when boys have been removed from a school in England and sent to a foreign school, for the sake of learning other European languages than that of their native land. The subjects and methods of instruction being arranged on a common basis, the pupil will have nothing to unlearn, and his progress in substantial knowledge will not be checked, while he is acquiring French and German by residence at Paris or on the Rhine. The whole course of teaching will occupy seven or eight years, of which two or three years may be spent at Chatou, near Paris, and the same amount of time at Godesberg, near Bonn, in the school conducted, respectively, by M P Barrère and Dr A Baskerville. A fourth will be established in Italy. The Head

Master of the London college is Dr Leonard Schmitz, late Rector of the High School of Edinburgh, with able assistants. A most characteristic feature in the course of instruction is the prominent place which is given to the physical sciences. By this kind of study, as well as by that of mathematics, it is sought to train the mind to accurate habits of reasoning, which the founders of the Spring Grove College esteem the most important object of education. The names of Professors Tyndall, Huxley, and Williamson, and Dr W B Hodgson, in the list of directors, are a sufficient guarantee for this part of the scheme. It seems calculated to remedy the great deficiency exposed by the late Report of the Public School Commissioners, and commented upon by Dr Faraday, Sir John Herschel, and the lecturers at the Royal Institution, whose essays on this subject have been collected, under the title of 'Modern Culture'. The study of Latin and Greek is nowise neglected at Spring Grove, under so eminent a classical scholar as Dr Schmitz; but it is to be commenced at a later age than usual, after mastering the grammar of the English language. Drawing, singing, drilling, and gymnastics form part of the regular course of instruction.

The opening ceremony passed off with entire success. The Prince of Wales arrived in a carriage-and-four at one o'clock, when a gun was fired, and the Royal standard was hoisted. He was received by Mr A W Paulton, the chairman, and several directors, with Dr Schmitz, who is one of the former schoolmasters of his Royal Highness, having taught him while at Edinburgh in his youth not many years ago. A procession was formed to conduct the Prince through the building. Having inspected every part, he came out in front and planted a tree – a *Wellingtonia gigantea*, or mammoth-tree of California – which will grow to an immense size and serve to commemorate his visit. He used a silver spade, which was presented to him by the directors. The college was then declared to be opened. The Prince of Wales and the Duc d'Aumale, who was also present, took luncheon in the dining-room with the directors and many distinguished guests. Mr Paulton was in the chair, and spoke, with his accustomed earnest eloquence, of the part taken by his deceased friend, Mr Cobden, in establishing the International Education Society. The Prince of Wales, in replying when his own health was proposed, said that Mr Cobden was a personal friend of his own lamented father, the late Prince Consort, who was himself most strongly impressed with the same views regarding the education of youth, and especially regarding the study of modern languages, which he (the Prince of Wales) thought quite essential. He gracefully bore testimony to the pleasure and benefit he had received from the instructions of his friend Dr Schmitz, at Edinburgh, and hoped the London College of the International Education Society would prosper in every way.

Bibby (1959) records that the first headmaster of the Spring Grove School, Leonhard (*sic*) Schmitz (1807–90), was born at Aix-la-Chapelle and educated in part at Bonn, and was formerly Rector of the

Edinburgh High School. Bibby (1956) notes that the school had an enrolment of 80 students in residence in the first term of the new buildings at Spring Grove.

The early years of the Spring Grove School witnessed an apparent struggle on the part of the directors (including the scientist T H Huxley) to establish a focus on science teaching in the curriculum. The Secretary of the International Education Society at the time, J F Tremayne, submitted a formal programme of science instruction to the governors covering each of the several years of instruction for the school programme. There is evidence (Bibby, 1956, 1959) that the first headmaster resisted the attempt to introduce up to three to four hours per week of science teaching, apparently in the belief that it would interfere with the teaching of the classics and the language emphasis that formed a central part of the early marketing of the school (Bibby, 1956). The syllabus passed down from the governors of the International Education Society was elaborate, with a proposed system of science electives in place for the fifth, sixth and seventh years.

Bibby (1959) further reports that the Spring Grove School was apparently able to move positively in the direction of an internationalist mission: 'The mission to which the school managed to achieve its internationalist aim is surprising. The boys must have come from wealthy [families]... but they were not restricted by nationality or religion or race'. However, Bibby cites from a local news-sheet of December 1870 (*Our Neighbourhood*) an occasion where the collection of students from around the world resorted to some rather extreme methods in settling their grievances with the school managers. As the local reporter recorded:

> For some reason – doubtless a proper one – the Principal of the International College, Spring Grove, deemed it necessary to stop certain holiday privileges to the pupils. A deputation to the gentleman, headed by a son of a well-known literary man, failed to get a rescind of the terrible denial: and hence a feeling of supposed injustice and ill-advised insubordination. Forming among themselves a Council of Resistance, the boys proceeded to purchase provisions in the shape of hams, preserved meats, bread, biscuits, jams, sweets, tobacco, &c, wherewith to stand the discomfort of a self-imposed siege. A portion of this had been smuggled into the rooms of the College, the remainder being granaried at a 'public' somewhere in the neighbourhood, to be delivered by ropes let down at night-time, as the wants of the garrison should demand. On the Saturday evening, a tumbling noise overhead awoke the officials to something unusual. Upon going to ascertain the cause it was found that the boys had barricaded the doors with chests of drawers and bedding, taking the dormitory-doors from their hinges, and adding them by means of

long screws, making admission impossible without the use of great force. In vain they were asked to surrender. The Principal was sent for, but could do nothing. A much-loved undermaster's appeal did not alter their determination. As a last resort, on Sunday morning, the aid of the police was sought, and they made short work of the mutineers. Bursting in the doors, they were assailed by brandy-balls from many a catapult! but the Helmet-and-Blue-cloth of law and order quickly brought surrender and subjection. A drum-head school martial proclaimed the dread sentence of expulsion to ten of the offenders, who were considered principals in the fitful fray – a severe punishment, but a lesson that will stand as a terrible menace to the boys. (cited in Bibby, 1959)

Another contemporary report described eyewitness stories of rather mercenary motives for the student unrest reflected in the placards displayed by the student mutineers:

'Smallberry Green in a state of siege' came like a clap of thunder upon us; but 'Blues to the fore' brought us speedy peace. Still, who shall gainsay the danger, or tell where the spirit of mutiny would stop? The International College in open rebellion, and armed with catapults and brandy-balls! – unfolding and flying the terrible banner – *Our Half-Holiday! No Uniform Caps! Unlimited Tobacco! No Surrender!* (cited in Bibby, 1956)

Stewart (1972) notes that the governors of Spring Grove School built extensive additional buildings in 1871, including a new wing to the original building and a gymnasium, at a cost of £10,000. Bibby (1959) listed the later cost of the extensions at £42,000, an investment that provided the boys with the 'rare luxury of baths with hot and cold water'. Stewart listed the pupils as coming from France, Germany, Italy, Spain, Portugal, the United States, India, Brazil, Chile, and Nicaragua. As noted, while the initial focus of the school was to be language instruction, science also came to the fore as a central part of the school's mission. He notes 'Thomas Henry Huxley... wanted to make science the backbone of the curriculum and proposed an ambitious scheme that would include physics, chemistry, biology, advanced social science and the natural history of man'. Stewart also noted that this 19th-century effort at establishing a linked group of schools was attempted later in the 20th century by Cecil Reddie of Abbotsholme and by Kurt Hahn. Stewart describes the Spring Grove School as 'a remarkable achievement, a product of the liberal intelligentsia for their children'.

An advertisement in the *Times* of 7 April 1880 indicated that the Spring Grove School had two laboratories for science teaching and baths with hot and cold water, which was, at the time, a rare luxury (Bibby, 1956). A contemporary description of the neighbourhood upon which the Spring Grove School was built can be found in a local directory of 1887 (cited by Bibby, 1956) described as 'a fashionable villa residency, nine miles from the metropolis, pleasantly situated on the western side of the London road', which Bibby notes would appeal to the 'respectable upper-middle-class parents for whose sons the school was designed'. The same local directory also indicates that Spring Grove had by then a staff of 14 masters including specialists in music, dance, French and German, and an enrolment of over 100 students (Bibby, 1956).

The English novelist, Maurice Hewlett (1861–1923), a former student of the Spring Grove School, presents some evidence that links the eventual establishment of the London College of the International Education Society with the earlier educational presentations and discussions of the Universal Exhibition in London of 1851:

> My father was an idealist of 1851; he showed the enthusiasm and nursed in his bosom the hopes and beliefs of the promoters of the International Exhibition of that year. There was a plentiful planting of foreign stock in England that year, and one of its weedy saplings was an International Education Company, which out of a magniloquent prospectus and some too-confident shareholders, bore the fruit, the London International College at Spring Grove. It never came to maturity, and is now dropped and returned to the ground of all such schemes. (cited in Bibby, 1956 and Hewlett, 1912)

Hewlett apparently spent several years at Spring Grove. In a quite morose recollection of his time at the College, he cited it as a 'barren, profitless time' (Hewlett, 1912) and observed only a marginal impact of internationalism at the time: 'The school-yard is taken for the world in small, and so allowed to be. There is no thought taken, or at least betrayed, that it is nothing more than a preparation for the world at large... There were no traces in my time of the Brotherhood of Man about it. A few Portuguese, a negro or two were there, and a multitude of Jews. But I fancy I should have found the same sort of thing at Eton'. Later in the same memoir, however, Hewlett notes that his own brother enjoyed his entire experience at the same school.

Unfortunately few, if any, historical documents exist that can be found to explain the demise of the Spring Grove School, which was apparently closed in 1889 and soon after transformed into the Borough Road Training College. For a period of over 20 years the intelligentsia of England struggled with the practicalities of schooling in the frontiers of international education, practicalities which, even to the present day, continue to represent a strong metaphor of the tension between the traditional objectives of a national educational system and the emerging realities of preparing students for an increasingly globalized society.

A new historical benchmark for international education

There were at least three other significant efforts towards schooling in international education before 1924, a date that has been traditionally accepted (Hill, 2001) as a historical starting point for international education in the West with the establishment of the International School of Geneva. In addition to the Spring Grove experiment, institutional efforts in the United States, West Bengal and Denmark have noteworthy stories that pre-date the founding of the Geneva school.

In 1910 Edwin Ginn, an educational publisher and peace philanthropist, established the International School of Peace in Boston (Scott, 1912; Meyer, 1949). The school was quickly transformed into the World Peace Foundation, which today has its offices in Cambridge, Massachusetts (Harley, 1931; Stomfay-Stitz, 1993).

In 1921 the Nobel laureate poet Rabindranath Tagore established an international school named Santinikentan, a distance of 99 miles from the Bengal capital Calcutta (Brickman, 1950; Scanlon, 1960). The motto selected for the school, which still operates today as an international university, was taken from an ancient Sanskrit verse: 'Yatra visvam bhavati ika-nidam – Where the world meets in one nest' (Kripilani, 1962).

The year 1921 also witnessed the establishment of the International Folk (Peoples) High School in Elsinore, Denmark (Carr, 1945; Stoker, 1933; Kenworthy, 1951) by Peter Manniche. Kenworthy, in the same work, notes that the purpose of the school included the aim 'to further international understanding and co-operation' and the teaching staff included Swedes, Germans, Danes and English professionals.

Conclusion

The complete stories of these other international schools and their role in the growth of international education in the first era of globalization still remain to be told. The first era of globalization alluded to by Friedman in the Lexus and the Olive Tree, did apparently produce notable attempts to expand the boundaries of national education and to strengthen the frontiers of international understanding. The Victorian experiment in international education, which for over two decades operated at Spring Grove outside Hounslow in England, should now, in the absence of competing historical evidence, be considered the 'first' international school of the modern age in the West, and a potential point of reference for further consideration as a significant benchmark in the modern history of the larger field of international education.

References

Bell, G (1863) Proposed international schools, *Journal of the Society of Arts*, **XI** (540), p 336 [27 March]

Bibby, C (1956) A Victorian experiment in international education: the College at Spring Grove, *British Journal of Educational Studies*, **V** (1), pp 25–36

Bibby, C (1959) *T H Huxley: Scientist, humanist and educator*, Horizon Press, New York

Bibby, C (1972) *Scientist Extraordinary: The life and scientific work of Thomas Henry Huxley, 1825–1895*, Pergamon Press, Oxford

Bohn, J (ed) (1865) International Education, *The Reader: A review of literature, science and art*, **V** (129), pp 678–79 [17 June]

Brickman, W W (1950) International education, in *Encyclopedia of Educational Research*, ed W S Monroe, Macmillan, New York

Brickman, W W (1962) International Relations in Higher Education, 1862–1962, in *A Century of Higher Education: Classical citadel to collegiate colossus*, eds W W Brickman and S Lehrer, Society for the Advancement of Education, New York

Carr, W G (1945) *Only by Understanding* (Foreign Policy Association Headline Series), **52**, Foreign Policy Association, New York

Deighton, L C (ed) (1971) *The Encyclopedia of Education*, Macmillan, New York

Dickens, C (ed) (1864) International education, in *All The Year Round: A weekly journal*, **XII** (281), pp 281–308

Friedman, T L (2000) *The Lexus and the Olive Tree*, Anchor Books, New York

Harley, J E (ed) (1931) *International Understanding: Agencies educating for a new world*, Stanford University Press, Stanford, California

Hewlett, M (1912) The Gods in the Schoolhouse, *The English Review*, **XIII** pp 43–51

Hill, I (2001) Early stirrings: the beginnings of the international education movement, *International Schools Journal*, **XX** (2), pp 11–22

Hobson, D (2001) *Who was Richard Cobden? Deluded activist or economic revolutionary?* [Online] http://www.assetpub.com/archive/gc/97–03gcfall/fall97GC054.html

Illustrated London News (1867) The Prince of Wales and the International Education Society, **LI**, pp 63–64 [20 July]

Kenworthy, L S (1951) The schools of the world and education for a world society, in *Education for a World Society*, eds C O Arndt and S Everett, Harper and Brothers, New York

Kripilani, K (1962) *Rabindranath Tagore: A biography*, Grove Press, New York

Meyer, A E (1949) *The Development of Education in the Twentieth Century*, Greenwood Press, Westport Connecticut

Scanlon, D G (1960) (ed) *International Education: A documentary history*, Columbia University, Bureau of Publications, Teachers College, New York

Scott, W (1912) *World Education: A discussion of the favorable conditions for a world campaign for education*, University Press, Cambridge, Massachusetts

Stewart, W A C (1972) *Progressives and Radicals in English Education, 1750–1970*, Macmillan, London

Stoker, S (1933) *The Schools and International Understanding*, University of North Carolina Press, Chapel Hill, North Carolina

Stomfay-Stitz, A (1993) *Peace Education in America 1828–1990*, Scarecrow Press, London

Chapter 2

The history of international education: an International Baccalaureate perspective

Ian Hill

Introduction

The International Baccalaureate (IB) Diploma Programme is offered in more than 1,100 schools in over 100 countries. Approximately 14 per cent more schools offer the programme each year around the world. It enjoys recognition for university entrance in all of the developed countries and in most of the developing world; as such, it represents the most widely known end-of-secondary school qualification not tied to a particular country. The International Baccalaureate Organization (IBO) now offers a series of three international education programmes for children from 3 to 19 (or more) years of age: the Diploma, Middle Years and Primary Years Programmes (IBO, 2002).

This chapter explores the creation and growth of the oldest of these, the IB Diploma Programme, from four perspectives. After identifying the rationale for its emergence, the discussion then moves to a consideration of the state of international education prior to this event. The third part traces briefly the evolution of the programme itself, from the first history syllabus, and considers the problems that had to be overcome. The final perspective proposes a model for international education and considers how well the IB Diploma Programme fits this model.

Rationale for the IB Diploma Programme

As a result of a 1962 conference of teachers of social studies in international schools, organized by the International Schools Association (ISA) in Geneva, the first IB course in contemporary history was developed. The conference of teachers made the following recommendation: 'The Conference asks ISA to issue a statement of educational aims acceptable to all member schools. It further requests that the development of a joint social studies final exam be explored by ISA as the first step toward the establishment of basic standards' (First Conference of Teachers of Social Studies in International Schools, 1962).

This outcome spurred the ISA Eleventh General Assembly (which took place at the same time) to recommend that the International School of Geneva takes steps to 'formulate an advanced level ISA examination in contemporary history (and political and economic affairs); and develop common standards for grading and marking systems' (ISA, 1962).

These proposals were put into practice. The 'common standards' led to the development of the IB Diploma Programme with the same external examinations taken by students across the globe. This new programme came about because teachers from a number of different countries wanted to address national bias in an attempt to develop an appreciation of the inevitable range of cultural perceptions of historical events. The parents (international civil servants) who dominated the executive committee of ISA supported the idea. They wanted for their children an education whose objectives reflected those of the organizations they served: the promotion of world peace and international understanding.

The need for an internationally recognized diploma was also an important motivating force for parents and teachers. It would serve as an international passport to higher education and therefore facilitate global mobility. Learning about other cultures and world issues, and being able to speak other languages, were important pragmatic elements. It was clear to the teachers that a new pedagogical approach was needed to promote international understanding, an approach that would cut through stereotypes and prejudices: critical inquiry coupled with an open mind willing to question established beliefs, willing to withdraw from conventional positions in the light of new evidence and experiences, willing to accept that being different does not mean being wrong. This was quite a change from the emphasis at the time on accumulating knowledge as fact by memorization.

An international university entrance diploma had already been mooted in 1925 by the International School of Geneva, in 1946 by the

Collège Cévénol, France (Collège Cévénol, 1946), in 1948 by the Werkplaats International Children's Community, Holland (Boeke, 1948), and in 1949 by the Conference of Internationally-Minded Schools (Conference of Principals of International Schools and Schools Specially Interested in Developing International Understanding, 1951). However, nothing came of these early ideas. It was the needs of an increasing number of international schools, together with formal aggregations to represent their interests, which laid the foundation for the historic decision to proceed in 1962.

The leverage of a number of highly placed international civil servants grouped in Geneva, ready to put their shoulders to the cause, was another important factor in bringing about the creation of the IB Diploma Programme. Heads of the International School of Geneva also played a vital role in enthusing and supporting the staff who were largely responsible for the first syllabi and examinations.

Most importantly, the situation at the International School of Geneva required attention. From the outset the school prepared students for the national university entrance examinations of England ('A' levels), France (*baccalauréat*), Germany (*abitur*), and Switzerland (*maturité*) and, later (in the 1940s), the American College Board Advanced Placement examinations (Mowat, 1968). Small groups of students were undertaking courses in classes grouped largely according to nationality; this led to unviable class sizes and cultural isolation. An international programme available in English and French also held the promise (alas not to be realized) of bringing together the separate English and French language sections of the school. The impetus for an IB Diploma gravitated around this institution together with the associations and conferences that brought other like-minded schools together. Thus, the IB Diploma Programme came about for ideological, utilitarian and pedagogical reasons:

- to provide a perspective that would promote international understanding, prepare students for world citizenship and promote peace;
- to provide a school-leaving diploma that would be recognized for university entrance around the world with common curriculum and examinations; and
- to promote critical thinking skills (rather than an emphasis on encyclopedic knowledge) via a balanced programme in the humanities, the experimental sciences and experiential learning.

International education by 1962

International schools had sprung up in different parts of the world to cater for the children of parents working outside their home countries, particularly for United Nations (UN) agencies and outposts. The longest surviving of these schools was the International School of Geneva founded in 1924, principally by UN employees. Its visionary head, Madame Maurette, stressed the ideological objectives of an international education. She argued that the students needed 'a complete and rounded view of the world, not only knowledge and understanding but the desire for peace, the feeling of the brotherhood of man' (Maurette, 1948).

UN Organization employees were also instrumental in founding the United Nations International School (UNIS) in New York. From the day it opened in 1947, the parents and staff of UNIS emphasized an international dimension in curriculum planning. The first objective for the new primary school was 'to try to give the child a sound education which, while preserving his native tongue, history and cultural background, will, at the same time, in the work and play of the school, free him of those prejudices and pieces of misinformation which separate peoples; so that wherever he may be in the future, he remains a good citizen of his own country; more important, a good citizen of the world' (Malinowski and Zorn, 1973).

Using material produced by the United Nations Educational, Scientific and Cultural Organization (UNESCO) on the teaching of geography (Ficheux et al, 1949) and history (Hill, 1953) for international understanding, together with assistance from Madame Maurette, in 1964 the school produced a social studies curriculum. It was high on the promotion of international understanding but not easy to put into practice, through lack of text books without a national bias and lack of teachers trained in the delivery of international curricula.

As other international schools grew in many parts of the world, teachers and parents became worried about the inappropriateness of national curricula for providing a truly international experience in the academic programme. The IB Diploma Programme was to respond in large measure to these concerns. Inevitably the increasing number of international schools (institutions with a wide variety of student nationalities) and internationally-minded schools (institutions with an international perspective) (Hill, 2000) began to aggregate as officially constituted associations.

Through conferences and workshops they sought to attract teachers across the world to discuss issues of international education. The Conference of Internationally-minded Schools (CIS) was formed as a result of a meeting convened by UNESCO in 1949. This is the first known official, intercontinental grouping to bring together schools with a common cause. Membership was open to schools that 'consciously aim at furthering world peace and international understanding through education' (Conference of Principals of International Schools and Schools Specially Interested in Developing International Understanding, 1951). The CIS organized a four-week 'course for teachers interested in international education' at the International School of Geneva in the summer of 1950. The course attracted 50 teachers and heads of school from many European countries, Asia and the United States and, by its end, agreement on a definition of international education was reached:

> It should give the child an understanding of his past as a common heritage to which all men irrespective of nation, race or creed have contributed and which all men should share; it should give him an understanding of his present world as a world in which peoples are interdependent and in which cooperation is a necessity.
>
> In such an education emphasis should be laid on a basic attitude of respect for all human beings as persons, understanding of those things which unite us and an appreciation of the positive values of those things which may seem to divide us, with the objective of thinking free from fear or prejudice. (Course for Teachers Interested in International Education, 1950)

This is the first known definition of international education devised by a group of school representatives from different countries meeting together. It foreshadowed the utilitarian (acquiring knowledge), pedagogical (understanding the knowledge) and humanistic impetus of the rationale behind the IB Diploma Programme.

Another official aggregation, the International Schools Association (ISA), was founded in Geneva in 1951 by international civil servants, all of whom were initially members of school governing boards. The ISA was established to fulfil pedagogical and administrative purposes:

- to develop close cooperation between existing international schools by means of regular or occasional consultations on educational or administrative questions;
- to stimulate, facilitate or carry out research work on educational or administrative questions;
- to promote the establishment of new international schools; and
- to publicize aims and principles of international schools (ISA, 1957).

The provision of an internationally recognized common curriculum and examination later arose from the first two purposes. Initially some international schools prepared all students for one national examination and relied upon 'equivalence' agreements (which were not always easy to negotiate) to secure university placements in other countries. For example, Atlantic College in Wales offered only English 'A' levels when it was founded in 1962, yet its students came from all over the world (Peterson, 1968). Others prepared a number of national examinations within one school such as the International School of the Hague (later to become the American School of the Hague), founded in 1953, where three national streams operated leading to the pre-university examinations of France, Germany and the United States (Knight and Leach, 1964). The United Nations International School (UNIS), New York, offered American Advanced Placement and English 'A' Levels (Malinowski and Zorn, 1973). Such schools felt they needed to offer a range of national courses because mutual recognition of end-of-secondary school qualifications was not well established. So schools began searching for an international programme that could be taken by all students and accepted around the world. It was the International School of Geneva that brought the stakeholders together and it was individuals such as Alec Peterson who contributed to this search both before and after the beginnings of the IB Diploma Programme.

Peterson was head of the Department of Educational Studies at the University of Oxford and the first Director General of the IB Organization from the mid-1960s. He worked on the first curriculum model for Atlantic College in 1962. Peterson was a staunch campaigner against what he regarded as the over-specialization of English education at pre-university level. In 1960 he published a report on behalf of the Oxford Department of Educational Studies, *Arts and Science Sides in the Sixth Form*. It is noteworthy how closely the content of the report resembles not only the philosophy but also the structure and pedagogical underpinning of the IB Diploma Programme, which began to be elaborated, quite independently, a few years later.

The report extolled the need for a broader education that still allowed for a degree of specialization. It spoke of the need for ethics in science and for humanities specialists to know something about the beauty of mathematics. It promoted critical analysis and learning to learn rather than encyclopedic knowledge and memorization. It proposed increasing the number of specialized subjects in the English sixth form from three to four, spread over the humanities and the sciences. A fifth block of time was to be added to cover religious and physical education, the creative arts and a new course of about 60 hours that would enable students to 'make a unity' of their whole learning experience. 'The fifth block should therefore include a course, similar to the best and not the worst of the *classes de philosophie*, on the methodology of the subjects' (Peterson, 1987). It is remarkable that this precursor of the Theory of Knowledge course should arise quite independently of the subject of the same name that was first suggested at a curriculum conference in 1965 before Peterson became involved in the curriculum side of the IB Diploma Programme.

Peterson had also shown interest in a range of assessment techniques that would gauge 'the whole endowment and personality of the student' (Peterson, 1987). He did not want good teaching to be distorted by intensive examination preparation. He thought highly of oral examinations with a visiting examiner (a hallmark of IB first language examinations for many years), of mixing a small amount of multiple choice testing with essays (still used in the IB Diploma experimental science papers), of assessing analytical skills and cultural sensitivity rather than factual recall, and of qualitative measures of affective development (identified particularly via the Creativity Action Service (CAS) requirement in the IB Diploma Programme). Peterson's ideas, though directed initially at a national system, were to have a profound influence on the IB Diploma courses.

Development of the IB Diploma Programme

During the early 1960s, teachers at the International School of Geneva, progressively assisted by other schools, developed the profile and subject syllabi of the IB Diploma Programme starting with the first history course. In June 1964 a 'Draft Proposal for an International Baccalaureate' was published in the *ISA Newsletter Bulletin*. It stated that the study of literature and philosophy of different cultures should be compulsory. (World Literature, as part of the first language, and the Theory of Knowledge with its philosophical links, are both obligatory subject requirements today.) The document went on to suggest subject offerings at a higher and lower level with a total of eight subjects to be studied covering the major disciplines.

At curriculum conferences in 1965, the number of subjects was reduced to six, plus a compulsory artistic activity, which later grew into Creativity Action Service (CAS). Theory of Knowledge was added as a result of a curriculum conference held at Sèvres, France in 1967. The research activity, the Extended Essay, was implemented in 1972 in its current form. So the profile of the Diploma became established: a first and second language, mathematics, a subject chosen from each of the groups of humanities and experimental sciences, and a further subject chosen from an electives group, which included at the time the arts, Latin and Ancient Greek. This provided sufficient breadth. The programme evolved throughout some 50 subject-committee meetings, which took place in different world locations from 1967 to 1975. But, if the project were to succeed, this development necessitated a structure and financial support, and there were issues to be overcome other than curriculum development.

In 1964, the ISA created in Geneva the International Schools Examination Syndicate (ISES), which officially became the IB Office in 1968. From its inception this body undertook marketing initiatives for recognition of the Diploma. Four main audiences were targeted: universities, ministries of education and national governments, examining bodies, and schools. University and government authorities needed to accept the proposed IB Diploma. While almost all international schools at the time were independent fee-paying schools, some were state-controlled institutions, which necessitated the agreement of education ministry officials before the IB could be accepted. Contact with examination boards was a delicate matter, because the IB could be seen to be drawing the best candidates from, for example, 'A' levels (England and Wales), the French *baccalauréat* and Advanced Placement (United States). However, the contact proved fruitful and also provided for an exchange of expertise when it came to examination procedures and the setting and marking of papers.

Parents, students, teachers and school administrators needed to be convinced that the curricula were relevant to international students and acceptable by the best universities around the globe; ideological objectives were not of themselves sufficient motivation. There is a pragmatic side to becoming informed about world affairs, to learning another language, to learning about other cultures: it can provide leverage when vying for business contracts in other countries and it can provide job opportunities, both of which are perfectly legitimate goals in themselves. It can also provide intellectual pleasure and fulfil pedagogical objectives in relation to critical analysis skills, depending on the teaching and learning process. UNESCO, the Twentieth Century Fund (now the Century Fund) and the Ford Foundation (Fox, 2001) variously provided sufficient financial support for the project during the period 1964 to 1976. From 1976, participating schools started to pay an annual registration fee and a number of governments also provided an annual financial contribution to the IBO.

The most difficult marketing period was, of course, at the beginning when the IB was an unknown quantity and had yet to prove itself. Two early publications helped to disseminate information, particularly to educational audiences, about the development of the untried IB Diploma: Martin Mayer's *Diploma: International Schools and University Entrance* (1968) and Robert Leach's *International Schools and Their Role in the Field of International Education* (1969). By 1975, heads, teachers, university admissions officers and government ministries were accepting the IB Diploma on the basis of its initial success in a number of schools around the globe.

So the IB Diploma Programme promised to respond to the dilemma of international schools by providing a common curriculum (initially available in English and French, then also in Spanish from 1982) with an international perspective, academic rigour, critical thinking and research skills, and emphasizing the development of the whole person: in sum, the creation of world citizens.

The IB Diploma Programme and international education

This section proposes a 'definition' of international education gleaned from sources other than the IBO, including UNESCO (1974), Muller (1986), Oxfam (1997) and the Department for Education and Employment of England and Wales (2000), and suggests to what extent the IB Diploma Programme fits this model. The discussion relates back to the ideology, utility and pedagogy that played important roles in the rationale for the IB Programme.

A formal curriculum comprises content (knowledge and concepts), skills and attitudes. Students in schools offering an international education programme should acquire, from a global perspective, *knowledge* about:

- social justice and equity;
- interdependence;
- sustainable development (a balance between economic growth, protection of the environment and a fair distribution of material wealth and the earth's resources);
- cultural diversity;
- peace and conflict;
- population concerns (migration, ethnicity, refugee issues);
- languages.

This is the 'stuff' with which students will work. There is nothing ideological about this content *per se*; it is rather utilitarian – useful to know, almost factual. Students then need *skills* with which to approach this material. The most important skill is the ability to analyse critically the information presented: to understand, for example, why cultural behaviour is different, to what extent nations are interdependent, which areas of sustainable development need most attention, how language is inextricably intertwined with culture, what are the ingredients of peace and of conflict, how can current events be analysed in terms of these areas of knowledge? This requires a pedagogical approach that places importance on critical thinking skills, working cooperatively, independent research, interdisciplinarity, developing the 'whole person', and learning how to learn.

Attitudes are the affective part of the 'whole person'. This is the ideology in international education:

- commitment to social justice and equity on a world scale;
- empathy for the feelings, needs and lives of others in different countries;
- respect for cultural diversity within and without one's geographical location;
- a belief that people can make a difference;
- concern for the environment on a global scale;
- commitment to sustainable development on a global scale.

The diverse cultural mix of an international school is helpful if it is properly exploited, but national schools can and do find substitutes to provide different cultural perspectives.

Many of the IB Diploma Programme subjects involve the introduction of the knowledge, skills and attitudes identified in the lists above to varying degrees. Students might, however, have more or less 'internationalism' in their complete programme depending on which courses they choose. This is an issue yet to be resolved. The current, obligatory Theory of Knowledge course (IBO, 1999) abounds with topic questions relating to intercultural understanding and values that clearly address the ideological level. The potential of the compulsory 4,000-word Extended Essay to be written on (transdisciplinary) global issues has yet to be realized. Where students are able to interact with other cultural groups in their local community or undertake projects of assistance in other countries via CAS, a real international dimension based on personal experience will have been achieved. Not all IB schools, however, are able to do this.

Conclusion

To conclude, let us consider the knowledge, skills and attitudes that the IBO seeks to develop in its three programmes: 'strong emphasis is placed on the ideals of international understanding and responsible citizenship, to the end that IB students may become critical and compassionate thinkers, lifelong learners and informed participants in local and world affairs, conscious of the shared humanity that binds all people together while respecting the variety of cultures and attitudes that makes for the richness of life' (IBO, 1996).

The concept of 'world citizenship' is fundamental to international education. It comprises three levels. First the utilitarian level of assimilating knowledge about content, then the pedagogical level of understanding and applying the content to events through critical analysis. Thus far students could be 'informed participants in local and world affairs', but they would not have attained the third level of having attitudes that lead to positive action for a better world. Hayden (2001) cautions us that the 'pragmatic dimension may be developed without the ideological dimension necessarily being nurtured'. Only when students are 'compassionate thinkers', 'conscious of the shared humanity that binds people together' and 'respecting the variety of cultures and attitudes that makes for the richness of life', will the possibility of establishing an ideology in international education exist. And this, the most important objective, can only be measured through the actions of individuals during their lifetime.

References

Boeke, K (1948) Letter to the Assistant Director General for UNESCO, 5 August, UNESCO archives, Paris

Collège Cévénol (1946) *Handbook*, November, Chambon-sur-Lignon, France

Conference of Principals of International Schools and Schools Specially Interested in Developing International Understanding (1951) Report of the Second Meeting, UNESCO archives, Paris

Course for Teachers Interested in International Education (1950) Final Report: Section I, International School of Geneva, 23 July–19 August, UNESCO archives, Paris

Department for Education and Employment (2000) *Developing a Global Dimension in the School Curriculum*, DfEE, London

Ficheux, R *et al* (1949) Some Suggestions on the Teaching of Geography, *Towards World Understanding series, no 7*, UNESCO, Paris

First Conference of Teachers of Social Studies in International Schools: Report (1962) International School of Geneva, 26 August–1 September

Fox, E (2001) The Emergence of the International Baccalaureate as an Impetus for Curriculum Reform, in *International Education: Principles and practice*, eds M C Hayden and J J Thompson, Kogan Page, London

Hayden, M (2001) International Education and the IB Programmes, paper presented to a meeting of the IBO Academic Advisory Committee, April: Geneva

Hill, C (1953) Suggestions on the Teaching of History, *Towards World Understanding series, no 9*, UNESCO, Paris

Hill, I (2000) Internationally Minded Schools, *International Schools Journal* , **XX** (1), pp 24–37

International Baccalaureate Organization (IBO) (1996) *Mission Statement*, IBO, Geneva

IBO (1999) *Theory of Knowledge Guide*, IBO, Geneva

IBO (2002) [Online] http://www.ibo.org

International Schools Association (ISA) (1957) *Sixth Assembly Minutes*, IB Organization archives, Geneva

ISA (1962) *Eleventh Assembly Minutes*, IB Organization archives, Geneva

Knight, M and Leach, R (1964) International secondary schools in *Education and International Life*, eds G Bereday and J Lauwerys, Evans Brothers, London

Leach, R (1969) *International Schools and their Role in the Field of International Education*, Pergamon Press, New York

Malinowski, H and Zorn, V (1973) *The United Nations International School: Its history and development*, United Nations International School, New York

Maurette, M-T (1948) Techniques d'éducation pour la paix: existent-ils? (Réponse à une enquête de l'UNESCO), Monograph. International School of Geneva, Geneva

Mayer, M (1968) *Diploma: International schools and university entrance*, Twentieth Century Fund, New York

Mowat, J (1968) Towards an international university entrance examination, *Aberdeen University Review*, **42**, pp 280–87

Muller, R (1986) *World Core Curriculum Manual*, Robert Muller School: Arlington, Texas

Oxfam (1997) *A Curriculum for Global Citizenship*, Oxfam, Oxford

Peterson, A D C (1968) Dainton and the International Baccalaureate, *Universities Quarterly*, **22**, pp 274–80

Peterson, A D C (1987) *Schools Across Frontiers: The story of the International Baccalaureate and the United World Colleges*, Open Court, La Salle, Illinois

UNESCO (1974) *Recommendation on Education for International Understanding*, UNESCO General Conference, Paris

Chapter 3

International education: a commitment to universal values

Charles A Gellar

Introduction

Surprisingly perhaps, the concept of an international education has had a long history. Certainly, prior to World War II, the realization of what war between nation states can bring in human misery and degradation was a major incentive in the desire of many liberal-thinking people to promote the concept of internationalism as a counter-balance to nationalism. As an essential element in pursuing and maintaining world peace, the education of the young, which focused on how nations and peoples can work in harmony to achieve international cooperation and understanding, became an important means by which to achieve this balance. At the forefront of this endeavour, the International School of Geneva was formed in 1924 with these aims in mind. As Paul Mantoux, the Director of the Political Section of the League of Nations succinctly put it in 1931: 'Brutal events have supplied evidence of a truth that had been slowly gaining ground, namely, the interdependence of nations and the need for establishing in the world an order and harmony hitherto lacking. It was not owing to some impulse of dreamy love for mankind in the abstract but rather for the sake of their own countries that the promoters of international education set to work'.

After World War II, many expressed similar views, for instance: 'The development of international-mindedness does not mean the abandonment of national-mindedness; if it means anything it demands an informed consciousness of the place of one's nation in a world society and the contributions it can make to a world society whose survival depends on the maintenance of peace and relief from the fear of war' (Kandel, 1952).

In the 1950s and 1960s, so-called international schools sprang up all over the world to educate the increasing number of children of the burgeoning internationally mobile diplomatic and business communities. But, to use a phrase of Michael Matthews (1989a and 1989b), such schools were much more 'market-driven' than 'ideology-driven', in the way that those of the earlier period had been.

The meaning of 'international'

Much has been debated and written about the nature of schools calling themselves international and whether the term 'international' has any meaning at all (Hayden and Thompson, 2000). Edna Murphy in a recent editorial for the *International Schools Journal* has perhaps had the much-needed last word on this particular approach (2000). Fortunately Ian Hill (2000), Deputy Director-General of the International Baccalaureate Organization (IBO), has pulled the proverbial rabbit out of the hat by suggesting that a more useful approach is to discriminate between those schools that are 'internationally-minded' and those, regardless of how they may designate themselves, that are not.

But what distinguishes an internationally-minded school from all others? In the author's opinion, there are two essential distinctions, one educational and the other ethical. Firstly, its curriculum emphasizes studies in world history and literature, world cultures, stressing the interdependence of nations and peoples, and de-emphasizing the study of such topics from the perspective of only one country or of a select region and secondly, its ethical aim is actively to espouse and uphold certain 'universal' values and to make them an integral part of the life of the school, its community and, particularly, the children in its care.

The curriculum in and of itself is obviously an essential component, and, as such, over the past half-century has been given the time and attention it fully deserves. Schools that have embraced the International Baccalaureate (IB) Diploma Programme, the IB Middle Years Programme (MYP), or IB Primary Years Programme (PYP), have certainly met the first requirement. Recipients of the IB Diploma have become preferred, even sought-after, candidates for admission to virtually all universities and colleges of higher education worldwide, particularly by some of the most elite institutions in the Western world. The original aim of the IBO to produce a universally accepted curriculum for entrance to higher education has been an unqualified success.

Movement towards universal values

But can university entrance be any longer the *sine qua non* in IB thinking? With the taking on of the PYP and MYP for children aged 3 to 16, an entirely new dimension has been opened up for the IBO. These new programmes are designed to instil in pupils the need to question and search for answers to important issues and topics, and not to concentrate on learning accepted answers. By this means, the somewhat vexing dimension of 'meaning' comes in. To know the answer is not the same thing as 'does it have any meaning in my life?'. Pure knowledge of a subject is not enough; it must be shown to be 'useful' to that person too: 'useful' in the sense put forward by Whitehead when he wrote (1929): 'If education is not useful, what is it? Is it a talent to be hidden away in a napkin? Of course it should be useful, whatever your aim in life. It is useful because understanding is useful... Understanding in the sense of "To understand all is to forgive all"'.

It appears that the philosophical imperative of 'usefulness' occasioned by the incorporation of the MYP and PYP will make it necessary for the IBO to take a fresh look at curricula research and reform, particularly at IB Diploma level.

The fact that the world is small, fragile, and its inhabitants increasingly dependent on one another, has become obvious to all. This realization has also made it imperative that international educators devote much more attention and resources to developing new curricula; courses that focus on issues and problems that are trans-national and trans-cultural, and that also examine and reflect upon the ways of thinking of those – the majority of humankind – brought up in the non-Western world of thought and experience. In the past, a number of attempts have been made. At an important meeting of heads of IB schools in Princeton, New Jersey in 1980 the then Director-General of the IBO, Alec Peterson, presented his arguments for making the Theory of Knowledge (TOK) course the linchpin of the entire IB Diploma curriculum. The author remembers questioning him on the fact that the title of the course implied a Western way of looking at knowledge, and that there was a need to bring in Eastern ways of thinking about the subject. Much to the author's chagrin, the IB examiner in philosophy interrupted the discussion to announce boldly and authoritatively that Eastern philosophy was not philosophy at all and had no place in the TOK course! 'Finita la commedia'. This bias continues.

Some years ago, a course of studies was proposed by the same Alec Peterson to be called 'The Culture of Cities'. The idea was that students from one school would study the history, economics and cultural life of their own city and then compare and contrast that with what had been discovered by students of schools in other cities. IB schools in New York City, Copenhagen and Tehran were approached to pilot the scheme. In those pre-Internet days, student study trips to each of the cities in the pilot project were to be arranged. But even then a world crisis intervened (the fall of the Shah of Iran). In this age of easy electronic access and e-communality, courses of this kind involving schools in disparate parts of the world would be extremely rewarding to the participants and also be financially viable for many schools.

Another curricular proposal, which enjoyed much enthusiastic approval among educators at the time, was the Peace and Conflict Studies course, developed at Atlantic College and, sadly, never adopted by the IB Organization more widely. It has needed resurrection, and the programme developed by the International Schools Association (ISA)'s International Education System Pilot Project (IESPP) attempted to do just that by making 'Education for Peace' the cornerstone of international education in the schools that have been chosen to enter the project. Phil Thomas has lucidly and impressively presented the case for this ground-breaking endeavour in a series of articles (Thomas 1996, 1998).

But what of the second, the ethical dimension? It is the author's contention that the ultimate justification for espousing an international education for any and all rests on the universal values such an education engenders in its pupils. The history of the 20th century, and now the 21st with the recent tragic events in the United States and Afghanistan and, sadly, the anticipation of more misfortunes to come, have made many aware that what we truly value is far more important than the things we possess or have wished to possess. We in the West have been wallowing in the world of 'price' for far too long. It seems that the benefits of globalization are not taken to mean the encouraging of understanding, empathy, and the sharing of goods and ideas with other parts of the world, but the establishment of 'price' as the only criterion by which everything in the world is to be valued. The culture of perpetual economic growth needs to be questioned. Just where do the internationally-minded stand on these issues?

Educators and teachers of the present and of the past half-century, particularly in secular Anglo-American schools, have had a reluctance, even an aversion, to expressing explicitly belief in any values that could be interpreted as moral. This is despite the fact that schools must and do operate on the implicit assumption that truth, fairness and trust are fundamental to their success. It could be argued that the concept of universal values has been an anathema in some academic and even more polite circles for many years. The moral dilemmas presented in 20th century existentialist thought have had little impact on contemporary Anglo-American positivist and empiricist philosophical thinking.

But whether there is a philosophical justification for the belief that there are specific universal values that all human beings would adhere to, this issue has become a matter not of evidence, but of the survival of humankind. We may differ as to what might be labelled as universal, but certainly world peace, justice and fairness, and compassion for all human beings would be high on anyone's list. Some would argue that compassion is enough. The Dalai Lama in his recent book, *Ancient Wisdom, Modern World: Ethics for the New Millennium* (1999), sees that in all the world's major religions, each gives the development of compassion a key role. In his words, ethically wholesome actions arise naturally in the context of compassion. When we act out of concern for others, the peace this creates in our own hearts brings peace to everyone with whom we associate. The Dalai Lama emphasizes that all human beings desire to be happy and that happiness is characterized by peace. He proposes a spiritual revolution, based not on a universal religious principle, but on the premise that ethical conduct consists of not harming others. But how is one to teach such concepts?

The importance of teaching from a historical perspective has not been given the attention that it deserves, particularly in the teaching of science and mathematics where the human dimension has all but been excluded. Yet the need for integrity, objectivity, even courage, has been crucial in the pursuit of truth and the search for order, and teaching from a historical perspective would make this manifest. As an example of the importance of such concepts, what of the idea of 'beauty'? This is a concept that has played a very long and fruitful role in science and mathematics, yet for the uninitiated it seems 'curious' to say the least. Whitehead (1933), the outstanding mathematician that he was, even went so far as to say that in the contemplation of the beautiful: 'youth is peculiarly liable to the vision of that Peace [sic] which is the harmony of the soul's activities with ideal aims that lie beyond any personal satisfaction'.

Given this endorsement, there is a strong case for giving increased attention to the teaching of the arts, music and drama. All relate powerfully to the human condition and to the development of an ethical perspective. Most of the human qualities we most admire are best brought out in children by their involvement in such activities. In the arts, children can bear witness to what is best and what is worst in humankind, and confront the destructiveness of evil without enduring the almost unspeakable agony of its reality. To quote Whitehead again

(1933): 'Art heightens the sense of humanity... Art is civilization. For civilization is nothing other than the unremitting aim at the major perfections of harmony'.

Conclusion

International schools, even those offering an IB programme, can and do get by without the need to wrestle with or even debate the need for universal values, but internationally-minded schools cannot. It is hoped that those who are internationally-minded will work to insure that a clear and unambiguous statement of universal values is made an essential part of the ethos of international education; that a commitment to justice, peace, and compassion for all be openly espoused and made central in their thought and conduct.

References

Dalai Lama (1999) *Ancient Wisdom, Modern World: Ethics for the new millennium*, Riverhead Books, New York

Hayden, M C and Thompson, J J (2000) Quality in Diversity, in *International Schools and International Education: Improving teaching, management and quality*, eds M C Hayden and J J Thompson, Kogan Page, London

Hill, I (2000) Internationally-minded schools, *International Schools Journal*, **XX** (1), pp 24–37

Kandel, I L (1952) Education, national and international, *The Education Forum*, **16**, pp 397–407

Mantoux, P (1931) Foreword, in *International Understanding: Agencies educating for a new world*, ed J E Harley, Stanford University Press, Stanford, California

Matthews, M (1989a) The scale of international education, *International Schools Journal*, **17**, pp 7–17

Matthews, M (1989b) The uniqueness of international education, *International Schools Journal*, **18**, pp 24–34

Murphy, E (2000) Questions for the new millennium, *International Schools Journal*, **XIX** (2), pp 5–10

Thomas, P (1996) Preparing students for a better world: an International Education System, *International Schools Journal*, **XVI** (1), pp 24–29

Thomas, P (1998) Education for Peace, in *International Education: Principles and practice*, eds M C Hayden and J J Thompson, Kogan Page, London

Whitehead, A N (1929) *The Aims of Education and Other Essays*, Macmillan, New York

Whitehead, A N (1933) *Adventures of Ideas*, Cambridge University Press, Cambridge

Part B

CURRICULUM

Chapter 4

Defining 'international' in an international curriculum

Martin Skelton

Introduction

Any curriculum, new or old, sits in a particular context. Over time, the context changes and the curriculum has to adapt or increasingly become a museum piece. This chapter will discuss some of the contextual issues surrounding the development of an international curriculum.

The definition of curriculum

Attempting to find an agreed definition of 'curriculum' is not quite as hard as finding an agreed definition of an 'international school' (see below) but it is certainly difficult. Definitions of curriculum range from a series of statements about what must be learned (Ross, 2000) to a complex culture that includes the structure of knowledge, the specific content, the balance between subjects, the organization of the school day, the resources to be used, the teaching methods and the expectations of pupils and staff (Catling, 2001). Issues about the planned, delivered or received curriculum add further to the mix. Curriculum makers are largely responsible for the planned curriculum and partly responsible, by definition, for the delivered and received curricula. But how much detail should be contained in a planned curriculum is an issue that has to be decided by the curriculum maker.

The definition of an international school

Following Hayden and Thompson's lead (1995), almost everyone has stopped trying to define an 'international school'. There simply is not the space here to run the argument at length but anyone who works with international schools will know that 'The International School of X' may be a very, very different place from 'The International School of Y'. By 2000, Hayden and Thompson were advising that we might be better 'not... developing a network of international schools *per se*, but rather... developing a network of schools... which aim to promote international education' (Hayden and Thompson, 2000). Which, of course, prompts the question, 'What is international education?'.

In trying to answer that question it is common to speak of 'international-mindedness', which appears to mean something akin to the UNESCO declaration of 1996 (UNESCO, 1996). This declaration identifies issues such as a sense of universal values, valuing freedom, intercultural understanding, non-violent conflict resolution and so on. While such a definition is both worthwhile and helpful, it may be taking one step too far to assume that it is agreed by all of the stakeholders in international education.

The organization and working practices of international schools

Think about these few quoted statements:

> Relocated children need about eight months to adapt to their school. (Akram, 1995)

> All of my previous posts have involved moving into a post where there has been a lack of continuity amongst the staff. (in Hardman, 2001)

> There is less security of tenure for a headteacher in an international school than in most national schools: being fired is a frequent occurrence. (Blandford and Shaw, 2001)

> Research suggests two characteristics common to many effective schools. A focus on added-value student learning and an overarching consistency which contributes to a clear definition of 'the way we do things around here'. (Deal and Kennedy, 1983)

> Change takes time. (Fullan, 2001, and almost every writer on change)

Many children stay in international schools for no longer than two to three years at a time as their parents move from position to position around the world. Turbulence in student numbers is higher in international schools than in other schools. What these statements suggest is that individual schools trying to create their own curriculum might encounter some problems. There is no doubt that it can be done, as some outstanding international schools, teachers and principals have shown. But the way in which most international schools work means that it is difficult to construct a curriculum that delivers both a consistent focus on student outcomes (internationally-minded or otherwise) and help to teachers when the turnover of students, teachers, principals, board members and parents is as high as it is. Over the considerable period of time it takes to develop a curriculum in such schools, how can we be sure that the process both retains a sense of coordination and remains a keeper of the flame?

The definition of an 'international' curriculum

The inevitable lack of clarity about the definitions of 'curriculum', 'international school' and 'international education' helps to explain why the creation of an international curriculum has to be a work in progress. Somewhere in the web of interconnecting uncertainties, which surround the definitions of these three terms, sit a number of nodal points around which an 'international curriculum' can also be defined.

In the *International Schools Journal* of November 2000, Ian Hill argues that such a curriculum will:

- contain course content that provides an international perspective;
- recognize that the world is increasingly interdependent;
- provide activities that bring students into contact with people of other cultures;
- create a context for world peace by providing opportunities for many cultures to learn together in mutual understanding and respect.

But this is just one suggestion. There are a number of these nodal points, and not simply one. So there are likely to be a number of international curricula. The task of international curriculum creators, therefore, is not ever-increasingly to refine our work so that it gets closer and closer to an ideal model. It is to construct something that responds to a number of the contextual elements in international education and to try to engage in a process of continual improvement.

Let me add one further layer of complexity here. Any definition of an international curriculum implicitly suggests that such a curriculum is significantly different from a national curriculum. Is this so? It can be argued that an international curriculum shares (or should share) many of the aims, targets and procedures of national curricula. Perhaps it might be better to think of an 'internationally-minded' curriculum than of an 'international' one.

Recent brain-based evidence about learning

The last 15 years have seen an explosion of neurological research and a complementary explosion of advice to teachers on how to use the research to impact positively on children's learning in the classroom. The particular work of neurological researchers such as Howard Gardner (1993 and 2001), Michael Gazzaniga (2000) and others, together with the popularization of that work by authors such as Eric Jensen (1998) and many, many others, has opened up the 'black box' of the brain to far more than an input–output model of learning.

Much of that research and advice needs to be treated with caution by teachers in classrooms, partly because the evidence base from the neurological researchers is not yet as strong as it needs to be in some important areas, and partly because there has been the usual rush to jump onto a publishing or authorial bandwagon with some half-thought-out ideas. This is a shame, because some of the evidence and the conclusions that are being drawn from this research are very helpful to teachers. Some of the evidence validates teaching and learning strategies that have been used for some time; other evidence guides us into new understandings of what might need to happen in classrooms for effective learning to take place. Any curriculum writers hoping to help teachers to improve student learning must face up to the dual task of sorting out the neurological wheat from the chaff and then incorporating it into the curricula they produce.

The future

It is often said that the good news is that many schools are currently doing a very successful job of educating their children, while the bad news is that they are successful in educating those children to take part in a world of the 1950s and 1960s rather than that of the new millennium. This is an easy, if sometimes true, jibe. But then it is easy to see why educators look backwards, when the alternative is to look forward. It is much easier to be proved wrong trying to predict the future. For those involved in designing and creating internationally-minded curricula for primary and elementary aged children, the problem is even greater than for those designing late secondary or tertiary curricula. Most elementary children are unlikely to reach full working capacity for perhaps 20 to 30 years. How can we know what the world will be by then?

The response is that we cannot, but we must try. A curriculum that claims to help children develop the range of knowledge, skills and understandings appropriate for their future lives cannot fall back on the past entirely. The cutting edge of curriculum leadership as opposed to curriculum management is as sharp here as it is anywhere.

Three aspects of the future seem to receive common assent. First, the muscle economy is being replaced by the knowledge economy. As technology increases, the number of children likely to earn a living by using their muscular energy will continually decrease. Given the socio-economic pool that serves many international schools, this is likely to be even more so for the children who experience their education in this context. Second, the lifelong job is likely to be replaced by the portfolio of jobs. This might mean that a child currently in school will have four or five jobs over the length of their career; it might mean that at any one time they will have two or three part-time jobs. Whatever the portfolio looks like, such a future requires in all children a revised range of personal skills and attitudes that may have been in the possession of only a few in the past.

Third, the world is becoming more global. There are any number of examples of this, but perhaps the warning from a Japanese company to the British government that it will move its factory out of the United Kingdom unless the United Kingdom joins the European currency (*The Independent*, 2000) is one of the most potent. Or shall we look at the astonishing worldwide impact of the events of 11 September 2001? Or the fact that I am writing this part of the chapter in Saudi Arabia just one hour after having a cup of Starbucks coffee in the shopping mall where Saudi women were carrying home bags from fashion stores found around the world?

Increasing globalization is perhaps the single most important reason why we need to develop internationally-minded curricula. In such a world it is already essential to understand, relate to and coexist with other cultures whilst at the same time remaining a part of one's own. It will be even more important in the future.

Ascertaining the 'international' in all of this

To try to do this I am going to use the work of Ken Wilber (2000) as a framework. Wilber is a difficult man to pin down: whether as philosopher or psychologist he does not fit neatly into any single box. What does make him appealing is that he is one of the leading contemporary writers about *integral theory*. Wilber, and others like him, is working from a position where he attempts to see not what divides current and historical movements and ideas but what they have in common. I am going to use four of his ideas. In doing so, I am hoping that they will provide direction to the aim behind the heading of this chapter; one that, I hope, supports the view that internationalism is 'an integrating, rather than a differentiating, relationship' (Al Farra, 2000).

Idea 1

'... if we remain merely at the stage of celebrating diversity, we ultimately are promoting fragmentation, alienation, separation and despair. You go your way, I go my way, we both fly apart – which is often what has happened under the reign of the pluralistic relativists... It is not enough to recognize the many ways in which we are different; we need to go further and start recognizing the many ways in which we are also similar' (Wilber, 2000).

Here, it seems to me, is an argument that may both support and develop the commonly held legitimacy of 'independence' and 'interdependence'. The concepts of 'independence' and 'interdependence' feature in much current writing about international curricula, including that of Hill, quoted earlier. Both are amongst the guiding principles behind the International Primary Curriculum (IPC) with which I have been involved for the past three-and-a-half years. In the IPC we have set out with the aim of helping children to discover their own national and cultural identity, and to learn to live with those whose national and cultural identities are different.

If we are not careful, though, this apparently liberal and progressive approach will still result in division rather than union. The 'trick' in delivering a curriculum based on this dualistic approach is the development of tolerance, empathy and mutual understanding. We are trying to encourage the development of a view that says 'I am different and I have a right to be. You are different from me with the same rights, but we can live together'. What is wrong with that? It is certainly better than much that we have now. That may be true, but if we do not actually enable tolerance, empathy and mutual understanding to be developed, the net result will still be an awareness of differences rather than of similarity. Wilber challenges us to go further than this. We may well be more similar than we are different. Dylan Evans (2001), for example, quotes Paul Ekman's ground-breaking work that shows that the six basic emotions of joy, distress, anger, fear, surprise and disgust exist in all cultures.

I believe that it is important for us to encourage notions of 'independence' and 'interdependence'. But I am also coming to believe that these concepts are only likely to have the real power for change many of us invest in them if they are preceded by the knowledge and understanding that we are also very similar.

For the 'real school' international curriculum this certainly means that the 'international day', during which we celebrate our magnificent national dress or share our national cuisine, is not enough. Taking pride in providing a context in which children and students of different cultures and nationalities can coexist alongside each other may be limiting our vision rather than extending it. And it is easy to be placated by the existence of apparent interdependence without looking too closely at what is happening underneath. Perhaps the 'exit outcomes' we hope for should be bolder than this. Diversity certainly exists and we need to celebrate it. But similarities exist, too, and we need to make sure our knowledge and understanding of them coexists against concepts that stress an essential separation rather than a coming together.

Idea 2

'A "holon" is a whole that is a part of other wholes. For example, a whole atom is part of a whole molecule; a whole molecule is part of a whole cell; a whole cell is part of a whole organism. Or again, a whole letter is part of a whole word, which is part of a whole sentence, which is part of a whole paragraph and so on. Reality is composed of neither wholes nor parts, but of whole/parts, or holons' (Wilber, 2000).

Learning goals are important to any curriculum. They define what it is that the curriculum is expecting children and students to achieve at different ages and stages of their school career. They exhibit the purposefulness of the planned and delivered curriculum and express the school's intention towards the received curriculum. As current debates within the standards movement of the United States show, defining learning goals and standards is not an easy task. As Gandal and Vranek (2001) have pointed out: 'If the standards are ambiguous, they also offer no assurance that every student is learning challenging material. Too often, the standards we have reviewed tend to be imprecise and all-encompassing'.

If we can agree on what an 'international' element of the curriculum might be, and I am suggesting 'similarity, independence and interdependence', then we also need to agree that these desirable outcomes are not going to be achieved by osmosis. It is not enough to be well-intentioned. These 'international' elements of the curriculum need explicit learning outcomes, too. One useful way of defining learning goals clearly is to focus on 'knowledge', 'skills' and 'understanding'. This is not an unusual approach. But what frequently seems to be happening is that these separate kinds of learning goals are treated hierarchically. 'Learning for understanding' is clearly an important aim for the whole curriculum but it does not mean that understanding is somehow more important than knowledge. Wilber's notion of holons, or a 'holarchy' rather than a 'hierarchy', is helpful here, as shown in Figure 4.1.

Learning, and the application of that learning, is always a combination of knowledge, skills and understanding. Understanding emerges out of the combination of knowledge, plus skills, plus practice. What Guy Claxton (1998) identifies as 'slow thinking', out of which understanding eventually emerges, is actually the process through which the combination of knowledge, skills and practice develops, over time, a deepening understanding of key concepts, which then helps to further develop practice.

But knowledge, skills and understanding are not hierarchical; they are holarchical. One is not better than the others. As we move from knowledge to skills to understanding each *transcends but includes* the others. Understanding is not possible without continual reference to knowledge, skills and application. To develop understanding does not mean to leave knowledge and skills behind. It means to include them appropriately. Imagine trying to 'understand' the culture of a different country

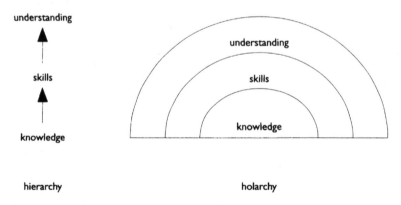

Figure 4.1 Relationship between holarchy and hierarchy

without any knowledge about the country or the ability to apply, compare and contrast that knowledge with other equally relevant knowledge. Just recently, I was walking around a historic monument, trying to 'make sense' of what I was experiencing. I was having some difficulty until by a stroke of luck I managed to join up with the fringes of a guided tour. What helped me begin to make sense of the monument was the information, the factual knowledge, the tour guide was providing about a period of which I knew relatively little. Only when the knowledge became part of my mental map was I able to begin to say to myself 'So that's why…'.

Becoming internationally-minded is, I believe, no different. Curriculum designers interested in defining the international aspects of the curriculum need to do so in ways that reflect the knowledge, skills and understanding involved in similarity, independence and interdependence at different ages and stages of a child's or student's school career. What curriculum writers must not do is to make assumptions that these ideas are only abstract and conceptual or that only abstract and conceptual ideas matter. Curriculum designers are right to focus on 'teaching for understanding' but things start to go wrong when teachers putting such methodologies into practice begin to devalue the knowledge component. Within each understanding is nested both knowledge and skills.

Idea 3

This third idea is more complex and I risk doing it a disservice. It sits at the centre of much of Wilber's work over the past 20 years, during which he has spent time analysing many of the leading cross-cultural historical and contemporary movements, philosophies and trends. What he has set out to do, as you would expect of an integralist, is to see whether these movements and philosophies share anything with each other. Not, as he puts it, on the level of fine detail – partly because it would be an impossible task to look at the fine detail of each of these many groups of ideas, and partly because at a finely detailed level they are almost certain to be different. His work has been concerned with looking at the 'orienting generalizations' that underpin these movements. To put it very simply, we all know that composers of symphonic music have their own individual signature but we also know that all symphonic music shares some 'orienting generalizations'. Without them, we could not begin to talk of some music being symphonic and other music not.

There are a number of ways in which Wilber has identified such generalizations. First, he distinguishes between 'left-hand' and 'right-hand' paths. Left-hand paths are 'interpretive, hermeneutic and about consciousness'. Right-hand paths are 'monological, empirical and about form'. He also distinguishes between the 'individual' and the 'collective', both of which can apply to each of the paths.

With so little space to explore this idea it is better to reproduce one of Wilber's own diagrams in order to conceptualize this order more easily. By looking at each of the writers and thinkers included in each quadrant (see Figure 4.2) it is relatively easy to form an idea of what he is trying to say.

Wilber then argues that none of these quadrants is independent of the others. To stay within one quadrant is to miss the full scope of what is possible and to deny the opportunity to reach what is possible. He quotes research by iSchaik Development Associates, which acts as consultant to UNICEF amongst others. In identifying a major reason for some of the past failures of UNICEF and the UN, iSchaik points out that 'UNICEF's activities have largely operated on the Upper and Lower Right-hand quadrants, that is the quadrants that are objective and exterior... and to a large extent ignored the interior and cultural quadrants'.

Of course, such a charge cannot be set only against organizations such as UNICEF. Nor is the criticism applicable to those who seek to bring

	left-hand paths	right-hand paths
	• interpretive • hermeneutic • consciousness	• monological • empirical, positivistic • form
individual	Freud C G Jung Piaget Aurobindo Plotinus Gautama Buddha	B F Skinner John Watson John Locke empiricism behaviorism physics, biology, neurology, etc
	I	it
	we	its
collective	Thomas Kuhn Wilhelm Dilthey Jean Gebser Max Weber Hans-Georg Gadamer	systems theory Talcott Parsons Auguste Comte Karl Marx Gerhard Lenski ecological web of life

Taken from *A Theory of Everything* by Ken Wilber. © 2000 Ken Wilber. Reprinted by arrangement with Shambhala Publications Inc., Boston, www.shambhala.com

Figure 4.2 Some representative theorists in each quadrant

about change from only the objective and the exterior. Similar criticisms can be levelled at those who aim to bring about change from the point of view of only the interior and the cultural. There are many examples of this in practice in education. At the macro level the initial introduction of the National Curriculum in England and Wales was undoubtedly objective and exterior. Even now, the increasing reliance on governmentally set targets for local authorities and then for schools in that context is further evidence that this is still the dominant mindset. There is a little evidence of a realization that making this count in the hearts and minds of individual teachers, the cultural communities of schools and the teaching profession, is also important but it is still unclear how much influence this view will have in practice.

It is not only at the governmental level that this happens. At the school level, there is plenty of evidence of both sides of the quadrant being played inappropriately. Boards of international schools are often criticized for trying to impose change through *diktat* and structural imposition. Heads can do likewise. It is one of the typifications of a 'masculine' rather than 'feminine' management style. But headteachers and teachers can also make the mistake of assuming that a focus on the left-hand quadrants of the interior and the cultural is enough. This 'Mom, Pop and Apple Pie' view of the curriculum says that as long as we all believe something to be true and keep reaffirming those beliefs to each other, then something good is bound to happen. In actuality, of course, such a view is as likely to be effective as plaintively asking the warring peoples of our nations 'But why can't you just get on?'.

If we believe that an 'internationally-minded' curriculum is important then we need to reject such simple and single-minded views and look at the development of such a curriculum from a four-quadrant point perspective. Yes, it is important that individual teachers should be given experiences through staff development that helps to encourage a personally held view that an international mindset is worthwhile. It is an important personal quality to look for when selecting candidates. It is equally important that the community of the school should develop such a mindset, too. We need to look at ways in which the culture of the school, the collective, is also internationally-minded. The international community needs to proclaim powerfully the beliefs that it holds. After all, it is one of the main purposes of the proposed 'Alliance for International Education' (Hayden and Thompson, 2000) that has been the major stimulus for this book.

But it is also important that we realize that changing the hearts of the individuals and groups with whom we work is not enough. Helping children to develop international mindsets of their own requires the structural components that are a hallmark of the exterior and the objective. The international elements of a curriculum need to be clearly articulated at a whole school level; they need to be assessed or judged, whilst accepting that much of the appropriate evidence will be soft rather than hard. They need 'an independent measure of educational quality' (Lowe, 2000). They need to be publicly accountable and capable of defence against external challenge. School structures, that support an 'internationally-minded' curriculum need to be as much systemic as they need to be emotional. Such right-hand processes, when combined with left-hand approaches, help the curriculum to become 'a process of guiding organizational energy rather than attempting to control and dominate' (Welton, 2001).

The 'international' elements of a curriculum can no more survive without a whole-quadrant approach than can anything else in the planned and delivered curriculum. We need to do everything we can to capture the hearts of teachers, students, parents, board members and others. We also need to do everything we can to make sure that such a worthwhile element of the curriculum is formally structured and formally accountable.

Idea 4

Wilber develops his four-quadrant view further. In looking at each quadrant, Wilber identifies a number of stages of development within each. These stages also form a 'holarchy' rather than a hierarchy. (Another way in which Wilber defines 'holarchy' is that it is a 'growth hierarchy'; successive stages are more developed than preceding ones but one stage is not 'better' than another; it transcends and includes what has gone before it.)

Each level of development in one quadrant also has its correlate level of development in the other quadrant. This is not necessarily a good thing. As Wilber says: '... this does not mean that development is nothing but sweetness and light, a series of wonderful promotions on a linear ladder of progress. For each stage of development brings not only new capacities but the possibility of disaster; not just novel potentials but novel pathologies; new strengths, new diseases'.

The aftermath of 11 September 2001 provides us with just one example of such potential disasters. Many in the world sit and hope that the development of the exterior and objective (in the form of weapons of mass destruction) will be paralleled by an equal development in individual and collective morality. When one exceeds the other, the imbalance is likely to be disastrous as we have already seen in the past.

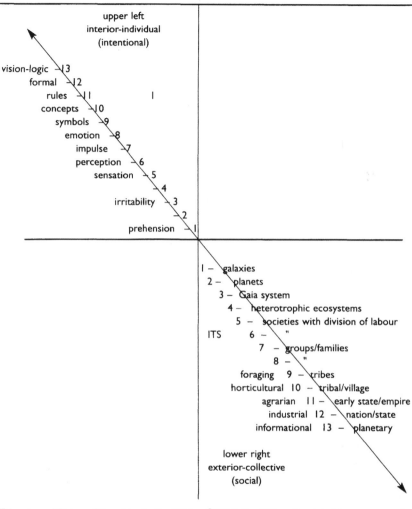

upper left
interior-individual
(intentional)

vision-logic 13
formal 12
rules 11
concepts 10
symbols 9
emotion 8
impulse 7
perception 6
sensation 5
4
irritability 3
2
prehension 1

1 — galaxies
2 — planets
3 — Gaia system
4 — heterotrophic ecosystems
5 — societies with division of labour
ITS 6 — "
7 — groups/families
8 — "
foraging 9 — tribes
horticultural 10 — tribal/village
agrarian 11 — early state/empire
industrial 12 — nation/state
informational 13 — planetary

lower right
exterior-collective
(social)

Taken from *A Theory of Everything* by Ken Wilber. © 2000 Ken Wilber. Reprinted by arrangement with Shambhala Publications Inc., Boston, www.shambhala.com

Figure 4.3   Two of the four quadrants

To give a brief flavour of this, Figure 4.3 shows the developmental holarchy of two of Wilber's four quadrants: the interior-individual and the exterior-collective.

The developmental changes in these two quadrants give us further insight into what an 'international' curriculum might be. The exterior-collective quadrant suggests that an understanding of 'nation/state' is a necessary part of the development of an international perspective. Curriculum writers or deliverers cannot just swoop on 'international' understanding and assume that focusing on it at length with apparently well-thought-out and structured activities is going do to anything at all. 'International' is, after all, 'inter' and 'national'. An international curriculum is one that makes it clear that a necessary part of the development towards 'international-mindedness' is an equally important, although not overwhelming, awareness and understanding of 'nationhood'. We cannot ignore the concept of nationhood or leave it behind if we also want to develop international-mindedness. 'International-mindedness' transcends but includes national-mindedness.

Equally, the developmental changes in the interior-individual quadrant tell us that children need to move through certain stages of individual development before they are ready to take on the complex ideas that reside within international-mindedness. The correlate is at least those of 'symbols', 'emotions' and 'rules'. In other words, even if we understand that nationhood is an integral part of international-mindedness, trying to do this at the wrong stage of a child's development would be a waste of time.

This is important for international curriculum writers. There is no point beginning to talk of 'international-mindedness' to my two-year-old granddaughter, and we need to avoid falling into the trap of believing that taking a child of that age to lots of foreign countries will somehow enable the development of such thinking. So the important issue is to define at which particular stage of a child's development such ideas can be introduced and what are the appropriate knowledge, skills and experiences that will give the development of 'international-mindedness' a chance.

Elementary, primary or early years curriculum writers have a particular job on their hands here. Much of the discussion of 'international-mindedness' seems to me to have been quite understandably hijacked by ideas and approaches that are appropriate to school-leavers rather than school beginners. Both left-hand and right-hand quadrants have supported this successful hijacking. I am only one of the many people who feels left-hand personal inspiration when I talk with some of the mature students about to exit formal schooling for the last time; and I am also one of many people who strongly supports the existence of a structured curriculum based on the IB Diploma Programme. This does not mean, however, that we can transport the concepts, methodologies and learning outcomes oriented towards 18-year-olds to a class of 6- to 12-year olds. What one needs is not necessarily needed by the other.

Conclusion

So what is 'international' about an international curriculum? First, it is an approach that sets out to develop understandings of our similarities, in addition to an acceptance of our differences and an ability to live together within those differences. Second, it is an approach that accepts the need to define the knowledge, skills and understandings that lead to an international mindset as rigorously as it accepts the need to define the learning outcomes for individual curriculum subjects. In doing so, it is an approach that is prepared to put as much energy into focusing on the detail of knowledge and skills as it does on enjoying the pleasure of eventual understanding. Third, it is an approach that is as much about developing a formal curriculum and supportive systemic curriculum and management structures as it is about creating an emotional and cultural awareness and attachment to international-mindedness. Fourth, it is an approach that accepts that the development of the knowledge, skills and understandings contained within the idea of 'international-mindedness' is necessarily different for children and students of different ages and at different stages of development.

Such a view of an 'international' curriculum also enables a positive response to the context set out at the beginning of the chapter. It enables schools and others to develop a response to the need for both a planned and delivered curriculum; it responds to the confusion of definitions about 'international schools' by supporting international-mindedness but extending the parameters to include 'similarity' as well as independence and interdependence; it allows evidence of recent brain-based research into learning to help make decisions about what is 'internationally' appropriate at different ages and stages; it provides the formal curriculum structures that are necessary in environments where the turnover of students, teachers, board members and others is so high; and it helps to ensure that the preparation of children and students for a 21st-century world is not left to hope and good intention but is founded on rigour and purposefulness.

References

Akram, C (1995) Change and adaptation: children and curriculum in international schools, *International Schools Journal*, **XV** (1), pp 39–53

Al Farra, S (2000) Images of International Education, in *International Schools and International Education*, eds M C Hayden and J J Thompson, Kogan Page, London

Blandford, S and Shaw, M (2001) The nature of international school leadership, in *Managing International Schools*, eds S Blandford and M Shaw, Routledge Falmer, London

Catling, S (2001) Developing the Curriculum, in *Managing International Schools*, eds S Blandford and M Shaw, Routledge Falmer, London

Claxton, G (1998) *Hare Brain Tortoise Mind: Why intelligence increases when you think less*, Fourth Estate, London

Deal, T E and Kennedy, A (1983) Culture and school performance, *Educational Leadership* **48** (8), pp 45–53

Evans, D (2001) *Emotion*, Oxford University Press, Oxford

Fullan, M (2001) *The New Meaning of Educational Change*, Cassell, London

Gandal, M and Vranek, J (2001) Standards: here today, here tomorrow, *Educational Leadership*, **59** (1), pp 6–14

Gardner, H (1993) *Multiple Intelligences: The theory in practice*, Harper Collins, London

Gardner, H (2001) *An Education For the Future*, presented to The Royal Symposium, Amsterdam [Online] www.projectzero.com

Gazzaniga, M (ed) (2000) *Cognitive Neuroscience: A reader*, Blackwell, Oxford

Hardman, J (2001) Improving recruitment and retention, in *Managing International Schools*, eds S Blandford and M Shaw, Routledge Falmer, London

Hayden, M C and Thompson, J J (1995), International schools and international education: a relationship reviewed, *Oxford Review of Education*, **21** (3), pp 327–45

Hayden, M C and Thompson, J J (2000) International education: flying flags or raising standards?, *International Schools Journal*, **XIX** (2), pp 48–56

Hill, I (2000) Internationally-minded schools, *International Schools Journal*, **XX** (1), pp 24–37

Jensen, E (1998) *Teaching with the Brain in Mind*, Association for Supervision and Curriculum Development (ASCD), Virginia, United States

Lowe, J (2000) Assessment and Educational Quality, in *International Schools and International Education*, eds M C Hayden and J J Thompson, Kogan Page, London

Ross, A (2000) *Curriculum Construction and Critique*, Falmer Press, London

UNESCO (1996) *Declaration and Integrated Framework of Action on Education for Peace, Human Rights and Democracy*, UNESCO Press, Paris

Welton, J (2001) Planning: the art of the possible, in *Managing International Schools*, eds S Blandford and M Shaw, Routledge Falmer, London

Wilber, K (2000) *A Theory of Everything*, Shambhala Press, Boston

Chapter 5

Criteria for curriculum continuity in international education

Helen Drennen

Introduction

In recent times, considerable effort has gone into meeting the challenge of creating curricula that incorporate objectives directly, or indirectly, related to the promotion of international-mindedness for students studying in both national systems and international schools worldwide. Curriculum and assessment authorities have sought to address the task, starting from a base of well-established curricula, through various approaches that have been described, elsewhere, as exportation and adaptation (Thompson, 1998). But very few examples exist of curricula that have been designed, *de novo*, to satisfy international education objectives. Examples of those that do are the International Primary Curriculum (IPC, 2002) and the three programmes that form the curricular portfolio of the International Baccalaureate Organization (IBO) (IBO, 2002a).

Even so, relatively little attention has been drawn to the problem that is of such crucial importance for teachers, administrators and curriculum designers throughout the world: that of providing, in curriculum terms, clear criteria for continuity and progression across the whole student experience of formal education from kindergarten to the point of school-leaving. The incorporation of such continuity criteria into the programmes of study for each of the phases of student learning, would seem to be an essential ingredient for the creation of specifications and schemes of work that help overcome the effects of the numerous discontinuities experienced by many students, arising from their circumstances. Thus, the transfer of students from teacher to teacher within the same school, from school to school within the same locality, from one national system to another, from one phase of education to another (primary to secondary, lower secondary to upper secondary) and between schools within an international school network, all present potential points at which student learning, and teacher planning, can suffer from a lack of coherence.

The introduction of the Primary Years Programme (PYP) by the IBO in September 1997, marked an important step in the development of its programmes of international education. Since that time, the IBO has offered three international programmes, the Diploma (introduced in 1969), the Middle Years (introduced in 1994) and the Primary Years, and the prospect of a continuous international educational experience from early childhood to school graduation has therefore become a possibility. Thus the concept of a consistent, broad-based international curriculum came into being (IBO, 2002b) and immediately the challenge of providing curricular continuity became a stark reality for those responsible for the implementation of the programmes for schools in both national systems and international networks. As a response to that curriculum challenge, teachers drawn from a wide range of educational contexts, together with curriculum designers with expertise across all phases of compulsory education, have sought to identify those features of curriculum design that are most likely to aid progression in learning for those students engaging in study through a curriculum designed to be international in character.

The purpose of this chapter is to share something of that process of identification more widely so that the criteria arising from the work undertaken can be subject to a broader base of debate and refinement, ensuring that their use in future curriculum development that aims to incorporate continuity and progression can be deployed in as wide a range of contexts as possible. In the future it is intended that teachers, students and parents should be able to draw confidently on a recognizable educational framework that offers, across each phase, a common specification of aims and values, within an overarching concept of developing international-mindedness.

The criteria

Within the IBO, the process of generating the newly developed sequence of programmes offered many insights into the nature of international education and the criteria on which a template for a continuum from ages 4–18 might be built. Essentially, the following list represents the set of provisional criteria that have been identified to date. Taken together they form a proposed template for the purposes of both planning for, and evaluating the effectiveness of, strands of continuity across the three age ranges. No singular approach to pedagogy is intended. Indeed, flexibility in responding to local requirements and interests is at the heart of their deployment in curriculum design so that the resultant outcomes, in curriculum terms, can provide appropriate access, for all students, to what is shared and what is different in human experience:

- developing citizens of the world – culture, language and learning to live together;
- building and reinforcing a student's sense of identity and cultural awareness;
- fostering the recognition and development of universal human values;
- stimulating curiosity and inquiry to foster a spirit of discovery and enjoyment of learning;
- equipping students with the skills to learn and acquire knowledge, individually or collaboratively, and to apply these skills and knowledge across a broad range of areas;
- providing international content whilst responding to local requirements and interests;
- encouraging diversity, and flexibility in pedagogical approaches;
- providing appropriate forms of assessment and international benchmarking.

Following the experience of those involved in the process of curricula construction under the auspices of the IBO, comments are offered under each of these criteria as an aid to understanding the basis on which they have been derived. Examples of the criteria in action drawn from the IBO programmes are offered for illustration purposes; their more general applicability remains to be tested through current initiatives by others addressing similar aims.

Developing citizens of the world – culture, language and learning to live together

As a starting point those involved in the curriculum construction process were unapologetically idealistic in believing that education can foster understanding among young people around the world, encouraging future generations to live more peacefully and productively than before. By emphasizing the dynamic combination of knowledge, skills, independent critical thought, and international awareness or intercultural understanding, the principles of educating the whole person for a life of active, responsible citizenship can be espoused.

Developing the capacity for critical examination of oneself and one's traditions, for living 'the examined life' as Socrates described it, is the starting point from which all follows (Socrates, in Plato). Encouraging students to examine critically their own and others' customs and traditions is a necessary element for an education that equips them to discern what is of value and what ought to be cherished and retained.

The concept of an international community is also a prerequisite and its chief purpose is to provide an educational environment in which anyone, anywhere, may participate, may contribute, and may be encouraged by all to grow individually, and with an understanding of others. The development of 'world citizenship' does not assume that local or national citizenship is not of paramount importance, and it should be recognized that students need to be helped to appreciate and understand the worth of human life wherever it is lived, and that there is a shared bond with all other human beings by virtue of our common humanity. Such a pluralist view is based on the tenet that human diversity is intrinsically valuable and that, because there is a plurality of human identities, interaction brings the potential for greater mutual understanding. Developing in students their ability to appreciate and to evaluate human diversity and its legitimate boundaries can strengthen their motivation to adapt and modify their behaviour accordingly (Orellana Benado, 1995).

Today, more than ever before, there is an awareness that many of the issues facing young people require collaborative global solutions, which extend well beyond parochial and national boundaries. The prevalence of discrimination, racism in all its forms, abuse of human rights, famine, poverty and environmental destruction, require a much greater understanding of what internationalism means in terms of our planet and its inhabitants. Significantly, in each of the three programmes, the learning experiences for students are designed to relate to the realities of the outside world. Much emphasis is placed on the goal of international understanding and a consciousness of common concerns as a basis for a more peaceful, sustainable future for all. The challenge is to foster development of citizenship at multiple levels – in the immediate community, at a wider national level and beyond, in an international sense, whilst at the same time encouraging the development in students of a sense of their own identity.

One of the practical ways in which citizenship can be developed is through an involvement in service to others, which requires both action and reflection. The inclusion of this area in the design of each IBO programme provides a variety of opportunities for translating theory into practice and for engendering the satisfaction that comes from giving, whether that be within one's family, the school community, the local community, one's country or the wider world community.

The description of the educational aims of the IBO, outlined by the founding Director General Alec Peterson in reference to the Diploma Programme, still holds true for the Diploma Programme today: '... to develop to their fullest potential the powers of each individual to understand, to modify and to enjoy his or her environment, both inner and outer, in its physical, social, moral, aesthetic and spiritual aspects' (Peterson, 1987). And today, as expressed in the IBO mission statement:

> Through comprehensive and balanced curricula coupled with challenging assessment, the International Baccalaureate Organization aims to assist schools in their endeavours to develop the individual talents of young people and teach them to relate the experience of the classroom to the realities of the world outside. Beyond intellectual rigour and high academic standards, strong emphasis is placed on the ideals of international understanding and responsible citizenship, to the end that IB students may become critical and compassionate thinkers, lifelong learners and informed participants in local and world affairs, conscious of the shared humanity that binds all people together while respecting the variety of cultures and attitudes that makes for the richness of life. (IBO Council of Foundation, 1996)

How effective this statement is needs to be judged by its translation into the curriculum and assessment of each programme and, in turn, in the teaching and learning that take place in classrooms.

'Is the IB just another variant of the proliferation of national systems around the world, or do we in fact provide a service that transcends such boundaries in ways that are unique? The answers to such questions depend to a large degree on our interpretation of "international" and how we choose to infuse it into our curriculum'. (Peel, 1997)

What is significant is the underlying concept of education of the whole person as a lifelong process, of which the formal years of schooling are but a fundamental part. Education for world citizenship needs to begin early, in fact as soon as young children can engage in storytelling, of home, of other places and of other people. The development of world citizenship needs to take place at every age.

Building and reinforcing a student's sense of identity and cultural awareness

Developing an understanding of the nature and value of one's own culture is a fundamental starting point for any educational programme claiming to be international. From here the role of the study of others' cultures can begin. This idea has been succinctly expressed by a former director general of the IBO, Roger Peel (1997):

> From my own perspective, the honesty of the IB stems from the fact that we require all students to relate first to their own national identity – their own language, history and cultural heritage, no matter where in the world this may be. Beyond that, we ask that they identify with the corresponding traditions of others. It is not expected that they adopt alien points of view, merely that they are exposed to them and encouraged to respond intelligently. The end result, we hope, is a more compassionate population, a welcome manifestation of national diversity within an international framework of tolerant respect. Ideally, at the end of the IB experience, students should know themselves better than when they started, while acknowledging that others can be right in being different.

Giving priority to students knowing and appreciating their own culture first is essential in fostering that initial sense of identity with one's own traditions, customs and mores, and the joy and immense satisfaction that they provide in growing up. Cultural roots are as important as our basic needs for survival: they dictate relationships whether they are with family, community, nation or the wider world. Most significantly, they also determine how communication with others takes place and how the experiences of living are shared. Less admirably, however, such roots are largely responsible for the ways in which people exploit, exert power and destroy others, which is why the study of culture and language is fundamental to learning to live together.

'Culture is a fundamental phenomenon. It affects not only our daily practices: the way we live, are brought up, manage, are managed, and die; but also the theories we are able to develop to explain our practices. No part of our lives is exempt from culture's influence'. (Hofstede, 1997)

How students' understanding of culture is developed is a major challenge for all curriculum designers. How a curriculum can present students with major issues, such as Hofstede's, for analysis into the concept of culture is a significant task (Hofstede, 1997). Such issues include:

● how power, authority and inequality are manifested in one's own culture and that of others;

- how one's own culture regards the relationship between an individual and a group and how such a relationship is regarded in others';
- the significance of gender in one's own culture and in that of others;
- how one's own culture and others' deal with life's uncertainties and ambiguities.

Developing an understanding of culture is critical in promoting an understanding of others and an ability to relate cooperatively with them. This is what each individual programme and the sequence of programmes seek to achieve – to enable students to develop an awareness of themselves first, while recognizing that others are different and that others 'can be right in being different' (Peel, 1997). Without an understanding of the importance of diversity of culture in human life and an openness to cooperative sharing of knowledge, students are unlikely to develop tolerance and an acceptance that life must be sustained through living together peacefully.

The role of language, one's mother tongue, and the study of other languages in this context have a special place in any programme's design. It is through language that we access our own and others' culture. The role of language acquisition and development from early childhood in order to foster bi- and multi-lingualism is fundamental to any sequence of programmes.

Fostering the recognition and development of universal human values

'… while we live, while we are among human beings, let us cultivate our humanity' (Seneca). It is important to acknowledge the diverse values that are inherent in the different cultures of the world. Most important in this acknowledgement is the value placed on human diversity and on intellectual, personal, emotional and social growth, enriched by a strong civic sense and involvement in the local and wider community.

In developing an awareness of the diverse values of different cultures, it is, however, fundamental that students are exposed to those human values that are recognized as universal; these are embodied in the Universal Declaration of Human Rights, adopted and proclaimed by the General Assembly of the United Nations (UN) in 1948. Implicit in the recognition of universal human rights is the value placed on the role of education (Article 26 of the UN Declaration) to foster understanding and respect for life on earth and for the best possible curriculum to be enjoyed by all who participate. Of similar importance is the recognition that in any school, the quality of the environment for learning is critical, as the values and attitudes of the school community will largely shape the kind of future in which young people will live. A school's commitment to social justice and equity will be easily apparent in the daily life, conduct, management and leadership of that school.

Stimulating curiosity and inquiry to foster a spirit of discovery and enjoyment of learning

Developing inquiry skills in the fullest sense is of fundamental importance in helping students at every age to expand their levels of knowledge and understanding. It is important to give central focus to the student as 'the knower', in constructing meaning from existing knowledge and personal experience through active inquiry.

In the IB Primary Years Programme, inquiry is the leading, but not exclusive, pedagogical approach; at the Diploma level, inquiry, interpreted in the broadest sense and involving analysis, evaluation and synthesis, is fundamental to reaching deep and rich levels of understanding. In the particular case of the Middle Years Programme the distinct focus of inquiry within the Approaches to Learning area is designed to enable students to understand the nature of learning and to develop an approach to their own inquiry and learning that incorporates, correlates and transcends academic subjects. A similar example exists for the Theory of Knowledge course in the Diploma Programme. More generally it would seem that an explicit awareness of subjective and ideological biases in one's own thinking, and in others, is essential to understanding knowledge. An explicit expectation is that successful inquiry will lead to responsible action initiated by the children as a result of the learning process, so that participation in such a programme will encourage the translation of knowledge into action and reflection. It is at that point that the principle of developing in young people 'not just the power to think, but the will to act', as described by Kurt Hahn (Peterson, 1987), comes to the fore.

Equipping students with the skills to learn and acquire knowledge, individually or collaboratively, and to apply these skills and knowledge across a broad range of areas

While much is yet to be understood about the full range of learning in which students engage, it is recognized that developing flexibility and adaptability in students as learners is a crucial dimension. The encouragement and empowerment given to the student for his or her learning is also fundamental, as is the recognition that individuals, as well as groups, are learners. Applying skills, and acquiring knowledge through individual subjects and through transdisciplinary study, integrating different approaches to learning, using information technology in learning, and acknowledging intercultural and intergenerational learning, have all been identified as elements of curriculum design that help to promote the kind of learning that encourages the diversity essential to the development of internationalism across programmes.

Providing international content whilst responding to local requirements and interests

The content provided in an international curriculum must be both global and local, because each programme needs to be based on the premise that students need to understand themselves and their indigenous local culture before they can appreciate others. The combination of global and local enables an appreciation of what is similar and different in others. In turn the development of both dimensions is to a large extent dependent on the contribution of teachers in selecting curriculum content, a process referred to by Hargreaves (1998) as 'creative professionalism'. Innovative and committed teachers from many different cultures have played a significant role in the development of the content of the IB programmes in stimulating curiosity, inquiry, reflection and critical thinking, together with a sense of empathy.

Encouraging diversity, and flexibility in pedagogical approaches

Acknowledging and accepting that pedagogical practices, whilst having many common features, are largely influenced by individual cultures, is integral to providing a flexible approach to teaching and learning. Teaching an international programme must allow for variety and difference in method since diversity has been identified as an essential ingredient for the promotion of an international attitude (Hayden and Thompson, 1998) and this is as important in teaching methodology as it is, for example, in the selection of content. A major consideration in this respect is the impact of ICT and the use that can be made of its enormous potential as a medium for increasing awareness of shared global interests and concerns, and for teaching across geographical distances and boundaries.

Providing appropriate forms of assessment and international benchmarking

Assessment is an integral part of any curriculum model and in an international context there are many issues and possibilities to explore where performance and measurement are interpreted differently across cultures. In order to be consistent with the twin aims of promoting internationalism and ensuring continuity, the arrangements for the assessment of student achievement should be based on as broad an approach as possible. For this reason a wide range of structures should be used across international education programmes and the choice of the ways in which they are deployed made according to whether they measure student performance satisfactorily and directly in relation to the stated objectives of a course. In general, assessment structures should support identifiably sound classroom practice by giving feedback to learning, in addition to providing appropriate forms of assessment and international benchmarking, whether or not it also leads to a formal qualification recognized worldwide, as does the IB Diploma for university entrance purposes.

Conclusion

As previously mentioned, the framework of criteria, stated and elaborated upon briefly, has arisen from one organization's attempt to provide a rationale for the process of curriculum design and review that will support the development of continuity and progression, alongside the imperative to make its programmes international. In applying that rationale several features have emerged as common responses shared across all its curriculum models. In summary each programme:

- requires study across a broad and balanced range of knowledge domains including languages, humanities, science and technology, mathematics and the creative arts, drawing on content from educational cultures across the world;
- gives special emphasis to language acquisition and development;
- provides opportunities for engaging in transdisciplinary learning;
- focuses on developing the skills of learning culminating in a study of the theory of knowledge in the Diploma Programme;
- includes, to a different extent, study of individual subjects and of transdisciplinary areas;
- provides students with opportunities for individual and group collaborative planning and research; and
- includes a community service component requiring action and reflection.

It may well be that interpretation of the criteria within the framework will turn out to be very different for those teachers, and others, charged with similar responsibilities for the design and implementation of continuous programmes of international education. It may also be that through their endeavours they will further refine the criteria that comprise the current framework. The ideas put forward here are designed to encourage and stimulate such debate and development in a wider community than has so far been the case, and are therefore contestable. In doing so the hope is that future generations of young people will engage in learning through programmes that are intentionally planned to promote the growth and development of both ideas and ideals, through the aims of enabling them to learn to live together with understanding, tolerance and acceptance, and at peace.

References

Hargreaves, D (1998) *Creative professionalism – the role of teachers in the knowledge society*, Demos, London

Hayden, M C and Thompson, J J (eds) (1998) *International Education: Principles and Practice*, Kogan Page, London

Hofstede, G (1997) *Cultures and Organizations: Software of the Mind. Intercultural co-operation and its importance for survival*, McGraw Hill, New York

IBO Council of Foundation (1996) IBO Mission Statement, IBO, Geneva

International Baccalaureate Organization (IBO) (2002a) [Online] http://www.ibo.org

IBO (2002b) Monograph 4 in IBO Monograph Series, IBO, Geneva

International Primary Curriculum (2002) [Online] http://www.international primarycurriculum.com

Nussbaum, M C (1997) *Cultivating Humanity – A Classical Defence of Reform in Liberal Education*, Harvard University Press, Harvard

Orellana Benado, M E (1995) Pluralism and the Ethics of Internationalism, *IB World*, 8, p 29

Peel, R M (1997) *Guide to the Diploma Programme*, International Baccalaureate Organization, Geneva

Peterson, A D C (1987) *Schools Across Frontiers – the story of the International Baccalaureate and the United World Colleges*, Open Court, La Salle, Illinois

Plato, *Apology 3A*, in *Cultivating Humanity – A Classical Defence of Reform in Liberal Education*, M C Nussbaum (1997), Harvard University Press, Harvard

Seneca, *On Anger*, in *Cultivating Humanity – A Classical Defence of Reform in Liberal Education*, M C Nussbaum (1997), Harvard University Press, Harvard

Thompson, J J (1998) Towards a model for international education in *International Education: Principles and Practice*, eds M C Hayden and J J Thompson, Kogan Page, London

United Nations (1948) *Universal Declaration of Human Rights*, United Nations, Geneva

Chapter 6

Cultural dimensions of national and international educational assessment

Roger Brown

Introduction

Much of the work on assessment in an international context to date has focused on types of assessment, such as external assessment versus internal assessment, or on whether assessment is norm-referenced or criterion-referenced. But there is an alternative perspective: one of culture and values. Over recent times authors such as Filer (2000) and Le Métais (1999) have offered a view of education and its assessment that is situated in culture, and the values exhibited by countries and their corresponding educational systems.

Culture and values

Culture has many different meanings and can be located in many different contexts. In this chapter culture will be taken to be the values, norms, institutions and modes of thinking to which successive generations in a given society have attached primary importance. This coincides with the definition developed by Trompenaars and Hampden-Turner (1997) that 'culture is the way in which a group of people solves problems and reconciles dilemmas', developed from the writings of Schein (1985). Hofstede (1991) observes that at the heart of culture are values, which are located within the individual as well as collectively located within society. And as Kluckhohn and others (1962) recognize, 'A value is a conception, explicit and implicit, distinctive of an individual or characteristic of a group, of the desirable which influences the selection from available modes, means and ends of action'.

Kluckhohn and others (1962) also indicate that affective, cognitive and conative (selection) aspects are all essential components of the notion of value. The values evidenced by societies and individuals are unlikely to change over time and consequently reflect a stable pattern of desired behaviours within a cultural group. But defining values is problematic: every author has their own way of defining them. Rokeach (1973), for example, states that 'A value system is an enduring organization of beliefs concerning preferable modes of conduct or end states of existence along a continuum of relative importance'. Allport (1961) states that 'A value is a belief upon which a man [sic] acts by preference', while Hofstede (1991) has defined values as a broad tendency to prefer certain states of affairs over others, a definition based on the work of Kluckhohn and others.

Assessment

In this chapter assessment will be considered within the context of certification purposes at the end of secondary school (which can include, for instance, examinations, coursework, oral examinations, and practical examinations). Such assessment has a number of effects on the teaching and learning process within schools, including the inevitable 'backwash effect' on what is taught and learned within the classroom.

Peterson (1987) noted that 'Examinations at the end of secondary education commonly serve one or more of three different purposes: certification, selection and motivation', while Lowe (2000) categorized two types of international examinations: firstly, those used to make international comparisons of achievement across nations, with perhaps the most well known being the recent Third International Mathematics and Science Study (TIMSS) conducted by the International Association for the Evaluation of Educational Achievement (IEA) and secondly, those that assess and certify individual achievement such as the International Baccalaureate (IB), International General Certificate of Secondary Education (IGCSE), and Advanced International Certificate of Education (AICE).

Kellaghan and Greaney (2001) contend that international comparative studies 'tend to promote uniformity in curricula, since common assessment procedures are used across countries' and, if we accept the authors' view that these tests promote a uniformity of curricula, then these tests will also promote one set of cultural values of the particular curriculum being used. Kellaghan and Greaney ask 'Will assessments promote a "one-world" view in which we will eventually witness the demise of national systems of education, which traditionally have focused on the transmission of national cultures?'

In this chapter, international assessment will be considered in the context of international programmes such as the Advanced International Certificate of Education (AICE), Advanced Placement International Diploma for Overseas Study (APID) and the International Baccalaureate Diploma Programme (IBDP), as opposed to international comparative studies such as TIMSS.

Values and national educational systems

A nation's cultural values are evidenced in their educational aims (Beyer and Apple, 1998; Moon and Murphy, 1999). The values expressed in curriculum documents may be similar between nations but will be derived from the country's cultural capital. On the other hand, an international curriculum would be expected either to carry the values of the host country where the curriculum was originally developed or to attempt to carry the values of internationalism, however this may be defined. Such educational values are evident in the official policy documentation produced by all national and international education systems, including those found in the context of national assessments (Beyer and Apple, 1998; Le Métais, 1999; Moon and Murphy, 1999).

National cultural values

Hofstede (2001), in his pioneering work of the early 1980s, described the differences in the thinking and acting of persons and businesses as a culture-dependent activity, which could be located in the cultural dimensions of:

- power distance;
- uncertainty avoidance;
- individualism versus collectivism;
- masculinity versus femininity;
- long-term versus short-term orientation.

Hofstede (2001) developed these dimensions from the work of Kluckhohn and others (1962), who believed that 'there is a generalized framework that underlies the more apparent and striking facts of cultural relativity'. It is suggested therefore that it is possible to establish a framework that will allow for the comparison of cultural differences and the similarities of different groups.

Hampden-Turner and Trompenaars (2000) used the pattern variables of Parsons and Shils (1962) to develop their dimensions of cultural diversity, which are:

- universalism versus particularism;
- individualism versus communitarianism;
- neutral versus emotional;
- specific versus diffuse;
- achievement versus ascription.

For Trompenaars and Hampden-Turner the distinctive part of culture is how these dilemmas are resolved, and their approach recognizes that the decisions we make are a function of our value systems that inform the choices we make. The work of Hampden-Turner and Trompenaars (2000) and Hofstede (1991) indicates that each culture exhibits certain preferences over others and as a consequence will favour particular modes of conduct and behaviours over others. But these dimensions of values are not mutually exclusive. Instead 'cultures dance from one preferred end to its opposite and back' (Hampden-Turner and Trompenaars, 1997). Education and educational assessment are directly related to a nation's culture (Le Métais, 1999) and therefore it would be expected that nations might exemplify different values in both their education and their assessment regimes. The existence of values within the assessment system has been recognized by authors such as Cresswell (1998) who noted that 'Values permeate assessment processes... The values of the designers and operators of educational systems influence every step of the assessment process and it is possible to identify two distinct aspects of the role of values in educational assessments: decisions concerning what is assessed, and judgments of the quality of student responses' (Cresswell, 1998).

Planel et al (2000) have also observed that 'Enshrined within the contents and form of national tests are the values of educational systems and cultures', that is to say that different national assessment systems are likely to display differing values in their assessments. Baumgart and Halse (1999), for example, found in their analysis of geography and society-and-culture multiple-choice examination papers from different national contexts, that on the surface they appeared to be similar. However, 'Although examination papers in Japan in particular but also in Thailand required an extensive knowledge base, they also required challenging levels of analysis, interpretation and translation. [On the other hand, for] Australian examination papers using multiple-choice format, answers did not require memorisation and could be inferred from skill-based interpretation and analysis of the data supplied'.

Such differences are indicative of the priorities (or value) placed upon certain forms of assessment over others; even though the questions are of a similar form the skills required to complete them are different. Similarly, West and Crighton (1999) noted that examination reform in Central and Eastern Europe used the work of 'UK or Dutch examination bodies rather than the US-based ones' as it was considered that the UK and Dutch examining bodies valued skills that were similar to those in Eastern Europe over those of the 'curriculum free' multiple-choice examinations prevalent in the United States at the time. West and Crighton (1999) also noted that 'Systems that offer a mixture of external and school-based assessment of national curricula, while less reliable, are closer to the educational values of the region [Eastern Europe] and therefore probably make up for in validity what they lose in reliability'. The work of West and Crighton (1999) would appear to provide further support to the notion that it is possible to develop a set of educational assessments that reflect the values of Western European culture, about which more will be written later.

Values existing in education

There exist many different sets of values in education, including moral, social and educational (Le Métais, 1999). Analysis here will focus on educational values and how they encourage certain types of educational assessment over others. Such values have been recognized by many authors including Bishop (1991); Ernest (1989); Hampden-Turner and Trompenaars (2000); Hofstede (1991); Leung (1998); Lim Chap Sam and Ernest (1997); Planel et al (2000); and Seah and Bishop (2000). Bernstein (1975 and 2000), meanwhile, has repeatedly stated that one of the impacts of education is that of cultural reproduction and he sees 'pedagogic practice as a fundamental social context through which cultural reproduction-production takes place' (Bernstein, 2000). Education is therefore a carrier of the values of the culture of a society and as such these values are transmitted from teacher to student, from school to teacher and from educational system to school. It is through this process that culture is maintained. Hofstede (1991 and 2001) has

Table 6.1 Dimensions of collectivist-individualist, power distance and uncertainty avoidance (adapted from Hofstede, 1986)

Collectivist societies have as a focus the student who learns how to complete tasks and will only respond to teachers when asked to do so. Larger classes will be split into smaller social groups, reflecting their particularist categories.	The focus in **individualist** societies is on lifelong learning and taking responsibility for one's own learning. Students are prepared to respond to open requests within the classroom. Groupings within the classroom will be based around the task being completed at the time, which represents a universalist perspective.
In **weak uncertainty avoidance** societies the students will work in unstructured learning situations. As teachers may not have all the answers, students are expected to seek out their own answers, and will be rewarded for innovative problem-solving.	In **strong uncertainty avoidance** societies the learning environment is more structured and assignments are therefore more detailed. Accuracy is also a key feature of such environments and the use of academic language is preferred.
In **small power distance** societies the focus is on initiative in classrooms and students demonstrate a willingness to present their point of view openly. Students develop their own problem-solving techniques and classrooms will encourage a two-way dialogue between students and teacher.	In **large power distance** societies the teacher is the focus of classroom interaction, will initiate discussion and will describe the methods to be used in the solution of problems.

demonstrated how cultural dimensions operate within the schooling system. The dimensions of collectivist-individualist, power distance and uncertainty avoidance are summarized in Table 6.1.

How these cultural dimensions are exemplified in assessment

The development of educational assessment will involve the resolution of dilemmas on how to assess and what to assess, and any assessment model produced is therefore likely to represent a compromise between the differing priorities of the groups involved in the development of that model. One of the most significant challenges faced by any educational assessment institution is that of ensuring validity and reliability of assessment as well as the authenticity of such assessment. That is, ensuring that the assessment is valid for the group of students taking the examination, is reliable and assesses in a way that recognizes the diversity of pedagogies and teaching methodologies used in a particular culture. How the assessing organization deals with these challenges reflects the choices made (or what is valued). Given that different countries have differing value systems, as shown by Hofstede (2001) and Trompenaars and

Hampden-Turner (1997), it is reasonable to assume that they will develop different assessment models that reflect these values.

Fan (1999) provides an example of the difficulties involved in assessment from a cultural perspective in the form of a question on lotteries in the United States, which he argues would not be suitable in China where lotteries 'were once regarded as a particular part of capitalist culture and strictly prohibited'. Thus if the use of certain contexts is encouraged in assessment, then the adoption of an international assessment system that encourages the use of contextual materials in assessment will require careful selection.

Assessment and values

Using the work of Hofstede (1991 and 2001), it is possible to describe approaches to educational assessment that arise from his dimensions of culture, as proposed in Table 6.2.

Table 6.2 Approaches to educational assessment

Collectivist	Individualist
Collectivism is about forming groups and is located in the domain of learning how to do and is seen as a means to an end where education is intended to make you part of the group. So assessment will focus on short answer questions or closed questions that are instrumental in nature.	Individualism is located in the creative domain and is focused on the student. Assessment therefore would be exemplified by the use of open-ended problem-solving tasks and assessment forms that would allow students to demonstrate creativity such as in interpretative works, essays and works of art. The assessment would also be relational in nature.
Weak Uncertainty Avoidance	**Strong Uncertainty Avoidance**
Assessment that represents this type of society would include open-ended unstructured tasks requiring problem-solving skills. That is, their assessment will encourage the use of risk-taking and would involve the use of oral assessments and presentations.	Assessment would focus on structured questioning where the questions would use academic language. Accuracy in responses would be indicated by the use of single response-type questions such as naming a geographical feature. That is, there would be a degree of certainty and expectedness about any assessment given
Small Power Distance	**Large Power Distance**
Assessment in a small power distance society would encourage open-ended assessment questions where students are expected to demonstrate the ability to solve unstructured problems. These societies will also encourage the use of oral assessments.	Assessment in this society would incorporate closed structured questions where the students are expected to perform a series of tasks within which a clear solution method is provided.

Table 6.3 Relationship between power distance and collectivist-individualist dimensions

	Small Power Distance	**Large Power Distance**
Collectivist	Assessment in collectivist societies with small power distance could involve the use of open-ended group tasks, where a group of students work on the task together. The assessment of the task would involve a group submission, and possibly include an oral presentation or performance.	Collectivist societies in large power distance relationships would tend to offer closed structured questions requiring short answers; the questions are instrumental in nature, and may include multiple-choice questions.
Individualist	Individualist societies in small power distance contexts would encourage open-ended assessment questions where students are expected to demonstrate the ability to solve unstructured problems. These societies will also encourage the use of oral assessments and students would be expected to demonstrate creativity such as in interpretative works, essays and works of art.	To reconcile these two opposing viewpoints of an individualist society with large power distance could require assessments that encourage some interpretation and creativity within a closed framework, where the students are constrained to interpret the question in one particular way even though there are other possible ways of completing the task.

What is evident from the work of Hampden-Turner and Trompenaars (2000), Hofstede (1991), Hofstede (2001) and Trompenaars and Hampden-Turner (1997) is that each country will exhibit different dimensions of culture, which will be reflected in their educational programmes. Hofstede (2001) uses a four-way matrix to describe the inter-connectedness between the dimensions of culture. A similar four-way matrix can be developed for assessment comparing the dimensions of culture and their corresponding assessments. So, for example, using the dimension of power distance and the collectivist-individualist dimensions, the matrix shown in Table 6.3 is produced.

International curricula

How then can an international examining body take account of national differences in educational values? Or should it offer its own set of educational values, which may or may not relate to those of a particular nation or group of nations?

International programmes leading to certificates such as the Diploma offered by the International Baccalaureate Organization (IBDP) and the

AICE Diploma provide a globally recognized qualification that will enable acceptance of the student into many universities throughout the world. Lowe (2000) has suggested that such programmes have become part of the 'global credentialism' where elites in one country can gain access to prestigious universities in Western European countries resulting in the maintenance of their positional advantage within their own country and in the wider global context.

Peterson (1987) describes in great detail the effort spent in trying to take the best of the national assessment systems of the early 1970s to develop the forms of assessment in the IB Diploma Programme. He cites a speech that he himself made to the Council of Europe in 1970 in which he stated that:

> Reviewing the state of research and innovation in Europe it would seem that the most promising line of development is the examen bilan. What is needed is a process of assessment which is as valid as possible, in the sense that it really assesses the whole endowment and personality of the pupil in relation to the next stage of his [sic] life, but at the same time sufficiently reliable to assure pupils, parents, teachers, and receiving institutions that justice is being done. Yet such a process must not, by its backwash effect, distort good teaching, nor be too slow, nor absorb too much of our scarce educational resources.

These sentiments are echoed on the IBO Web (reference) pages when it is stated that (IBO, 2001): 'The Diploma Programme incorporates the best elements of national systems, without being based on any one... Students who remain closer to home benefit from a highly respected international curriculum'.

Peterson (1987) acknowledged that a European perspective in the development of assessment for the IBDP is evident, and it is interesting to note that the assessment examples he uses are either European or US and as such conform to the Western European view of education and assessment. The Western European influence on the assessment of the IBDP can also be shown through the work of Hofstede and Trompenaars. Hofstede (2001) and Huntington (1998) demonstrate how Western European societies are individualist in nature, so that it would therefore be expected that there would be considerable similarity in assessment regimes and differences would be indicative of other cultural dimensions. Further consideration of Hofstede's data (2001) suggests that most Western European societies are likely to have a low uncertainty avoidance index as well as low power index values. Given these considerations, it is possible to suggest that the types of assessment preferred by Western European societies would be likely to favour:

- creative open-ended problem solving;
- unstructured tasks;
- interpretative and analytical skills;
- oral assessments;
- group work.

Hampden-Turner and Trompenaars (2000) suggest that Western European societies are more universalist than many of their counterparts. They state that a universalist society 'searches for sameness and similarity and tries to impose on all members of a class or universe the laws of their commonality'. Assessment bodies will therefore develop mechanisms to ensure that everyone is treated equally, and the use of some form of standardization of assessment will therefore follow. The standardization can be in the form of moderation of samples of work, or of norm-referencing of examinations, or even criterion-referencing where the specific intention exists of ensuring that all pieces of work satisfy the criterion stipulated in the specification.

When discussing individualism and assessment in the United States, Cambridge (2000) makes the following observations:

> Individualism can take different forms. It is remarkable that the educational system of the most individualist nation – the USA – requires college entry information in terms of norm-referencing. College application forms which solicit a recommendation from teachers frequently ask questions such as 'Where in the class would you place this student?' Interviews conducted by the author with teachers of International Baccalaureate Diploma Programme subjects, however, indicate that they are strongly influenced by the values of criterion-referenced assessment. This appears to exert a backwash effect on the assessment culture of IB schools, which tends to take the form of being strongly individualist, non-competitive and against norm-referencing, manifested as a preference not to rank students according to achievement.

A problem clearly arises in confusing individualism with universalism. Hofstede (2001) offers a way through this dilemma when he states that 'The individualist society tends to be universalist'. There is no doubt that the United States is an individualist culture, but the emphasis, at least when most of the surveys of that country were completed on multiple-choice testing, is on a universalist perspective of assessment where multiple-choice tests allow only one correct response and the comparability of students is easily achieved.

Conclusion

Taking account of national cultural differences in international assessments

Can an international assessment exist that is truly reflective of the values of all cultural groups? It would appear from the evidence offered here that each nation will have differing values and therefore it is difficult for an international assessment system to reflect the values of all nations. But if an assessment system has sufficient flexibility within it, then it may be able to be adapted to match more closely the values of a particular group. This could be achieved by a combination of internal assessment (or course work) and external assessment components. An internal assessment component can provide flexibility for the matching of cultures and assessment, in a way that is not possible with the necessarily more standardized approach of external assessment.

It is evident that for those international programmes in which there is a diversity of assessment there is the opportunity to match the dimensions of culture as outlined by Hofstede (2001). There is also no doubt that ensuring that students, teachers and other members of the school community come into contact with other forms of assessment within a structure that is seen as supportive will help to create a recognition of the possibilities offered by other systems and therefore other cultures.

The 'international' in international assessment

International assessment will include a range of forms of assessment (including oral, written, multiple-choice, external and internal), which provide the opportunity for students to become aware of the different ways in which their knowledge is both valued and assessed. Such diversity of assessment allows students to experience what Peterson (1987) described as assessment of the entire person. Such assessments will not only incorporate subject-based assessment but will also value non-traditional areas of the curriculum by recognizing students' performance in these areas. Broadening the forms of assessment allows for cultural diversity, encompassing the broader perspective of internationalism; in other words it provides students, within the assessment regime and through the inevitable backwash effect of assessment, the opportunity to experience the cultural values found in groups that are different from their own. Similarly there is the need to vary the context within the assessment task; that is when real life contexts are used, these contexts should provide opportunities for students to experience a variety of cultural contexts as well as to consider the alternative viewpoints that may result from such contexts.

It also needs to be recognized that, just as different cultural groups of students may have preferred ways of being assessed, so can the 'users' of the certification process within national cultures value certain types of assessments over others. It is therefore important that the examining body recognizes the importance of this dimension of its assessment regime and provides a comprehensive, culturally sensitive overview of its assessment strategies and the philosophies underpinning these assessments.

Assessment that is international in outlook will therefore recognize the broad range of forms of assessment that are valued by different cultural groups. Furthermore these assessments will be designed to support the development of intercultural understanding while recognizing the differing cultural contexts of further and higher education institutions.

References

Allport, G W (1961) *Pattern and Growth of Personality*, Holt, Rinehart and Winston, New York

Baumgart, N and Halse, C (1999), Approaches to Learning across Cultures: the role of assessment, *Assessment in Education*, **6** (3), pp 321–39

Bernstein, B (1975) *Class, Codes and Control 3: Towards a Theory of Educational Transmissions*, Routledge and Kegan Paul, London

Bernstein, B (2000) *Pedagogy, Symbolic Control and Identity*, Rowman and Littlefield, Maryland

Beyer, L E and Apple, M W (eds) (1998) *The Curriculum: Problems, politics and possibilities*, SUNY, Albany

Bishop, A J (1991) *Mathematical Enculturation: A cultural perspective on mathematics education*, Kluwer Academic Press, Dordrecht

Cambridge, J (2000) Globalization and the seven cultures of capitalism, in *International Schools & International Education: Improving teaching, management & quality*, eds M C Hayden and J J Thompson, Kogan Page, London

Cresswell, M J (1998) What are examination standards? The role of values in large scale assessment, Paper presented at 22nd International Association for Educational Assessment (IAEA) conference, Beijing

Ernest, P (1989), The Knowledge, Beliefs and Attitudes of the Mathematics Teacher: a model, *Journal of Education for Teaching*, **15** (1), pp 13–33

Fan, L (1999) Applications of Arithmetic in US and Chinese Textbooks: a comparative study, in *International Comparisons in Mathematics Education*, eds G Kaiser, E Luna and I Huntley, Falmer Press, London

Filer, A (ed) (2000) *Assessment: Social practice and social product*, Routledge and Falmer, London

Hampden-Turner, C M and Trompenaars, F (1997), Response to Geert Hofstede, *International Journal of Intercultural Relations*, **21** (1), pp 149–59

Hampden-Turner, C M and Trompenaars, F (2000) *Building Cross Cultural Competence*, John Wiley and Sons Ltd, Chichester

Hofstede, G (1986) Cultural Differences in Teaching and Learning, *International Journal of Intercultural Relations*, **10** (3), pp 301–20

Hofstede, G (1991) *Cultures and Organizations*, Harper Collins Business, London

Hofstede, G (2001) *Cultures Consequences: Comparing values, behaviors, institutions, and organizations across nations*, Sage Publications, Thousand Oaks

Huntington, S P (1998) *The Clash of Civilizations and the Remaking of the World Order*, Touchstone Books, London

International Baccalaureate Organization (2001) [Online] http://www.ibo.org

Kellaghan, T and Greaney, V (2001), The Globalisation of Assessment in the 20th Century, *Assessment in Education*, **8** (1), pp 88–102

Kluckhohn, C and others (1962) Values and Value Orientations in the Theory of Action: An Exploration in Definition and Classification, in *Towards a General Theory of Action*, eds T Parsons and E A Shils, Harvard University Press, Cambridge, Massachusetts

Le Métais, J (1999) Values and Aims in Curriculum and Assessment Frameworks: a 16 nation review, in *Curriculum in Context*, eds B Moon and P Murphy, Paul Chapman Publishing, London

Leung, F (1998) The Traditional Chinese Views of Mathematics and Education: Implications for Mathematics Education in the New Millennium, in *Rethinking the Mathematics Curriculum*, eds C Hoyles, C Morgan and G Woodhouse, Falmer Press, London

Lim Chap Sam and Ernest, P (1997) *Values in Mathematics Education: What is planned and what is espoused?*, British Society for Research into Learning Mathematics (BSRLM), University of Nottingham

Lowe, J (2000) International Examinations: the new credentialism and reproduction of advantage in a globalising world, *Assessment in Education: Policy principles and practice*, **7** (3), pp 363–77

Moon, B and Murphy, P (eds) (1999) *Curriculum in Context*, Paul Chapman Publishing, London

Parsons, T and Shils, E A (eds) (1962) *Towards a General Theory of Action*, Harvard University Press, Cambridge, Massachusetts

Peterson, A D C (1987) *Schools Across Frontiers. The story of the International Baccalaureate and the United World Colleges*, Open Court Publishing, La Salle, Illinois

Planel, C, Broadfoot, P, Osborn, M, Sharpe, K and Ward, B (2000), National assessments: underlying cultural values revealed by comparing English and French national tests, *European Journal of Education*, **35** (3), pp 361–74

Rokeach, M (1973) *The Nature of Human Values*, Free Press, New York

Schein, E (1985) *Organizational Culture and Leadership*, Jossey-Bass, San Francisco

Seah, W T and Bishop, A J (2000) Values in mathematics textbooks: A view through two Australasian regions, 81st Annual Meeting of the American Educational Research Association, New Orleans

Trompenaars, F and Hampden-Turner, C M (1997) *Riding the Waves of Culture*, Nicholas Brealey Publishing Ltd, London

West, R and Crighton, J (1999), Examination Reform in Central and Eastern Europe: issues and trends, *Assessment in Education*, **6** (2), pp 271–89

Part C

PROFESSIONAL DEVELOPMENT

Chapter 7

The role of continuing professional development in the improvement of international schools

Jackie Holderness

Introduction

This chapter will consider the importance of individual professional development for international schoolteachers, within the larger framework of international school staff development. It will firstly address issues relating to initial and in-service teacher education for international schoolteachers and investigate concepts and models of Continuing Professional Development (CPD), before considering the role of research in CPD. In particular, the role in school improvement of action research by individual members of staff will be explored. Finally, because many international schoolteachers need to study through distance-learning methods, this chapter will investigate the challenges of attempting further and higher studies at a distance, while working full-time; a model of CPD that has become increasingly popular among the international school fraternity.

Professional development versus staff development

It is important to distinguish, for the purposes of this chapter, between professional development and staff development. Continuing

Professional Development (CPD) tends to be individual- and teacher-centred, and continues during a teacher's career. CPD relates, therefore, to improving the individual's practice within the classroom, or as a curriculum leader or team member. While a few headteachers may resent individuals seeking to pursue their studies above and beyond whole-school in-service education of teachers (INSET) or staff development, most recognize the importance of teachers remaining professionally fulfilled and know that successful teachers are those who strive to keep up-to-date and who remain as learners themselves. As Peterson (1987) pointed out, the teacher has far more lasting an influence on students than does the syllabus. Whatever the syllabus may be, a teacher who has had an opportunity to develop as a reflective practitioner is more likely to make sense of it to the students in their care.

Let us first examine what *professional development* may mean. Within the domain of language teaching, Nunan and Richards (1990) see it as a continuum from training to development. They suggest that teachers move through three distinct stages of professional development, each one epitomized by the following questions:

- stage 1: teacher training [What do I teach? What can I use to teach?];
- stage 2: developing competence [How do I teach? How can I teach better?];
- stage 3: teacher development [Why do I teach what I teach? Why do I teach as I do?].

Hopefully, enquiring, reflective and lifelong learners continue to ask themselves these questions on a regular basis. Sotto (1994) makes a similar point, saying that 'it is not enough to go into a classroom with a set of objectives, lesson notes and an overhead projector... effective teaching is much more a matter of trying to understand how people learn'. Teachers who see themselves as learners are more likely to achieve such an understanding than colleagues who see themselves as teachers only.

By contrast with professional development, *staff development* has a broader goal, which is to bring staff together to ensure unity of purpose, ethos, policy and practice. Bennett (1996) stresses the value of this in helping teachers to manage change more effectively: 'In the... pursuit of individual and organisational health and a continuous climate of improvement, it will be important that professionals value each other's strengths and recognise the need to shape collectively a future which takes account of their conflicting worlds and seeks reconciliation through shared perceptions'.

Bennett goes on to identify a premise that is central to this chapter in pointing to the role of the teacher as researcher. Understanding the here and now of the classroom, through observation and reflection, is the first step in that direction.

School development, enhancing the quality of provision and experience within the school for students, staff and parents, is wider still and usually includes planning for both whole-school staff development and individual and professional development. As Hayden points out elsewhere in this volume, the motivation for any of the above may be driven by needs (such as accreditation requirements, marketing pressures or examination goals) or wants (such as a school striving to enhance certain features of the environment or pedagogy, or an individual wishing to seek greater responsibility or explore new ways to teach). International teachers have both needs and wants and remain in need of development in the two spheres, referred to by Hayden as the technical/pragmatic and the ideological/professional. McClelland and Varma (1996) have researched and described how these wants and needs change with the age and experience of individual teachers. The initial stages of a teaching career, for instance, tend to be characterized by anxiety, idealism and the desire to make a difference to the world.

Internationalism and globalization

At this point, it is important to identify the differences between internationalism and globalization, because international schoolteachers encounter both on a daily basis. Let us say that internationalism is about the interaction and interchange between nations and national identities, whereas globalization can be said to ignore national boundaries and identities in order to serve a single, often corporate, identity.

Another dichotomy teachers have to address, in the day-to-day running of the international school, is the issue of conflicting loyalties to the international and to the local; to commonality and to uniqueness. Globalization seems to involve two cultural forces: integration and segregation. The first, a centrifugal kind of force, pulls together people with common values, behaviours and perspectives; the second, a centripetal force, makes distinctive, and differentiates people into small groups.

While encouraging a world view and a culture of internationalism, it is vital to celebrate each individual's cultural heritage and identity. By so doing, teachers can become what Henderson (1968) called 'terrestrial teachers'. Steiner (1996) suggests that 'The terrestrial teacher... has [a] threefold sense of identity and aims to develop such an identity in children and young people'. This identity needs to be, Steiner suggests:

- strong, confident;
- open to change, constantly developing;
- receptive towards other identities, ready to learn from them and quick to identify commonalties.

Steiner (1996) goes on to emphasize that anyone learning to be a teacher should understand the role of identity in learning and 'have the right and the duty to reflect upon and discuss these broad concepts so that they can become a "global teacher"'. If teachers in training were indeed trained to see themselves as terrestrial or global teachers, then the vision of many international educators could become a reality. This vision is captured by Gellar (1993) in arguing that '... any school in the world, public or private, can be international'.

Determining the 'international' in initial teacher education

In 1998, Peel suggested that the task before international education was to ensure:

- shared responsibility;
- global standards in examinations;
- training of teachers and examiners.

Yet most newly appointed international teachers, leaving their home countries to enter the world of international schooling, are likely to have had little preparation for, or induction into, their new life. If internationalism is a mindset as well as, hopefully, a permeative feature of an international school curriculum, it would appear that headteachers should find the time and money to encourage new staff to 'think internationally'. 'We would define international by what schools do in nurturing (multicultural) understanding; that co-operation, not competition, is the only viable way to solve the major problems facing the planet, all of which transcend ethnic and political borders' (Gellar, 1993).

Any initial training would need not so much to prepare teachers for what has been termed the 'global village' as for a network of different and diverse villages. One of the most challenging aspects of international education is finding texts, activities and materials that are genuinely international and not tied to some narrow national agenda or view of learning. Ideally, for all student teachers Initial Teacher Education (ITE), or Initial Teacher Training (ITT), would strive to achieve truly international, multicultural understanding. Courses would explore principles of international education and discuss global curriculum developments. In a war-torn world, it would make sense to introduce peace studies and intercultural understanding. Deeper understanding of different educational cultures, learning and teaching styles, and other issues in comparative education would help students to put their own teaching into context. Initial training in English as an Additional Language (EAL) is essential but rarely thorough enough for teachers who are preparing children to enter a multilingual society.

It would be helpful if ITE/ITT providers were to collaborate with organizations such as the International Baccalaureate Organization (IBO) to design courses that could be taken by teachers who are hoping to work in an international school or who have already been appointed to do so. Formal school placements in international schools may be difficult to organize in the context of national teacher training programmes because of prescriptive national requirements. However, it would be interesting to see schools that have been accredited by the European Council of International Schools (ECIS) offering school experience in exchange for teaching assistantships. Exchange programmes between international schools, such as cross-cultural exchanges or cross-regional exchanges would enable teachers to establish professional 'buddy' networks. Schools could be accredited as training institutions, along the lines of beacon schools in the United Kingdom (Rudd, 2001). There is certainly scope for formalization/accreditation to show that one has taken steps to develop into an international schoolteacher.

Accredited, short, pre-service courses may be the way forward here, with teachers building up credits through a professional portfolio of in-service days, international conferences or articles published in, for instance, *The International Educator*, *IS magazine*, *International Schools Journal*, or the *Journal of Research in International Education*. Further qualifications, such as certificates, diplomas and Masters or Doctoral degrees, could all contribute to the creation of a professional profile in international education, which reflects lifelong learning in a global classroom.

The 'international' in continuing professional development

According to Jarvis (1983), the desire to learn throughout one's career is intrinsic to being a professional. Lifelong learning is more than a mere slogan. It is essential to any professional group, especially in a world where changes are inevitable, rapid and demanding. Yet Fullan and Hargreaves (1996) claimed that the 'the focus on the link between teacher development and educational change is barely fifteen years old'. They suggest that 'successful change involves learning how to do something new', highlighting the link between study and improvement. They go on to assert that teacher development is 'tantamount to transforming educational institutions'.

The last 20 years have seen an increased emphasis on international schools becoming more effective and accountable through greater investment in the personal and professional development of their staff. Schools have begun to appoint coordinators for professional development and to highlight links between teacher appraisal and staff development. Despite teachers representing the largest slice of a school's budget and being the most influential factors in a child's memories of school, until relatively recently insufficient attention has been paid to teachers in the international school literature (Matthews, 1989). The focus of the literature has tended to be upon the students and the curriculum, even though the success of both of these rests upon the calibre and professionalism of the teachers. Schools determined to ensure quality staff development may already be addressing these issues. When schools value, support and develop their staff, they are actively engaged in enhancing the ethos and quality of teaching and learning. They are involved in an enterprise to help individuals achieve their full potential. They encourage teachers to grow professionally and personally, recognizing that the investment of time, money and the effective management of the process are worthwhile. They know that with more fulfilled and professionally challenged staff, they can expect more informed teaching and learning, which is likely to improve school results and thereby raise parent satisfaction.

While the overall picture of CPD in international schools has not been a consistent one, input such as ECIS global and regional conferences have successfully contributed to a stronger commitment to both professional and staff development in this context. Figure 7.1 identifies a number of opportunities for staff development and CPD, which may be available to those employed in international schools.

Because they are often on short- or fixed-term contracts, international school teachers may feel uncomfortable about asking for funding for CPD and may content themselves with whatever INSET the school organizes. This may lead to their feeling vulnerable about career prospects, should they wish to return to their home country. Staff in international schools may feel at a disadvantage compared with their

---

Whole-school INSET

- Heads identify a need (eg based upon ECIS accreditation recommendations or staff survey), then call in an 'expert' from overseas.
- Several, even all, members of staff are encouraged to attend a conference (eg the annual ECIS Conference).
- Staff expertise within the school is encouraged and members of staff asked to lead school-based INSET.

Individual CPD

- Teacher applies to attend short, off-site, professional course (subject-based, age-related or personal fulfilment).
- Teacher chooses sabbatical study to gain further qualifications (eg EdD, MA, Diploma or Certificate).
- Teacher seeks further qualifications as above but chooses a part-time, distance learning programme.
- Teacher chooses course or sabbatical for personal fulfilment, without a career focus or qualifications.

Figure 7.1   Opportunities for staff development and CPD

colleagues back home because of the difficulties of keeping up-to-date with new developments. They worry that trends are passing them by, and find it more difficult to access materials and courses to sustain the notion of lifelong learning. It is likely they may not be sufficiently linguistically proficient to study in the host country and, for those who are English-speakers, the nearest English-speaking centre of higher or further education may not offer suitable courses or reflect and accept their educational background from another country. Some international teachers may seek out opportunities to study education more deeply in order to overcome a sense of isolation caused by feeling that they are cut adrift from what they would regard as their educational 'roots', while others may seek consciously to 'internationalize' their experience by choosing further study in a different national context.

Interestingly, the fear of becoming out-of-date or isolated may drive international teachers to devote more time and energy to CPD than that spent on CPD by many educators who have remained in their home context. International educators recognize the need to keep abreast of developments in education, hence the large numbers attending annual events such as the ECIS conferences. Conferences that draw together schools in a specific region or with global representation are often very stimulating, as much because of the networks between colleagues that they help to establish as the professional debates and INSET on offer.

To supplement or replace attendance at conferences, many international schools favour short INSET staff development events, such as a weekend workshop on a particular theme. Such opportunities, while valuable, usually only respond to immediate school/staff needs that may be short-lived or personally unsatisfying to individual colleagues. Such INSET tends to focus on immediate pragmatic needs, such as implementing the Literacy Hour in a British-type international school, a subject-specific IB workshop or ESL support. As Hayden points out elsewhere in this volume, however, international schoolteachers also have professional needs. They want to analyse their practice, debate new ideas and feel they are growing as educators.

My own experience may be relevant here as a case study. After seven years teaching in a British-style international school, during which time the school provided a wide range of in-service courses from 'Primary Science' to 'Dealing with Dyslexia', I was ready to pursue further educational studies. The only option available, at that time, was to return to the United Kingdom and take a full-time Master's degree. The year's sabbatical leave I took was professionally rewarding and stimulating. It was impossible, however, to research my own or my school's practice within the international context. I had to 'borrow' local schools' pupils and colleagues for my observations and interviews. Naturally, I returned to my international school revitalized with new ideas, but the long-term effect upon my own school and school development was uncertain because my colleagues had no collegial sense of ownership of the research. They had not participated in, or discussed, its process. I had studied and discussed my reading with fellow students but had been unable to share my research with my own international school community. How much more effective is likely to be the kind of action research where one reflects on one's own practice while still *in situ*.

The 'international' in educational research

Most research begins with questions about a current state or set of circumstances, such as 'What if?', 'How can?' or 'Why does?'. These questions are large enough to be relevant to any school in any context. They form the basis for what Senge (1992) called the 'learning organization'. Without reflective professionals and strong research evidence, educational practices are subject to mythologies, ideologies and fashion trends. Cohen and Manion (1994) say that more research into education is to be encouraged, because 'it will enable educators to develop the kind of sound knowledge base that characterises other professions and disciplines, and one that will ensure education a maturity and sense of progression'.

There is an increasing amount of research on international schools going on now, thanks at least in part to the development of, for example, the International Baccalaureate Research Unit, Masters and Doctoral programmes at universities in different parts of the world, studies being undertaken by university researchers, and ECIS Research Fellowships. Even though it could be argued that the outcomes of such research have not always been widely disseminated, the body of research is growing, which has meant that international teachers now have access to research that can inform much-needed debate into uniquely international school issues.

The 'international' in action research

Educational research has become increasingly concerned with the efforts of individuals to challenge their own practices and assumptions and to reflect-in-action, a concept developed by Schon (1987), amongst others, and known as 'action research'. This type of research can be defined as a way of approaching everyday experience and systematically assessing what is happening in a classroom or school. It implies a professional desire to improve or change a situation or behaviour and should be collaborative, involving the researcher's colleagues. Some evaluation of the improvement is also needed, as the basis for planning further improvement. With a similar focus on improvement in situations, experiences or behaviours, Kemmis and McTaggart (1998) explain that action research is 'a method for practitioners to live with the complexity of real experience, while at the same time striving for concrete improvement'.

We could argue, therefore, that every reflective international schoolteacher is an international education action researcher, because action research involves examining one's professional practice within a collegial framework and exploring ways to improve that practice. Interestingly, any practitioners involved in action research who want to reflect upon an issue in their own school need to apply the questions that are now familiar to many primary international schoolchildren and their teachers who are following the IB Primary Years Programme, as shown in Figure 7.2.

As members of staff in a school, we could apply these questions to any area of school life that has been identified in the school development plan. We may find it relatively easy to answer the first questions but the last question 'How do we know?' brings us back to the role of research in school development. Only by studying and understanding the current situation, and by collecting and analysing data, can we know what needs changing, why it needs changing and how we can start to change things most effectively.

Questions for learners

What is it like?

How does it work?

Why is it like it is?

How is it changing?

How is it connected to other things?

What are the points of view?

What is our responsibility?

How do we know?

Figure 7.2 IB Primary Years Programme questions for learners (Bartlett, 2001)

Although much educational research is recognized as being designed to be of practical use, it is essential for teachers to be able to articulate academic studies with real-life research into education: 'There is an attractive pragmatism in educational research, which prefers to reward approaches that work, rather than those which are canonical within a particular theoretical sub-culture' (Labaree, 2000).

Where professional development is encouraged on a whole school basis, for instance as part of the school development plan, it suggests that the leadership of the school has recognized the inter-connectedness of individual staff development and the whole-school's needs and quality. Reflective practices, where the teacher becomes a learner/enquirer/researcher, will support improvement in classroom practice while at the same time often fostering increased collaboration with colleagues. The professional growth fostered within a group of researchers is likely to have a direct influence on teachers' teaching skills and strategies and to lead to improved learning outcomes and possibly also to refinements in curriculum, policy and management. For this reason, many headteachers encourage staff to embark upon higher degrees and upon school-based action research.

International school action researchers appreciate their unique situation; they want to understand more deeply the complexities of teaching within a multicultural setting and work to improve their practice. Action research projects enable teachers to ensure personal relevance and to make certain that theories explored are tied to the concrete reality of the international school context.

The 'international' in distance learning

There are many myths about distance learning, which may lead to teachers having mixed feelings about it. Some see it as too impersonal, too unstructured, too dependent on the self-discipline of the learner and too isolating. The images conjured up include, perhaps, Australian outback radio classes or early UK Open University packs and television lectures. Holmberg (1991) saw distance learning as a 'didactic conversation' but recommended that some face-to-face contact be built into any distance-learning course in order to promote emotional involvement because, he asserted, 'emotional involvement promotes learning'.

Herein, indeed, lies the strength of the Open University model of study. One central feature of its distance-learning programmes is the intensive summer school, a model that has been used by other universities including Bath and Oxford Brookes in their Master's courses for international schoolteachers. Such summer schools are useful not merely for allowing transmission of, or access to, knowledge but, most powerfully, when used 'for intensive discussions, exchanges of ideas, joint problem-solving, illuminating what students have already learnt from other aspects of their study, critical questioning, reflecting on the value of research results, and applying acquired knowledge. Communication and debate are in the foreground; training in academic dialogue is what is required' (Peters, 1998).

In recent times, in order to enable this academic dialogue to continue at a distance, the Open University and other universities have harnessed new interactive Internet technologies 'to enrich and enable distance learning by creating a web of student-to-student communication' (Daniel, 2000).

A distance-learning programme is ideal for the international school-teacher who does not want the upheaval of a full year's sabbatical leave. Taught elements may be compressed into intensive residential learning experiences, sometimes followed up by distance-learning materials and assignments or online conferencing. The majority of the distance-learning study time is by private study, reading, action research projects and tutorials, using e-mail to communicate with tutors and interactive Web sites to discuss ideas and support each other. The model of learning is autonomous, self-guided learning, in which students will make their own learning decisions.

This brings us to another feature of staff development that is very important. The subject to be studied has to be relevant and should emotionally involve the students. Most distance-learning courses enable students to tailor-make their own assignments to suit their particular context. Their choice of focus, and emotional involvement with it, will help to sustain them despite the distance between themselves and their peers or tutors.

We are witnessing the arrival of 'virtual universities' where students can control the pace and growth of their learning and mix different modes of pedagogy, combining online, face-to-face and independent study. Distance education has become an important approach to lifetime learning. A distance-learning, part-time, course has appeal both for students, who do not have to disrupt their family or home lives, and for schools, who find it is economically attractive because it does not necessitate supply cover or lead to discontinuity amongst the staff. We need to recognize the value of distance learning in professional development, especially for international schoolteachers.

Based on my own experience, teaching on a distance-learning programme, I would suggest that certain features of distance learning contribute to its effectiveness. These are as follows:

1. The length of the study period, which may be at least two to three years at Master's level and four to five for a Doctorate. Shorter INSET experiences, however intense or interactive, cannot compare to the longer engagement with educational ideas offered by a higher degree course. Short courses may focus more on the improvement of teaching skills or raise awareness of innovations but cannot serve as teacher or staff development. Longer courses address issues, professional attitudes and judgments, and encourage deeper and broader understanding. Research by Vulliamy and Webb (1991) has provided evidence that longer programmes, such as a two-year part-time study, had a significant effect on the thinking and confidence of the participants.

2. The increasingly interactive nature of distance-learning programmes, made possible by new technologies, has enabled tutors and students to communicate more easily, conducting the 'didactic conversations' referred to by Holmberg (1991). The original Latin term for 'tutor' meant in fact 'protector' and the individualized tutor–tutee relationship, so central to traditional British university life, has an important part to play in reducing students' isolation and giving them the academic confidence they need. This ensures what Moore (1993) calls the smallest 'transactional distance' for distance learners, where transactional distance is a function of three variables: characteristics of students, teaching goals and content, and teaching methods and culture.

3. The use of school-based assignments, central to most distance-learning programmes, means that students are required to develop the skills of a reflective practitioner. By analysing current practices and searching for ways to improve them, students become agents for school development. Because students are responsible for choosing their area

of study, there can be no guarantee that the area investigated will benefit the school directly. However, many students choose to negotiate their project title with their headteacher or the coordinator for school development. This means that the area selected for study is likely to be of mutual benefit to the student and the school, possibly even furthering the School Development Plan. Where the benefit is not mutual and students pursue an area purely for their own interest, the value of the experience may, however, be equally high. Although the task may be triggered off miles away, the outcomes are likely to be observed most keenly in the student's own classroom.

4. Intercultural learning and communication occurs. Distance learners tend to come from a wide range of cultural backgrounds and, if they are international teachers, may well be living far from their heritage culture. They will be Third Culture Teachers (TCTs), as opposed to Third Culture Kids (TCKs) (Langford, 2001). Whether discussing education online or at a residential summer school, international teacher students bring their rich intercultural awareness to bear upon the debate.

There are, of course, challenging aspects to distance learning, including the following:

1. Discipline and organization are frequently cited as problematic. Juggling work and study, family and friends, is clearly difficult for many students. Time is the chief issue in the sense of, for instance, scheduling, managing and finding blocks of time for study.
2. Keeping track of deadlines and structuring study are often mentioned as hurdles to be overcome by distance learners, with particular reference to 'starting and finishing'.
3. Communication problems specifically related to distance include accessing information required for the research, such as current research resources. There may be feelings of working in isolation and a lack of collegial feedback.

Fortunately, most distance-learning programme designers are aware of these dangers and have evolved systems of support and flexibility so that students can travel on their CPD journey at a pace that is manageable for them.

Conclusion

There would appear to be general acceptance of the idea that reflective practice, lifelong learning and the refinement of one's professional practice is essential to professional growth. International educators generally recognize the need to keep abreast of developments in education. International education has strengthened its own professionalism, thanks to academics and curriculum developers working in the field, the IBO, ECIS conferences, ECIS fellowships and the involvement of international school heads in peer-assessments or ECIS accreditations. Additionally, the growing body of research into international schools has meant that international teachers have access to results that can inform much-needed debate into uniquely international school issues.

It is for these reasons that school boards may partially subsidize or even fully finance their staff to follow professional development courses. Such commitment to teachers' long-term professional growth can be helpful in attracting an otherwise potentially transient staff to stay longer and yet feel professionally fulfilled. It is also likely that award-bearing courses will enhance the professional profile of members of staff and demonstrate the school's commitment to lifelong learning at all levels.

By changing and improving staff we can change and improve schools. There is a link between individual and school development, as shown by Eraut (1994) and Day *et al* (2000). Headteachers know that their teachers are worthy of nurture and development and believe that they will become better teachers as a result of conducting further study and action research. Finally, therefore, to consider whether studies at a far-flung institution have a positive impact on an international school, we can turn to two teachers who took up the challenge of action research and survived 'the loneliness of the long distance researcher'. These teachers have examined the impact of their studies upon themselves and their schools: 'My research into teaching and learning styles has been shared with colleagues and helped us all in understanding East/West cultural differences'; 'The quality of teaching and learning has improved because I am much more aware of why I do things the way I do... am I catering to a different learning style? Am I declaring my objectives clearly enough? Does the student know why she is performing the experiment? Are my students analysing their work enough? A horde of such queries that the reading, discussions and writing on the MA have raised in my mind (and) keep the process of teaching and learning, as I go along, challenging and stimulating'.

Ensuring that we remain challenged and stimulated helps us to sustain our passion for teaching. Ultimately, it is this passion for teaching that drives change and improvement, as Whitaker (1995) notes: 'Teaching, like learning, is an infinitely intricate and precarious activity. There are no simple solutions, no quick fixes and no easy remedies. There are only ideas and opportunities and efforts'.

Action research enables teachers to engage with those ideas, identify those opportunities and channel those efforts effectively. Whitaker continues: 'Change will not be accomplished by spectacular reforms... Change and development will be achieved through the often small but painstaking and dedicated steps of those who, as educators, have a passion for their craft, who love the learning process with all its confusions and messiness and who are committed to the causes of the pupils they teach'.

References

Bartlett, K (2001) International Curricula: more or less important at the primary level?, in *International Education: Principles and practice*, eds M C Hayden and J J Thompson, Kogan Page, London

Bennett, C (1996) *Researching into Teaching Methods: In colleges and universities*, Kogan Page, London

Cohen, L and Manion, L (1994) *Research Methods in Education*, Routledge, London

Daniel, J (2000) Can you get my hard nose in focus? Universities, mass education and appropriate technology, in *The Knowledge Web: Learning and collaborating on the Net*, eds M Eisenstadt and T Vincent, Kogan Page, London

Day, C, Fernandez, A, Hauge, T E and Moller, J (eds) (2000) *The Life and Work of Teachers: International perspectives in changing times*, Falmer Press, London

Eraut, M (1994) *Developing Professional Knowledge and Competence*, Falmer Press, London

Fullan, M and Hargreaves, A (1996) *What's Worth Fghting for in Your School?*, Teachers' College Press, New York

Gellar, C (1993) Editorial, *The International Schools Journal*, **26**, p 6

Henderson, J L (1968) *Education for World Understanding*, Pergamon Press, Oxford

Holmberg, B (1991) Testable Theory based on Discourse and Empathy, *Open Learning*, **6** (2), pp 44–46

Jarvis, P (1983) *Professional Education*, Croom Helm, London

Kemmis, S and McTaggart, R (1998) *The Action Research Planner*, Deakin University Press, Deakin

Labaree, D F (2000) Educational Researchers: living with a lesser form of knowledge, in *The Life and Work of Teachers: International perspectives in changing times*, eds C Day, A Fernandez, T E Hauge and J Moller, Falmer Press, London

Langford, M (2001) Global Nomads, Third Culture Kids and international schools, in *International Education: Principles and practice*, eds M C Hayden and J J Thompson, Kogan Page, London

McLelland, V and Varma, V (1996) *The Needs of Teachers*, Cassell, London

Matthews, M (1989) The scale of international education. Part 1, *International Schools Journal*, **17**, pp 7–17

Moore, M (1993) Theory of transactional distance, in *Theoretical Principles of Distance Education*, ed D Keegan, Routledge, London

Nunan, D and Richards, J C (1990) *Second Language Teacher Education*, Cambridge University Press, Cambridge

Peel, R M (1998) International Education Comes of Age, *International Schools Journal*, **XVII**, 2, pp 12–17

Peters, O (1998) *Learning and Teaching in Distance Education: Analyses and interpretations*, Kogan Page, London

Peterson, A D C (1987) *Schools Across Frontiers: The Story of the International Baccalaureate and the United World Colleges*, Open Court, La Salle, Illinois

Rudd, P (2001) *Beacon Schools: Further external evaluation of the initiative*, NFER, Slough

Schon, D (1987) *Educating the Reflective Practitioner: Towards a new design for teaching and learning in the professions*, Jossey-Bass, San Francisco

Senge, P M (1992) *The Fifth Discipline: The art and practice of the Learning Organisation*, Century Business, London

Sotto, E (1994) *When Teaching Becomes Learning*, Cassell, London

Steiner, M (1996) *Developing the Global Teacher*, Trentham, Stoke-on-Trent

Vulliamy, G and Webb, R (1991) Teacher research and educational change: an empirical study, *British Educational Research Journal*, **17** (3), pp 219–36

Whitaker, P (1995) *Managing to Learn*, Cassell, London

Chapter 8

Professional development: an international schools' perspective

Neil Richards

Introduction

Professional development in schools is big business; the ever-increasing mound of professional development invitations that land on any senior administrator's desk attest to this fact. There are courses to suit every school's pocket and needs, as well as courses to cure every malaise known to education, including a number not yet identified by the researchers. Most do not carry health-warnings, yet the request to 'post this in the faculty room' is as insidious as a virus, and in the frontier territory of international education, purveyors of snake oil abound.

As a major determinant for the direction and ethos of a school, professional development cannot be ignored; it is a part of the basic fabric of whole school development, and, deep down where responsibility lurks, you know it does you good. Or do you? Most school administrators would surely admit to a twinge of unease when the experts, for a small fee of course, are willing to dispense their words of wisdom. Whilst enthusiastic converts to new methodologies or educational theories can energize staff in a variety of ways, not all of them are necessarily productive. Furthermore, professional development that is squandered, or subsequently ignored, can be more damaging to the long-term health of a school than having no professional development at all, as teachers lose confidence in the school's capacity to adapt or innovate.

However, the importance of structured professional development for a school cannot be overstated. There is a symbiotic relationship between the teacher, international schools and international education. Crucial to the health of this relationship is the provision of opportunities for a constant flow and interchange of ideas, and it is within this context that the importance of professional development is apparent.

A model for professional development

The model in Figure 8.1, based upon fields of congruence, will be used in this chapter as the basis for the examination of the relationship between the school, the teacher and international education.

There is an obvious professional overlap of the school, the teacher and international education in its broader sense, as well as, presumably, a measure of philosophical congruence: this is represented by the field marked A. The school and the teacher have areas of interaction that are not necessarily related to any vision of internationalism, but could revolve around internal issues, school procedures, and career/school expectations: this is represented by field B.

The international school and the proponents of an international education, such as the International Baccalaureate Organization (IBO), the International Schools Association (ISA) or the accrediting agencies, should have a shared vision, or at least a significant degree of contextual overlap, in their philosophies of international education and global citizenship. This may be less easy to demarcate, but is represented by the

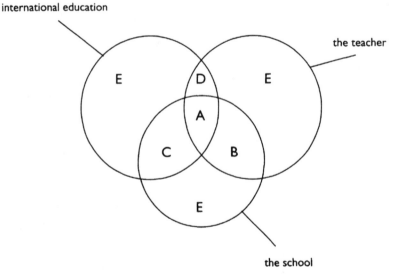

Figure 8.1 A model for professional development

field marked C. The model also acknowledges the relationship between the wider world of international education and the teacher, which will almost certainly extend well beyond the school, and the lifespan of a contractual period. This is represented by field D.

Finally, each of the three elements has broader areas of interest and responsibilities that are substantially independent of the others. The agencies of 'international education' have their world constituency; the teacher has his/her future career; the school has a tradition and a future development based upon the unique requirements of the locality in which it is based. These independent factors are represented by the fields marked E.

The three elements in the model (school, teacher and international education) are each dependent upon the other two, and it is upon the success of the interrelationships that the concept of international education is shaped. Professional development strategies and programmes are the means through which these relationships are enhanced and, I would suggest, they provide the vehicle for the reflective and creative dimension that is necessary for international education to continue to meet the needs of the global society.

Culture and climate

Organizations, whether global or local, have essential characteristics that create identity and a sense of belonging, and it is now commonplace to refer to this unique blend of characteristics as a 'culture'. As organizations grow and develop, cultures evolve, but it cannot be assumed that any one culture is necessarily the most effective for achieving a desired outcome merely because of its evolution. In the first place the phrase 'desired outcome' is fraught with difficulty in the context of an international school, and secondly the growing acceptance among international schools of externally developed but internally applied curricula could seriously compromise the traditions of many of these schools. Put simply, the traditional, evolved cultures may not necessarily be the most appropriate vehicles for a philosophy of internationalism such as that espoused, for example, by the IBO, and reflected within its curricula. Indeed, schools may actually undergo some sort of identity crisis as cultural structures are bent to accommodate new curriculum models. Or, conversely, some schools may find it expedient to bend the new curriculum to fit the old shape. In either scenario, something must surely be lost in the process.

Climate, on the other hand, might be considered as a prevailing trend of opinion or feeling in a community or organization, and is a much more immediate indicator of organizational health and efficiency. An organization filled with disgruntled, or confused, personnel will function inefficiently, no matter how ingrained the operational culture. Differences of opinion are the lifeblood of an effective teaching staff, but ultimately clear directives, with sound rationale, have to be given and followed in order for the school to operate effectively.

In every school, both 'culture' and 'climate' are affected by, and impact upon, the efficacy of the teachers. However, and even more fundamentally perhaps, it is the school administration that must deal with the angst of self-doubt, as the gurus of internationalism proffer their wares.

To effect a change in a school culture can be a slow and often painful process. The ground has to be thoroughly prepared with the stakeholders of the school, and the teaching staff need to be convinced of the benefits of change, as well as given the means to implement change effectively. Implementing change through administrative edict has not, in my experience, created a climate of receptiveness, and good ideas will wither on the vine if the soil is arid and devoid of nutrients.

Professional development must be woven into the very fabric of strategic planning, since the teachers are the instruments through which successful cultural change can be accomplished. No matter how well constructed are the administrative structures, or well articulated the rationale for change, the ownership of development must be shared with the teaching staff as a whole. There is no better example of this than the way in which the Primary Years Programme (PYP) of the IBO has developed out of the International Schools Curriculum Project, which was, in its turn, developed out of the experiences of a group of dedicated and visionary practitioners. The PYP programme is expanding rapidly, changing school cultures in the process, but fundamental to the success of this rapid growth is its insistence upon quality control, by granting authorization only after staff training and a period of successful implementation. This insistence upon quality control must lie at the heart of school development, and planned professional development is the foundation upon which school development is built.

Applying the model

The common ground: field A

This is possibly the area of greatest controlled integration, and for the most part represents the implementation of external programmes or curricula within a school. Such implementation is usually dependent upon very clear criteria and standards, with a high degree of external moderation and control. Programmes such as those of the IBO are the classic examples of this, but international schools often take on a variety of national examinations such as College Board examinations of the United States, or the International General Certificate of Secondary Education (IGCSE) emanating from Cambridge, United Kingdom. Both US and UK curricula are common, and many international schools are obliged to provide elements of the national curriculum requirements of the countries in which they are located. Interestingly, the obligation to provide a variety of external programmes, either to suit the requirements of the community or to fulfil the legal requirements of local authorities, has helped in the development of the concept of the 'eclectic' school.

The 'eclectic' school

It is not unusual for international schools to boast of an 'eclectic' approach, based upon the best educational practices from around the world (frequently a mix of British and US approaches, perhaps more diversified over recent years by antipodean influences). Selecting the best sounds eminently sensible, and it has a fine ring to it, but what does it mean? Does it mean that the school will continue to sift through the educational developments that emerge from national systems from around the world and that this is the basis of the school philosophy and vision? Or does it mean that individual teachers or administrators, through personal conviction and the exercising of will power and persuasion, hold the key to the development of such schools? Surely, any planning on the basis of waiting to see what comes around the next corner, or waiting to see what turns up with the next new staff intake, is extremely suspect.

In some ways the 'eclectic' school is the most accommodating of all school cultures, since it provides a safe setting for a variety of individualistic approaches. Whilst it may well be the most comfortable culture for experienced teachers, it offers scant support for new teachers, or teachers of limited experience, or for teachers unfamiliar with a Western-style pedagogy. The teacher does not merely pass on curriculum content, or provide training for the students, the teacher fashions the curriculum out of the content; in many ways the teacher is the curriculum, and therefore can never be wholly independent of it.

Eclecticism, it seems, is more a description of what currently exists in many international schools, rather than a strategy for development, and whilst it is perfectly understandable given the historical context within which many international schools have grown, it must surely be time to review such cultures.

Features of effective congruence

It is in the provision, and service, of externally developed curricula that professional development seems to be at its most focused. External agencies are clear about the outcomes they require and provide constant feedback as well as in-service training to ensure that the curriculum is delivered effectively. Schools are equally focused on the need to perform at a satisfactory level within the parameters of the external requirements and provide the necessary support, and pressure, to ensure that the teachers are on task. The key features of this effective congruence may, therefore, be identified as follows:

- Curriculum objectives, and desired outcomes, are well articulated and accepted.
- Resources are provided to achieve the objectives.
- Professional development is considered a vital factor in the achievement of the objectives.
- There is an external audit.
- The outcomes reflect upon each of the three elements of school, teacher and international education.

Since such features can be applied equally to a whole school strategic development, there should be no surprises in any of the above. However, it is by looking for evidence of such features in the other areas of congruence in the model that we may reveal inconsistencies of approach that could undermine this whole school development. Just how clear we are about our school-wide objectives and the various concepts of internationalism, and how well integrated these are with the three elements in the model, is open to a great deal of conjecture.

The school and the teacher: field B

It ought to be a safe assumption that all international school teachers have been trained somewhere and are certified practitioners, although from personal experience I know that this is often not the case. Many schools have strict employment criteria with regard to qualified teachers but a significant number, having to survive in challenging local conditions, are required to be slightly more generous in their interpretation of such qualifications than they might otherwise wish to be. An academic degree, even a higher degree, does not necessarily contain a pedagogical component. Neither should it be assumed that good learners are good teachers; higher degrees may look good on a school profile, but they should be treated with a healthy circumspection.

Even where all teachers hold a qualification in education, it cannot be assumed that the pedagogical backgrounds of the teachers are compatible. The national education cultures that give rise to the various teacher-training programmes can be quite different. It is ironic that two of the national systems that use English as the mother tongue (United Kingdom and United States), have quite distinctive educational cultures, and yet these two cultures have dominated the development of the international schools. (Try discussing 'grading' with a mixed group of US and UK teachers!) Our staff rooms, however, are often filled with a variety of cultures and nationalities and, although there is a heavy bias towards a Western pedagogical tradition, there are, especially in developing countries, significant numbers of 'other' representatives. These 'others' may well face pedagogical, pastoral, administrative and psychological challenges that are quite distinct from their 'Western' colleagues, and as such have the potential to compromise much more than desired classroom management techniques.

Adapting to a new school culture can be a painful experience. Changes in routine, regulations, communication and planning are easily accommodated, but less easy to absorb are changes in such things as pastoral approach and responsibility, assessment methodology and pedagogical 'style'. These latter three, in particular, are important in determining the profile of a teacher, and are, therefore, intrinsically bound up with a teacher's self-efficacy; there is a heavy price to pay if the school culture undermines it. Unfortunately, a review of the historic growth of international education would seem to indicate that there is no 'philosopher's stone' to transmute the 'national school teacher' into the more mythical 'international school teacher', other than 'experience' itself, with all the vagaries and chance opportunities that this implies. Flexibility seems to be one of the most eagerly sought after attributes in international teachers, but how flexible can our schools afford to be in return?

School cultures

Schools have a responsibility to identify the essential elements of their unique cultures, and to anticipate where problems of teacher compatibility may occur. Such essential elements may be determined by programmes such as those offered by the IBO, in which case, and as already noted, there are professional development opportunities of which a school can avail itself on a reasonably regular basis (the congruence of aims represented by area A on the model).

However, there may be other elements in a school's cultural make-up that are not so readily supported by professional development

opportunities elsewhere, and it is incumbent upon the school administration to identify these and provide for them in any strategy for
professional development. The three areas of 'pastoral approach', 'assessment methodology' and 'classroom management' have already been
suggested as possible areas of 'cultural' confusion, and expectations in
these areas must be articulated if school policy is to be implemented
effectively. Other areas for attention may be highlighted by the school's
philosophy and mission statement, but knowledge of a culture is not the
same as acceptance or adoption of that culture; the teacher, just like the
expatriate, can coexist quite happily with others, within a cocoon of
personal conviction, provided they are left to their own devices. Others
may not be so fortunate; a lack of confidence could lead to a different
kind of alienation within a staffroom or classroom.

School climate

My own research into staff morale and job satisfaction in an international school (Richards, 1997) suggests that numerous factors
undermine the idea of staff unity, not least of which are the different
teaching methodologies and previous school experiences of the teachers. Where pedagogical differences occur, this can lead to damaging
perceptions, within a school community, about teacher 'types', or worse
still about national or racial stereotypes. Teachers, as we know, can be
solitary creatures, and are well able to apply a whole range of defensive
techniques when threatened, though internationalism is unlikely to
flourish successfully in such an unhealthy climate.

It seems clear, however, that professional development has a profound
importance beyond its effect upon an individual teacher's career, or even
upon the performance of that teacher in the classroom. Holly and
Southworth (1993) suggest that staff development is one of the foundation stones of the developing school, and it is within this context of the
developing school, I would suggest, that professional development is best
applied. That is, as the means to develop the staff as a whole, in support
of the culture, stated philosophy and objectives of a school.

The features of congruence identified earlier are no less important
here; the curriculum objectives and desired outcomes must be clearly
articulated and understood. This must extend beyond the requirements
of the 'formal' curriculum, and embrace all aspects of a school's operations, especially, I would suggest, the approach to the social and
emotional development of the students. The resources must then be
provided to achieve the objectives. Professional development opportunities must be made available, either from external sources or from

within the structure of the school, to provide the teacher with the skills and understanding to integrate effectively. Finally, there must be a means to audit the effectiveness of the school's support for the teacher. Upon the success of such integration rests the reputation of the school and ultimately of international education itself.

The development of shared goals, responsibilities and the collaborative approach are difficult enough to apply in schools with a large degree of staff homogeneity and stability. In international schools, however, with their diversity of teacher backgrounds, a high staff turnover, and relatively frequent leadership change, that difficulty is greatly compounded. The tension between school philosophy and culture (represented and promoted by the school leadership/administration), and the philosophies and methodologies represented by the teaching body, creates the professional climate within our schools. Where there is a high degree of congruence, there is likely to be good morale and a high level of job satisfaction, but if this congruence does not exist, not only could it cause an unhealthy professional climate, it could also undermine the trust within the community of stakeholders.

It is, of course, possible for a school to have a high level of staff morale in situations where congruence does not seem to occur naturally, and where individual teachers, through personal charisma or through solid experience, instil a high degree of confidence in their respective classrooms. However, in such circumstances, the school administration may well be beset by anxious parents, who would have difficulty identifying the context for these individualistic approaches, and who might view progress through the school as something of a lottery. It would certainly be difficult to justify such a situation as being a natural and healthy consequence of school policy.

It is the prime responsibility, I would suggest, of all school administrations to identify the main features of a school's culture, and to provide full support to the staff, as a body, to achieve an understanding of the implications of the culture, and the expectations of the teachers within such a school culture. How well this is brought about will determine the professional climate.

The international school and international education: field C

'There is no such thing as international education, only international schools'. A statement such as this neatly sidesteps the semantics and problems of definition that surround the term 'international education'. Each school could then be defined through its own philosophy and mission statement, where they exist, or through school traditions, leadership, client groups, curricula, or a whole range of characteristics that make up each school's unique identity. By extension, it would follow that 'international education' could only be applied within the broadest possible terms if the aim is to include all, or even most, so-called international schools within its orbit.

Perhaps this is the crux of the problem associated with definitions of international education: they attempt to define what is, rather than what ought to be. Although it is recognized that within this very fluid world of international schools some common characteristics, or even some form of collective administrative expediency, may lend itself to suggest distinct sub-groupings – such as American international schools, United World Colleges, or 'IB schools' – it is rare to find international schools making conscious efforts towards homogeneity. Even the United World Colleges, with their common philosophy and tight, mutually supportive infrastructure, are, in a variety of ways, quite disparate institutions. The characteristics of the thousands of existing institutions, each of which seems to define internationalism through its own mutations, are impossible to package neatly. In which case, perhaps we should stop trying to apply this bottom up approach.

If, however, a broadly acceptable definition could be produced on the basis of what an international education ought to offer, rather than on what it seems to be, the direction for international school administrators would be a little clearer, and the planning of professional development a little more focused. It would certainly help clear the muddied waters that swirl around our international schools and their communities.

It is also time, perhaps, to accept that the word international is, in a great number of schools, descriptive of the student body rather than of the philosophy or the curriculum. In such schools, to be sure, an international dimension is created out of the interaction of students and the community (Hayden and Thompson, 1995), but it seems to be less of an issue of school culture, and more of an issue of school climate. School culture is often of national origin, and this affects such fundamental things as the administrative and curriculum structure, the assessment methodology and the pedagogical expectations.

Historically, where a deliberate attempt has been made to avoid a national connection, the resulting mix has usually been an Anglo-American cocktail. More recently, however, international schools have the example of the full IB curriculum before them, which, although arising out of Western pedagogy, has its own distinct identity based upon an articulated philosophy of internationalism. Not only this but, increasingly, well-established schools of a whole variety of academic persuasions are looking to embrace the IBO curricula. Surely, the IBO is now in a unique position to determine the form and future direction of international education.

The congruence of the school and international education in the model, I would suggest, is a crucial one. It implies integration, not overlap, and both the school, and more importantly the organizations in leadership positions such as the IBO, should recognize that each is buying into the philosophy of the other, and that the curriculum that is delivered becomes a fusion of the two. Taken a step further, it implies that it is a responsibility of both partners to clarify context as much as content and logistics, and this can only be done through the development of a shared vision of international education, supported by a structured staff professional development programme to achieve that vision; in short, adopting the very features of congruence that work so effectively in the application of external examination curricula within international schools.

The teacher and international education: field D

Is there really such a creature as 'the international teacher'? Despite many decades of international education, the chief requirement of teachers in international schools seems to be that they be flexible; chameleon-like in their ability to adapt to the educational environments in which they find themselves. Even so, there is no shortage of teachers who have made careers in international education and it seems unlikely that the supply will dry up.

As things stand many teachers, although certainly not all, are able to avail themselves of professional development opportunities, some of which have components on international education (although this frequently focuses on trying to understand what the phrase means). However, I believe that the establishment of an international teaching qualification is long overdue. As more and more schools seek an international dimension, it would make sense for an international agency, such as the IBO, to collaborate with a university (or universities) to provide an 'international teacher' training programme and qualification. Such a course would, perforce, be based upon the features of effective congruence suggested by the fields in the model. International curriculum objectives and outcomes would have to be clearly identified and be broadly accepted; resources, including expertise, would need to be made available; the outcomes would have to be of benefit to schools, teachers and 'international education' itself.

One of the greatest benefits would be to enable teachers from a variety of backgrounds, and especially those from developing countries, to break into international education and to contribute with confidence to its development. As a prerequisite many schools would have to break away from their educational chauvinism, adopt a philosophy-driven recruitment policy and, more importantly, provide the professional support that will enable these teachers to adapt to, and give of their best within, the educational culture of an international school. However, it remains for the agencies of international education to provide the real leadership, by articulating the context within which the special qualities and skills that are required by our teachers are used, thus ensuring that international education breaks down more barriers than it erects, and truly becomes globally significant.

Conclusion

To suggest that there is only one version of international education is neither appropriate nor possible. There are, and will continue to be, many differing interpretations of what constitutes – as well as what ought to constitute – an education of this type. Perhaps we are in need of new terminology, a taxonomy of international education based upon the curriculum objectives of the various 'types' of international schools. Perhaps we should dispense with the term 'international' altogether – it only confuses the issue – and begin to define our schools in other ways.

Clearly, however, professional development must cover all fields of congruence highlighted by the model, and this professional development needs to be applied within the clearly defined culture of the school. It cannot be limited only to the support and implementation of externally devised curricula: the relationship between the school, the teacher and the wider world of international education must be understood sufficiently to enable school strategists to provide the context within which professional development makes sense and has real impact.

The teacher, as a member of an organization, should have the opportunity to contribute to the school's development, but for this contribution to be productive, rather than counter-productive or tangential, it must be based upon mutual support and an understanding of the school's culture and objectives. Thus, one of the prime duties of a school administration, if it wishes to implement a professional development programme, is to clarify these objectives, and explain the rationale upon which they are based. To this end, internally provided opportunities for professional growth may be more important than those applied externally, but an understanding of the school's philosophy and ethos is an important prerequisite for teachers before embarking on courses elsewhere.

Further, as strategies for development are articulated, a school should be clear about the expectations it has of its teachers; whether, for example, these should include a minimum level of competency in information technology, or an understanding of the practical application of English as a second language (ESL) in the mainstream classroom. Professional development must have concrete aims, and once identified the expectation must be that they will be applied and lead to improvement. A school that invests in professional development within a strategic vacuum is wasting resources, and teacher time and effort.

Finally, the agencies that support international education must, I would suggest, look beyond the clean boundaries of the formal curriculum, and become a little more fastidious in their expectations of member schools, and more demanding of the international perspectives found within.

It would be a pity, indeed, if international education were to continue to be shored up by eclecticism and flexibility... with a dab or two of snake oil for those creaking joints.

References

Hayden, M C and Thompson, J J (1995) Perceptions of international education: a preliminary study, *International Review of Education*, **41** (5), pp 389–404

Holly, P J and Southworth, G (1993) *The Developing School,* Falmer Press, London

Richards, N (1997) A case study of the implementation of change and its effect upon the job satisfaction and morale of local-contract teaching staff in an international school, MPhil thesis, University of Bath

Chapter 9

International education: pragmatism and professionalism in supporting teachers

Mary Hayden

Introduction

Professional development is a concept widely recognized by teachers and administrators, whether in national systems or within the network of international schools and colleges around the world – even though the term 'professional development' itself may not necessarily be used in all contexts, and other terms such as in-service training, continuing professional development, staff development and lifelong learning all spring to mind. Likewise, the forms it takes will vary, from the heavily formalized, with detailed structure, prescribed outcomes and clearly specified consequences, to the very informal, where the learning or development occurs so gradually that it is barely observable on a day-to-day basis. It may be based on external input, or it may be internally driven in a way advocated by Powell (2000), which 'pervades the entire life of the organisation... (building)... a culture of reflective teaching practice'.

Opportunities to engage in professional development – in one or other of its forms – abound, although some will find such opportunities more accessible or attractive than others, and the particular nature of the professional development deemed appropriate will vary according to the context in which individuals are employed, the nature of their responsibilities, the stage of career reached and future career aspirations. What is

all-important is matching the type of professional development opportunity to the need, whether that need relates to support in refining the
way in which a particular task is deployed, or support in questioning the
very nature of the task to be undertaken.

It may, on occasion, appear to a casual observer that the role of a
teacher or administrator most resembles that of a circus plate-spinner
whose skill is in rushing from pole to pole, ensuring that all plates stay
spinning at the same time. To apply the analogy to the context of professional development, there will be types of professional development that
enable the spinner to learn how to keep the plates spinning for longer
periods of time, or to reduce the amount of running between poles and
re-spinning required (doing the same things better), and there will be
types of professional development that encourage the spinner to reflect
on whether the plates are of the most appropriate size, or the poles of the
most suitable length, or the layout and number of poles most appropriate for the task – or even whether plate-spinning is an appropriate
exercise in which to engage. Fitness for purpose is clearly a key concept
here, with the professional development in question likely to be of most
benefit when it clearly meets its purpose, however explicitly or otherwise this may have been stated.

This chapter will explore a range of issues relating to professional
development within the context of international education. Beginning
with a number of general considerations relating to professional development, it will then focus on its manifestation in the context of
international schools, before concluding with a consideration of the role
professional development may play in promoting international education.

Defining 'professional development'

As already intimated, the concept of professional development has been
interpreted at different times and in a wide range of contexts in a
number of different ways. For the purposes of this chapter, a broad definition will be adopted that views professional development as being
relevant at different stages of an individual's career, as suggested by Dean
(1991): 'Professional development is career long, starting with initial
training and continuing until retirement. It is an active process. The
teacher must actually work to develop. Development does not happen
merely as a result of years of teaching'.

The definition will also be broad in the sense of going beyond those
that focus on the main purposes of professional development as the

acquisition of subject or content knowledge and teaching skills (Hoyle 1980, Joyce and Showers 1980) and, rather, will share the view of Day (1999), who argued that:

> Professional development consists of all natural learning experiences and those conscious and planned activities which are intended to be of direct or indirect benefit to the individual, group or school and which contribute, through these, to the quality of education in the classroom. It is the process by which, alone and with others, teachers review, renew and extend their commitment as change agents to the moral purposes of teaching; and by which they acquire and develop critically the knowledge, skills and emotional intelligence essential to good professional thinking, planning and practice with children, young people and colleagues through each phase of their teaching lives.

It is evident, if such a notion of professional development is accepted, that it relates to every dimension of a teacher's professional life – as it is clear that this professional life is a complex one. Different teachers will deploy their roles in different ways, according to such factors as the context in which they are employed, the age group and other characteristics of the children in their care, the image of their own role as teacher, and their own personalities. Such differences notwithstanding, teachers are not generally perceived purely as deliverers of knowledge. As Day (1999) points out: 'Successful teaching will always demand both intrapersonal and interpersonal skills, and personal and professional commitment. It is a synthesis of the head and the heart', before going on to say that 'teachers... stand at the interface of the transmission of knowledge, skills and values'.

This last concept – values – is an interesting one in the context of international schools. In any school context a particular set of values will underpin the educational experience of its students. Such values may be made explicit in the mission statement and rigorously and consistently upheld throughout the school; alternatively they may not be made explicit but rather be implicit in everything that happens; they may be consistently applied, or they may vary among teachers, administrators and, indeed, all those involved in the school community. What is clear is that, as Watson and Ashton (1995) point out, education cannot be value-free. As Halstead (1996) put it: 'The values of schools are apparent in their organisation, curriculum and discipline procedures, as well as in the relationships between teachers and pupils. Values are reflected in what teachers choose to permit or encourage in the classroom, and in the way they respond to children's contributions to learning'.

Teachers, standing as Day (1999) has said 'at the interface of the transmission of knowledge, skills and values', are clearly crucial in conveying

– overtly or otherwise – a certain set of values to the students, in the context of the role they deploy as, for instance, teachers of mathematics, or kindergarten teachers. In other words, in addition to the role that teachers have as what might be described as 'technician', encouraging the development of cognitive and affective knowledge and skills, they also act – intentionally or not, overtly or otherwise – as role models (positive or negative) for those students in their care. Thus the school, through its value system and its policies, can influence every dimension of a student's life. As Jackson et al (1993) pointed out:

> To anyone who takes a close look at what goes on in classrooms it becomes quickly evident that our schools do much more than pass along requisite knowledge to the students attending them... They also influence the way those students look upon themselves and others. They affect the way learning is valued and sought after and lay the foundation of lifelong habits of thoughts and actions. They shape opinion and develop taste, helping to form likings and aversions. They contribute to the growth of character and, in some instances, they may even be a factor in its corruption.

The balance to be found in any individual between the roles of 'teacher as technician' and 'teacher as role model' may vary according to their particular responsibility, the cultural context, their personality and the characteristics of the students being taught. How, then, does this dual role relate to the discussion of professional development? The answer to this question lies in a consideration of how professional development is, or should be, used to support both aspects of a teacher's professional life: professional development for the teacher as technician, and professional development for the teacher as role model. The question could be asked in any context, national or international. This chapter, however, will focus on the context of international education and, in particular, on what might make professional development in this context different from professional development in any other. Before embarking upon a discussion of professional development in the context of international education, however, it may be helpful to consider briefly what we mean by international education and the role of the teacher in promoting this form of education.

International education and the role of the teacher

Much has been written about the concept of international education and its relationship to the context of international schools (see, for example, publications edited by Hayden and Thompson, 2000 and

2001). For the purposes of this chapter, it will be taken that the two terms do not go hand in hand, that international schools may or may not promote international education, and that international education may also be promoted within national schools. So far as international schools are concerned, many will claim in their mission statements to be promoting international education in the sense of encouraging students to develop attributes such as open-mindedness, tolerance, and respect for others, although it may not be too harsh to argue that some such claims exist more as a marketing strategy than as a reflection of a genuine commitment to such values by the school in question. There are many, however, including those referred to by Hill (2000) as 'internationally-minded' schools, which do actively promote what has been described as the 'ideological' dimensions of international education (Hayden, 2001) or, perhaps, 'education for international understanding'.

Such an ethos notwithstanding, it is also the case that such schools have to incorporate a 'pragmatic' dimension into their programmes and philosophy, in the sense that they have to recognize the need to prepare students on a practical as well as ideological basis for life after the school gates close metaphorically for the last time. Thus in addition to promoting what might be described as 'internationally-minded values', many schools will enter students for externally and internationally recognized examinations. There may be tensions inherent from time to time in juggling these two dimensions, but programmes such as those offered by the International Baccalaureate Organization support schools in balancing the dual role by themselves offering a blend of the pragmatic and the ideological, in the sense of promoting high academic standards while at the same time encouraging the development of attributes relating to the promotion of international understanding.

So far as the pragmatic dimension is concerned, students develop knowledge, understanding and skills, and demonstrate their knowledge, skills and understanding through, for example, accredited forms of assessment. From an ideological viewpoint, students in many international schools are encouraged to develop at an affective level those attributes found in many mission statements, including open-mindedness, empathy, respect for and interest in others, sensitivity, tolerance and flexibility. Too little research has been undertaken as yet with respect to the 'ideological' dimensions of international education to know to what extent such claims are actually realized in practice, and whether students emerge from schools that promote such values actively demonstrating the desired characteristics (Hayden, 2001).

At the moment we have only anecdotal evidence on which to base our perceptions, since even end-of-school programmes that claim to promote such attributes do not make formal judgments about the achievement of such qualities in their overall assessment schemes. A lack of hard evidence, however, does not mean that such attributes are not developed by many international school students, and one interesting question in this context relates to which factors associated with the international school experience are influential in the development of such attributes.

Clearly at least one likely influence is the teacher as a role model, as discussed above, exemplifying the values promoted by the school, which include those relating to the promotion of international education. Thus, while a teacher may have responsibility for a specific area of the curriculum, or a particular age group of children, it might be assumed that a teacher in an internationally-minded school would be actively encouraged also to play the part of role model for the promotion of international education. It is against this background and assumption that the next section will consider the place of professional development.

Professional development in international education

International education, it is argued, is concerned with the promotion of education for international understanding, and the 'teacher as role model' plays a crucial part in the development of relevant attributes in students. At the same time, the 'teacher as technician' supports the development of more cognitive dimensions of students' development. What, then, is the role of professional development in supporting the development of both dimensions of a teacher's responsibilities? In the broad definition adopted in this chapter, professional development could be considered to begin at the stage of initial training to teach, going on to include dimensions such as induction at a new school, appraisal, in-service courses, external programmes, and other opportunities that may be engaged in throughout the teacher's career. The following sections will focus on the three stages of initial training, induction, and those dimensions of continuing professional development that relate to the more established teacher. In each case, consideration will be given to the extent to which support appears to be provided for the teacher as both technician and role model.

Initial teacher education

It would almost certainly be safe to assert that the vast majority of teachers and administrators currently based in international schools worldwide have had no specific training to teach in that context before embarking upon their international school experience. In many (though not all) cases they will have been trained to teach, but this training will have been framed within a national context and the individual will have learned *in situ* 'how to teach in an international school' only after taking up their first such post. Some may find the challenge of adaptation more straightforward than others; a UK-trained teacher, for instance, taking up a post in a British international school, staffed mostly by British expatriates and catering largely for temporarily-displaced British expatriate children, is likely to face less of a challenge than a UK-trained teacher moving to a non-British international school catering for children from many national and linguistic backgrounds.

It might seem logical for such courses to be designed, but if training specifically related to international school teaching were to be provided, what form would the 'international' dimension take? One feature that springs to mind is practical preparation in terms of awareness-raising of different cultural contexts and educational practices (Joslin, 2002). While such a course would be likely to be generic in content and therefore not tailored specifically to any single context, it could nevertheless raise sufficient issues to help the new international schoolteacher to adapt more easily than might otherwise have been the case. It could also focus on the 'teacher as role model for international education' dimension, assuming that training in national contexts had already taken place and the 'technician' dimensions had therefore been developed. There is, however, little evidence of such professional development opportunities being available currently in the international school arena – perhaps linked, at least in part, to the challenges this would raise in requiring agreement on what precisely it is that such training would be preparing teachers *for*. Nevertheless, it is an area that could usefully be developed.

Induction

The variety of manifestations of professional development may continue early into the career of an international-school teacher, in the form of arrangements for induction by the school in which the individual takes a first teaching post. The extent to which such provision exists clearly varies, with some schools organizing quite detailed, formalized induction programmes for new staff, while others are more inclined to assume that the individual will 'pick things up' and ask for help as needed.

When formalized programmes exist, they may focus on different dimensions such as induction into the way the school works, into the ways of a particular department, into teaching itself (if the teacher is new to teaching, or relatively inexperienced), or into living in the local community. Although this dimension may be peculiar to international schools, it will be crucial in some contexts if the school is not to run the risk of the teacher being distracted from settling in professionally to the new post by being unsettled personally through not becoming integrated into the local community – whether that be the nearby city or the expatriate compound. The extent to which there is an 'international' thread running through such programmes would seem to vary according to the particular type of induction provided but, on the whole, provision tends to be very much a response to a practical need rather than explicitly linked to the promotion of the value systems of international education. Again, this is an area where greater support could be provided for the teacher as role model in promoting the values of international education.

Continuing professional development

For established teachers – those who have some experience of teaching, have been inducted into the ways of the local community and the school in which they are based, and are feeling reasonably confident about their capabilities – there may be two broad potential mindsets with respect to professional development. One mindset views the process of learning to teach as an ongoing one, believes that there is always something new to be learned, and perceives there to be value in finding out about new possibilities and new challenges, while considering how these might be adapted with benefit to the individual's own context. Another mindset favours the view that learning to teach is a 'one off' activity, that once the skill is acquired there is no necessity for further learning to follow, and that professional development opportunities are to be resisted where possible or tolerated where unavoidable. Those in the latter position, who perhaps fit the oft-cited reference to an individual who claims to have 25 years of experience but, in fact, has had one year of experience repeated 24 times, are probably relatively rare; as Holly and McLoughlin (1989) point out: 'The isolated practitioner, schooled and "certified", ready to "sink or swim" for the next thirty years, is soon to be extinct'.

Such teachers may well be in a minority in the context of international schools: perhaps because of the many new challenges regularly arising in the international school context, perhaps because venturing to teach outside one's own national system appeals to a certain type of individual. Whatever the reason, it would probably be fair to say that the majority of international schoolteachers are open to the professional development opportunities increasingly available from many different sources worldwide. Indeed, it would be virtually impossible for any teacher in an international school, or indeed in a national school in the developed world, to have resisted entirely the professional development opportunities thrust upon them in recent years by the introduction to the school context of, for instance, personal computers, e-mail and the Internet. Opportunities available to international-school teachers could be considered to cater broadly for two categories of needs, which will be considered in the following sections.

Pragmatic needs

Professional development provision in the early stage of an individual's career would appear to be a response largely to the practical needs of those new to their roles. Professional development opportunities for the more established international schoolteacher, meanwhile, tend to cater for a wider variety of wants and needs at differing levels. In some cases they are essentially practical responses to a situation where the need for learning and development of skills is clear. Such wants and needs could arguably be classified (to use the term used earlier in the context of the student experience) as 'pragmatic', in the sense of relating in some way to a perceived potential practical benefit to the individual in question.

One example here, perhaps, is the further qualification (such as a Master's degree or Doctorate), the award of which is expected to lead to an improvement in career prospects. Others might include some form of accreditation that an individual has participated in a workshop or training of some kind: even a statement of attendance might be perceived to have some benefit in this sense. Such pragmatic needs in the international education context tend to be satisfied by the provision made by external agencies such as universities, and other institutions such as the International Baccalaureate Organization (IBO), Cambridge International Examinations, Fieldwork, the Principals Training Center (PTC), European Council of International Schools (ECIS) and regional organizations of international schools. Such provision is 'international' in the sense that programmes offered are internationally, as well as nationally, recognized, that they have international, as well as national, currency (they are transportable from school to school and country to country), and they are flexible in terms of availability and opportunities for engagement.

Professional needs

Not all types of professional development arise, however, in the context of such pragmatic responses to need. What might be referred to as 'professional' wants and needs include those dimensions of professional development related directly to the increasing of the individual participant's own expertise, understanding or awareness, and improvement of practice for its own sake. Motivation for participating in such opportunities may not be extrinsic in the same way as it is for those opportunities described above as pragmatic (there may be no certificate, or no obvious path to promotion, for instance), but may be extrinsic in a different sense, perhaps of participation being a requirement of the school (such as a teacher having to learn how to apply information technology to teaching, or being expected to attend a workshop or conference). Alternatively, the motivation may be entirely intrinsic, as an individual seeks out opportunities willingly for the enjoyment and personal/professional satisfaction anticipated from participating. Or it may be somewhere in between the two: when, for instance, opportunities are offered and financed by the school as perceived benefits to the teacher.

It is also the case that what have been described as the pragmatic and professional dimensions of professional development can and do overlap, so that while someone's main motivation for engaging in a professional development opportunity may be the anticipated intrinsic satisfaction of understanding their subject area more completely, on occasion the pragmatic benefit of some form of accreditation will also follow. Or the other way around. I have been amused on more than one occasion to be told by an international-school teacher that, having embarked upon a Master's programme in order to gain an additional qualification with a view to enhancing their career prospects, they have been surprised to find that the course is actually also interesting and relevant to their practice!

If the international dimensions of the pragmatic aspects of professional development are essentially also pragmatic (in terms of recognition, transportability and flexibility) what, then, characterizes the international dimensions of the 'professional' aspects of professional development? It could be argued that many dimensions of professional development offered to teachers in international schools, including those schools promoting international education, actually focus rather heavily on the role of the teacher as technician. Whether in terms of ECIS and other workshops and conferences, PTC courses, IBO workshops, or in-service courses offered within schools, much professional development emphasizes issues relating to pragmatic or technical aspects of a teacher's role.

That is not in any sense to denigrate this dimension of a teacher's responsibility. Whatever the ideological underpinnings of a school's basic philosophy, there are few, if any, schools that can ignore the harsh reality of needing to satisfy university admissions tutors, prospective parents and others through external yardsticks understood in the international marketplace. Greenberg (1983) was not writing of the international school context when he noted that increasing accountability in education (where the teacher is expected to 'produce' a satisfactory 'product') introduces a new ideological basis into staff development, but his words might sound familiar to many teaching in at least some international schools when he refers:

> ... to the technology of pedagogy, and to the conceptualisations undergirding that pedagogy, which have begun to dominate the language and the scene in both policy and practice domains. Since the origin of public demands for 'accountability' we have been overrun by the 'technology' of behavioural objectives, minimum competencies, mastery learning, individually prescribed instruction, basic skills, and standardised test score competitions. At times, it seems that measurability has become more important than substance, and that results of normative tests have replaced values as the prime determinants of curriculum.

Even if Greenberg's perception has only a faint echo in the international school context, there may be implications for the international dimension of international education. What is international about professional development in the pragmatic context is described above as being essentially related to pragmatic dimensions such as transportability. In the 'professional' context, it could be argued that the international dimension also relates to very practical needs such as, for instance, better understanding of how Chief Examiners set and interpret their mark schemes, or how better support can be provided for globally mobile students. Important though such dimensions of professional development undoubtedly are, professional development of this type is, arguably, catering for the instrumental, 'technician'-focused dimensions of a teacher's responsibility. It might appear that professional development in the international school context, both pragmatic and professional, is seen as being international largely in the sense that it relates to development of the technical skills required to function effectively in an international context.

Professional development for international-mindedness

A school that claims to value music as part of its curriculum may well advertise the good results consistently achieved by its students in this area. It will probably ensure that it appoints teachers likely to be able to support the achievement of such consistently good results, and that it supports such teachers in keeping their skills honed through professional development opportunities of various types. If, on the other hand, a school claims to value 'international-mindedness' and to promote these values as a major part of the curriculum, what equivalent support can be provided for its teachers? Since every teacher acts as a role model, presumably every teacher should, in such a school, be a role model in terms of 'international-mindedness'. But, while professional development support may be provided with respect to the technical dimensions of a teacher's role, it appears that little support is provided with respect to the 'international-mindedness' dimension of this role.

It might be argued that it is sufficient for a school to appoint the 'right person' who will automatically and instinctively deploy the desired role and, undoubtedly, personal attributes in addition to technical skills will be considered in making an appointment. Assuming, however, that new recruits already have the desired attributes on appointment, just as they may already have a track record of encouraging students to achieve good results in, say, biology, a question might be asked as to what professional development opportunities are available to support them as they progress through their school career, as they would be to support a biology teacher progressing through their career. The answer to this question might be 'relatively little'.

Conclusion

Clearly it is easy to point to need without making constructive suggestions as to how that need might be met and, while it is fairly straightforward to provide support in the technicalities of, say, teaching mathematics effectively, the form in which support for teachers as international role models should be developed is less clear. It is almost certainly the case that, while such professional development does not have a high profile in a formal sense (in the way that, for example, professional development for the more technical dimensions of a teacher's role has a high profile through workshops and conferences), there is much in the way of informal professional development happening within schools, in the sense of relatively inexperienced teachers learning from more experienced teachers as role models.

If, however, the promotion of international education is as valued as a consideration of international school mission statements would suggest it is, perhaps more effort needs to be made to raise the profile of support provided for teachers in encouraging the promotion of such a value system. Exactly what form such support might take is debatable but, unless a higher profile is established, it may well appear that this very important dimension of international education remains undervalued compared with its more pragmatic counterpart. To take the earlier distinction made between pragmatic and professional aspects of professional development, it might be that some teachers would welcome such support for reasons related to their own professional satisfaction, while others would feel the need for a pragmatic incentive to encourage participation. The notion of some form of accreditation of what might be described as, say, an 'Advanced International Education Teacher' (akin to the Advanced Skills Teacher concept recently introduced in England and Wales) may seem to be taking the idea too far, but such accreditation would at least have the virtue of recognizing the centrality of this dimension of a teacher's role in the promotion of international education. Bajunid (2000) argues that:

> as the world enters the next millennium, teachers and educational leaders must play positive and effective leadership roles in society... Teachers and educational leaders must inspire themselves with great ideas such as goodness, truth, justice, liberty, equality and beauty (Adler, 1981). As teachers and educational leaders are inspired by lofty ideas and ideals so will their students be inspired. As they clarify their thinking and opinions and take their stand based on knowledge and clarified values, they will educate a new generation of students who will be committed to making the world a better place, a more enlightened place where mankind exercises stewardship roles with human dignity and justice.

If teachers in internationally-minded schools are, indeed, to play this crucial role they will need professional development support, provided in such a way as to promote the ideals of international education to which so many international schools aspire.

References

Adler, M J (1981) *Six Great Ideas*, Macmillan, New York

Bajunid, I (2000) Rethinking the work of teachers and school leaders in an age of change, in *The Life and Work of Teachers: International perspectives in changing times*, eds C Day, A Fernandez, T E Hauge and J Moller, Falmer Press, London

Day, C (1999) *Developing Teachers: The challenges of lifelong learning*, Falmer Press, London

Dean, J (1991) *Professional Development in School*, Open University Press, Buckingham

Greenberg, J D (1983) Connections and tensions: preservice-beginning teaching-inservice, *Journal of Teacher Education*, **34** (2), pp 38–43

Halstead, J M (1996), in *Values in Education and Education in Values*, eds J M Halstead and M J Taylor, Falmer Press, London

Hayden, M C (2001) International Education and the International Baccalaureate Programmes, unpublished paper presented to the International Baccalaureate Organization Academic Advisory Committee, 5 April 2001

Hayden, M C and Thompson, J J (eds) (2000) *International Schools and International Education: Improving teaching, management and quality*, Kogan Page, London

Hayden, M C and Thompson, J J (eds) (2001) *International Education: Principles and practice*, Kogan Page, London

Hill, I (2000) Internationally-minded schools, *International Schools Journal*, **XX** (1), pp 24–37

Holly, M L and McLoughlin, C S (eds) (1989) *Perspectives on Teachers' Professional Development*, Falmer Press, London

Hoyle, E (1980) Professionalization and deprofessionalization in education, in *World Yearbook of Education*, eds E Hoyle and J Megarry, Kogan Page, London

Jackson, P W, Boostrom, R E and Hansen, D T (1993), *The Moral Life of Schools*, Jossey-Bass, San Francisco

Joslin, P (2002) Teacher relocation: reflections in the context of international schools, *Journal of Research in International Education*, **1** (1) [in press]

Joyce, B R and Showers, B (1980) Improving in-service training: the messages of research, *Educational Leadership*, **37** (5), pp 379–85

Powell, W (2000) Professional development and reflective practice, in *International School and International Education: Improving teaching, management and quality*, eds M C Hayden and J J Thompson, Kogan Page, London

Watson, B and Ashton, E (1995) *Education, Assumptions and Values*, David Fulton Publishers Ltd, London

Part D

THE ORGANIZATION OF SCHOOLS AND THEIR COMMUNITIES

Chapter 10

Atolls, seas of culture and global nets

Keith Allen

Introduction

The juxtaposition of the words 'education' and 'community' is not new. The 1930s' Cambridgeshire Village Colleges of Henry Morris, for example, arguably launched the concept of 'community education', which was the subject of further considerable debate in the United Kingdom during the late 1970s and early 1980s as many educators appreciated that schools could no longer operate as islands of airy academia within an ocean of employment (see, for example, Allen *et al*, 1987). Comprehensive intakes, wider views of the nature of education, appreciation of the value of vocational preparation and economic realities, all led towards greater school-community links. Such growth in the imperative of what might be described as the 'external relations' of the school has been seen in other countries too.

This chapter will attempt to flag some of the issues facing *international* schools in relation to the communities within which they operate. It will end with a few thoughts on *internationally-minded* schools. The concept of 'community' recurs throughout. Schools *are* communities, schools *exist within* communities, schools *serve* communities, schools *form* communities, and schools *interact with* communities. What then do we mean by 'community' in these contexts?

Community, culture and values

Traditionally, 'community' relates to elements of 'commonality'. Dewey (1916) stated that people live in communities because of the things that they have in common, and lists 'aims, beliefs, aspirations, knowledge, a common understanding, and likemindedness'. Later writers emphasized the idea of networks within communities. Eggleston (1967) stressed the idea of association: 'a complex network of contractual agreements or collaborations for specific tasks in modern industrial societies'. Taking these two together, a community could be seen as a network of reciprocal social relationships.

More recently, Kennedy and Roudometof (2001) have emphasized that the concept of 'community' has changed and continues to evolve. In early societies, 'community' was restricted to individuals having face-to-face contact. With the development of the printed word and the legislature of the nation-state, 'communities' expanded. Now, communications technology and mass transport conspire to allow the conception of 'transnational communities' – communities that are not defined by location. Kennedy and Roudometof explain 'communities' as 'units of belonging whose members perceive that they share moral, aesthetic/expressive or cognitive meanings, thereby gaining a sense of personal as well as group identity'. They go on to argue that 'this identity demarcates the boundary between members and non-members'.

The concept of 'community' is closely allied to that of 'culture'. For Trompenaars and Hampden-Turner (1997), culture is the way in which a group of people solves problems and reconciles dilemmas. Echoing this view are the ideas of culture as 'community of practice' or 'shared world view in action'. Culture incorporates a social identity (Who am I? How do I differ from others?), a social memory (What are my roots?), a range of cultural practices (How do I behave?) and strategies for adaptation (How do we respond to change?). 'One's own culture provides the "lens" through which we view the world; the "logic"... by which we order it; the "grammar"... by which it makes sense' (Avruch and Black, 1993). The concept of 'culture' then leads to that of 'values'. Roger Brown suggested that culture is involved in the maintenance of current value systems and is a vital tool in ensuring that they will continue (Brown, 2000). George Walker has also focused on values (see, for example, Walker, 1999), adding that values form the core of a culture.

Throughout this chapter, I will be viewing communities as symbolic constructs founded on some kind of common culture through shared values. Within a community, meanings are negotiated and various social arrangements are built. Communities *may* be located in a closely defined physical space but, increasingly, they are delocalized.

I believe that it is also important to appreciate that each school will have its own culture. An important task of each international (or internationally-minded) school is to determine the appropriate culture (and values) for the school. This is no easy task but, if we are to understand the interactions between schools and their wider communities, we do need to have a clear view of the community that we are setting up within the school. Gautam Sen has suggested that the culture of the school covers norms, values, attitudes, assumptions and beliefs (Sen, 2001). These lead to several dilemmas, four of which are identified by Cambridge and Thompson (2001) as follows:

- the relative importance of cognitive and affective goals;
- encapsulated versus inclusive missions;
- the tension between international-mindedness and a globally-branded commodity; and
- issues of economic privilege, access and equity.

Schools exist within communities

In relation to the local community, many of the issues relating to *culture* discussed in the previous section apply. One key issue seems to be the *cultural* distance between the school and its immediate environs. International schools normally have student bodies that are significantly different from the local community within which they operate. We can imagine them as atolls in a coral sea. They have links, but different ways of life – different cultures.

This is not just a phenomenon of international schools. Many selective *national* schools (internationally-minded or not) may be described in this way. In applying to send their children to selective schools, parents are making a choice based on the notion that the selective system will reap benefits for their children that would not be apparent in a non-selective system. Frequently, this choice has an economic cost, but the benefits are perceived to outweigh such costs. The school may be chosen for many reasons. It might be seen as providing a higher quality product: it may, for instance, be better resourced. It may be seen as reinforcing privilege, in terms of the 'old school tie' opening avenues that are limited, or absent, within non-selective institutions. It may just promote separateness, ranging from separate-sex education, through religious schools to schools that restrict, through economic or other factors, entry to a sector of society. Whatever the distinction, these schools will have a cultural divide between themselves and sectors of their community. In many cases, the school will not discourage this view of separateness, being aware that it is a valid marketing tool.

In relation to international schools, the situation is slightly altered. Many are selective and are naturally keen to endorse their 'superior' product, especially in competitive market situations. But there is a tension between the commonly-held aims of 'international education' and both the reinforcement of privilege and the promotion of separateness. Selection and inclusion are uncomfortable bedfellows. An important task for the managers of many international schools is to find ways to make them more compatible.

One strategy for the school could be to find ways of generating *greater* links with the local community. International schools that echo the International Baccalaureate Organization (IBO)'s mission of '... respecting the variety of cultures and attitudes that makes for the richness of life...' (Walker, 2000a), face the imperative of developing *active* links with the community (Allen, 2000). But this raises the possibility of 'culture clash'. As Gautam Sen has suggested, just through offering international programmes, schools change their own ethos and culture *and* change the educational culture of the country in which they are located (Sen, 2001).

Sen goes on to suggest in the same work that cultural interfaces such as those between school and community can be seen as *conversations*, and international education can be represented as a 'grand conversation between civilizations'. This suggests that a balance needs to be made; that the exchange is between equals. Does it imply that 'Asian values' (for example, along the lines of those outlined by Zhou, 1996) should form part of the culture of schools in East Asia, or that Islamic values should be assimilated into the operational structures of international schools in the Middle East? Mark Cooray (1996) has pointed out that cultural mixing is inevitable when different groups are exposed to one another's influence. I believe that, if schools *can* integrate their learning experiences with the local community, a conversation of cultures can occur and that this will facilitate international education.

Let us think for a moment about *multiculturalism*. For Stephen Castles 'multiculturalism represents a kind of corrective to assimilation approaches and policies' (Castles, 2000), while Steven Vertovec (2002) distinguishes between 'weak' and 'strong' multiculturalism. The former is where cultural diversity is accepted in our private lives while a high degree of assimilation (monoculturalism) is expected in the public domain. The latter is when cultural differences are recognized in the public sphere as well as in the private. The concept of *weak* multicultur-alism in relation to international schools reminds us of Susan Zaw's description of 'a substantial monoculturalism as to values, mitigated by tolerance of exotic detail' (Zaw, 1996). If this is our chosen path, it begs the question as to its cultural foundations. Brown has suggested that our educational curriculum 'can either carry the values of the country in which the curriculum was originally developed or it can attempt to carry the values of internationalism' (Brown, 2000). I would suggest there is a third dimension: that of incorporating significant contributions from the host culture.

The most widely utilized international curricula are from the West. They incorporate Western values. Are these appropriate for international schools? Doubt comes from many quarters, not least from two giants of Indian 20th-century history, Rabindranath Tagore (Sudarshan, 1998) and Mahatma Gandhi (Sen, 2001). Tagore suggested that:

> We have for over a century been dragged by the prosperous West behind its chariot, choked by the dust, deafened by the noise, humbled by our own helplessness and overwhelmed by the speed. We agreed to acknowledge that this chariot-ride was progress, and the progress was civilisation. If we ever ventured to ask "progress towards what, and progress for whom", it was considered to be peculiarly and ridiculously oriental to entertain such ideas about the absoluteness of progress. Of late, a voice (Gandhi) has come to us to take count not only of the scientific perfection of the chariot but of the depth of the ditches lying in its path. (Tagore, in Sudarshan, 1998)

Gandhi, meanwhile, asserted that 'I do not want my house to be walled in on all sides and my windows to be stuffed. I want the cultures of all lands to be blown about my house as freely as possible. But I refuse to be blown off my feet by any of them' (Gandhi, in Sen 2001). As George Walker has pointed out, the spread of Western culture is *not* accepted in many environments, as it 'is being fiercely resisted by the strengthening of local cultures' (Walker, 2000b).

What about the idea of identifying 'international values'? The concept is supported by several documents. The 1995 Commission on Global Governance called for efforts to 'foster global citizenship' and to trans-form a 'global neighbourhood' into a 'universal moral community' (Sudarshan, 1998). Kevin Ryan, amongst others, has attempted to iden-tify 'moral laws' that are cross-cultural and 'universal truths' (Ryan, 1997), but these seem much too general to be useful (for example, one of his 'moral laws' is 'some degree of honesty'). Nevertheless, Hayden and Thompson (2000) argue that we *can* move towards the 'convergence of social and cultural values'.

Empirical evidence that this occurs can also be seen from the writings on those described as Third Culture Kids. Authors point out that students *do* find 'cultural balance' (Pollock and Van Reken, 2001), develop transcultural skills (Willis, Enloe and Minoura, 1994) and adopt an 'international "third culture"' for school (Langford, 2000). But, as Samia Al Farra (2000) has warned, 'many people... in the Arab world... perceive internationalism as a threat, as an invasion by Western values in particular'. Both of these ideas (Western-based international school cultures and global 'third culture' systems) are bound to widen the cultural distance between many international schools and the communities within which they exist. Would incorporation of local values and customs help? In the context of East Asia, this has been suggested by Professor Zhou Nanzhou. Arguing that 'culturally, the East and West are compatible and complementary rather than contradictory and mutually opposing', he suggests that education can make a great contribution to humanity if 'the East and West could learn and benefit from each other' (Zhou, 1996).

So where does this leave us? Our 'atoll' school is surrounded by a stimulating, but distinct, sea of cultures. The people of the atoll can adopt a significantly 'monocultural' system (with a few exotic details) or work towards a multicultural approach. If they succeed in following the difficult path towards *strong* multiculturalism, they may find that interactions with the sea of cultures outside fits neatly into this system, with the local communities merely representing an additional handful of equally valid cultures. On the other hand, if they follow the easier monocultural path, they have to choose the 'flavour' of monoculture. Emphasis on either the 'Western' or 'global' paths is more likely to lead to 'culture clash' with the community than adapting the school culture to some key values found within the local community.

Surely, the antithesis of international education is to allow our students to contravene local norms. Yet this is what we may see happening in practice. For example, several friends in South-East Asia have quietly and patiently pointed out that some of our 'Western' students' behaviour was offensive. This was especially true of 'overt sexual behaviour', but it extended into other fields too (dress, for example). If the school is hidden away from the gaze of the host community, such behaviour may be acceptable. But if a school is going out of its way to promote active links between itself and the host community, such attitudinal and behavioural differences cannot be hidden.

Before leaving this discussion on the cultural dilemmas facing schools that wish to exist in harmony with their local community, I would like to raise an issue relating to one part of the local community – the parents who send their children to the school. Several pieces of research (such as that of Bell, 1988) have shown that a coherent ethos between the school and parents is a prime factor in school effectiveness. This provides challenges for international schools as they deal with parents from diverse cultural backgrounds (arguably, more diverse than other sectors of the local community). Mary Langford suggests that parents need to be 'coached' as to what their role can and should be in an international school (Langford, 2000). But, with turnovers as high as 20 per cent per annum, this can be a monumental task. Is it possible? Is it even morally acceptable within a philosophy that values diversity?

Whether we accept the idea of coaching or not, schools should try to understand the cultural roots of parents. According to McLean's classification, those from collectivist states readily accept the demands of the school, while those from democratic-participatory systems expect to be represented in the general decision-making process of the school. In contrast to both of these, parents from 'communalist-localist' cultures expect to *control* the school (McLean, 1995). If we can understand and work from this understanding, we *may* be able to reduce the infamous frequency of Head-Board conflicts in our international schools. Just as importantly, we may also find ways to serve *all* parents appropriately.

The degree of distinction between different parents' attitudes could also be explored using Hofstede's dimensions (Hofstede, 1986). For example, parents from cultures involving *small power distances* might be expected to side with the student in teacher/student conflict, while those from *large power distance* cultures would naturally support the teacher. Such differences can generate significant issues in international schools. I remember the case of a student who had cheated in an examination. His father was called in to the school, in the expectation that he would support the school in its action against his son. But the father was aghast at the idea of discipline being meted out to his son: 'He should be congratulated for finding a way of getting full marks, rather than being punished', was his response.

International schools have two main tasks in relation to parents. One is to find ways of understanding their different attitudinal approaches. The second is to develop a range of organizational structures so that *all* parents can be involved in some way (Hornby, 1999). Both depend on the cultural interface between school and community.

Schools form communities

International schools still form a minority in relation to the number of *national* schools in a region. This can easily lead to a sense of isolation that is ameliorated by forming associations with other international schools, although we also need to be aware that fruitful associations *can* (and should) be made with non-international education providers. The associations between international schools range from the global to the local and from those with a high degree of exclusivity to those with open membership. Such partnerships and alliances have clear benefits, but there are also costs. Traditionally, playing an active part in a widespread coalition has involved international travel. The cost, both financial and ecological, of sending staff to conferences and workshops is often prohibitive, as is the option of sending significant numbers of students to equivalent events. But, when we get there, we might find that the agenda is heavily skewed towards the 'majority' and that the interests of the minority, such as Southern Hemisphere schools, schools in developing nations or small schools, are rarely addressed. I believe that there is a strong need for a move towards *regional* rather than global alliances. That is not to say that global communication is unimportant, but to a large extent this can be achieved through electronic means rather than through long-haul travel.

There is, however, a tension between the need for collaboration and the demands of competition within regional associations (Hall, 1999). If there are several international schools in a city, they may be reluctant participants in cooperative ventures if they are competing for the same market. In Bangkok, during the 1990s, there had been a rapid expansion of international schools. Largely for historical reasons (and because of former Thai laws), many were closely affiliated with one *national* education system such as the United States, United Kingdom, France, Taiwan or Japan. But none of these schools could operate with a student population made up of only the nationals of those countries, and there were students of many other nationalities looking for international education within Bangkok. So the schools were in competition. The regional affiliations that developed in this context were three-fold. Firstly, there were 'exclusive' associations, such as the group of British schools in South-East Asia. This produced a relatively homogeneous group, which had issues in common, where individual members were relatively distant from each other (so competition for students did not occur). Secondly, there were 'broad-based, wide-ranging' affiliations, such as EARCOS (the East Asian Regional Conference for Overseas Schools). Although linked to the United States, this organization embraced a wide range of schools. But, because it was so large, issues specific to one locale were largely avoided. Thirdly, local associations developed, but initially these were of a competitive nature and, typically, allowed students to compete with each other in sporting tournaments.

It was only when the Asian financial crisis hit all schools in the region that we started to develop a real degree of cooperation between schools. I remember hosting the first meeting between the 'big four' international schools in Bangkok. The meeting was cautious: we wanted each other's help, but we did not want to give away any competitive advantage that we had. It was like a game of poker. But, over a series of meetings, and with the group expanding to include more and more international schools, although we reserved the right to exclude schools from our discussions, the atmosphere relaxed, a little. Some schools were still very cagey in explaining how they were going to adjust teachers' salaries (we competed for staff as well as students). Some seemed incredibly honest, while some were economical with the truth. Some accepted that they faced an enormous crisis; others pretended that they were immune to the collapsing currency. The end result was beneficial (from my perspective), but it was a precarious balancing act. There was clearly a much greater sense of partnership between those schools that were confident of their market niche. They saw greater benefits in collaboration than the risks of non-communication. For schools that were less secure, the association was a gamble. They were the real poker players. They desperately needed market information, but were in a make-or-break situation. Several did not make it.

A much more assured local association is ACBIRP, the association of International Baccalaureate (IB) colleges of the River Plate region. Based in Buenos Aires, but including representatives from Uruguay and further afield in Argentina, it is a thriving, long-standing enterprise. Its vigour can be attributed to several factors. Firstly, there were strong people involved. Secondly, it was large but compact (Buenos Aires having more IB schools and colleges than any other city in the world). Thirdly, it had power. Its power derived from a combination of its numerical strength, that it was 'the voice in the wilderness' (representing as it did 'minority' interests amongst international schools worldwide such as a Southern Hemisphere academic year and Spanish-medium education) and that it had effective channels of communication with global organizations (for example, the Regional Director for IB Latin America was a member of the group).

ACBIRP flourished with collaboration easily out-manoeuvring competition. There were events for students, workshops for teachers and conferences for administrators. It could address issues that were of real interest for schools in the area. It provides a model for other regions to emulate. I would like to see our 'atoll' schools forming federations to facilitate regional cooperation. But this will require those regional groups to be 'empowered' or 'liberated' by the global (or macro-regional) providers of education (IBO included). As George Walker has written (Walker, 2000b), 'IBO offers an education system throughout the world, but not for the world'. Each region needs to sculpt this education system to local needs. Walker, in the same work, agrees that the IB Middle Years Programme and IB Primary Years Programme are 'likely to be more regionally influenced in their development' than the IB Diploma Programme. We need to look for ways of developing the Diploma Programme for regional relevance, but there will always be a tension between the 'standardization' requirements of a global passport to tertiary education and local variability.

Schools interact with communities

It is evident that schools are sensitive to events within their communities. It is equally obvious that, in the light of globalization, *all* schools are influenced by events on a global scale. It is also clear, however, that such events are much more likely to affect *international* schools. This connectedness manifests itself in several different areas. Firstly, as the students have personal connections with many countries around the world, there is always the possibility that an event thousands of kilometres away can have a direct impact on some students. Events occurring halfway round the world can have a *personal* meaning for an international student. Schools need to be sensitive to these events and their import.

Secondly, as international schools enrol students whose parents work in the world of international business, economic changes in the families' host country may have a significant impact on the school. In the 1980s, there was a trend, for example, *against* posting US families to Singapore. Often, one parent would be deployed there on a two-months-on-two-months-off contract, with the family staying in the United States. This had an immediate impact on enrolment of US students in international schools in Singapore. In my current school, students fly in from around the world to study in Oxford. We are susceptible to aspects as diverse as economic stability in Brazil, exchange rates between the United Kingdom and Russia, and educational 'fashions' in China. We must accept that developments in information and communications technology means that 'international' students may live in relative social isolation from the communities that are geographically close to them, while enjoying 'social nearness and closeness to others living thousands of miles away' (Kennedy and Roudometof, 2001).

The third level of impact is in relation to changes on the *global* scale. Much has been written about globalization recently. Anthony Giddens defines it as 'the intensification of worldwide social relations which link distant realities in such a way that local happenings are shaped by events occurring many miles away and vice versa' (Giddens, 1990). Held and collaborators write: 'Globalization may be thought of initially as the widening, deepening and speeding up of worldwide interconnectedness in all aspects of contemporary social life, from the cultural to the criminal, the financial to the spiritual' (Held *et al*, 1999). Globalization has, of course, a huge impact on the nature of, and operation of, international education. Glenn Rikowski (2001a) has stated that 'educators are implicated in this process, like everyone else. The school or university is no hiding place'. He goes on to suggest that teachers are the most critical workers in relation to globalization as they have a special role in shaping and developing the single commodity on which the whole capitalist system rests: worker power (Rikowski, 2001b).

Just as importantly, globalization changes the whole concept of *community*. It raises the possibility of wider, and yet more diverse, communities: 'everyone is compelled to live with, and negotiate the paradoxes and complexities arising from, the simultaneous exposure to local/national and global influences' (Kennedy and Roudometof, 2001). But, at the same time, it causes realignment. Anderson (1993) suggested that the mobility afforded by globalization would lead to stronger feelings of nostalgia for the homeland. Kennedy and Roudometof report that this *is* the case as migrant communities, and we deal with these in international schools, 'opt for the perpetuation of active transnational linkages between homeland and host country'. This presents several challenges for those working in the context of international education. As Cambridge and Thompson (2001) have pointed out, international education 'can be interpreted as an ideological construct which promotes hyperglobalism'. Yet, 'the essential pro-democratic logic of internationalism stands in sharp contrast to the logic of globalization' (Jones, 1998). Are we agents of globalization, products of it, or both?

John Lowe (2000) referred to the notion of globalization as a 'net'. Locations that are distant geographically are connected by the net. But it is important to appreciate that the net also has holes. It consists of two populations: those that are included in the web of connectedness and those that are excluded. As international schools, we are on the network. But if we have strong links with our host community, that connects us to the holes. We have to juggle with global connections while retaining a foothold at the local level. The national and transnational are part of the same picture as we are caught in a dialectic of sub-nationalism and supra-nationalism.

Our ability to function on the strings of the network has implications that are awe-inspiring. For example, the power of the Internet means that schools no longer need to restrict their student enrolment to those who physically set foot in the school. Although much of the current work in distance learning seems to involve tertiary level studies, schools *are* exploring the options. In 1997, the International School of Kuala Lumpur was seriously affected by families moving away from Malaysia due to the pollution from fires in Indonesia. This could have been disastrous for the school. But they kept in touch with students through the ether: setting work, commenting on work done, establishing banks of resources, and so on (Farnham, 1997). Does such a situation suggest that competition for places at international schools might, one day, be 'global', in the sense that students in a particular city could enrol in schools either in their own city, elsewhere in their country or anywhere around the world without leaving their home?

Recently, my current school embarked on a similar project for some students who were only able to afford to spend a short time in the United Kingdom. Through the Web, we set up schemes of work that students engaged in prior to visiting Britain. This work was supported by asynchronous teacher support: students posted work and the teacher in Oxford responded within a day. Subsequently, the students visited England for face-to-face sessions and relevant fieldwork, before returning to their home countries to write their final papers.

There is, then, the possibility of 'virtual schools'. George Walker has talked of a school in northern Scandinavia that has students but few teachers sufficiently experienced to teach the IB programme. Most of the staff are located elsewhere but are in contact with the school via the Internet (Walker, 2001). But the students do not all need to be present together. Using ideas such as the School of the Air (Alice Springs), the University of the South Pacific (functioning across 33 million square kilometres and 12 island nations), the African Virtual University and the Islamic Virtual School, groups of students can mix with each other, and with learning managers, through the Internet. Surely, this is *one* future of international education. It seems especially relevant for those international education providers who wish their 'product' to be available more widely, either geographically, or within communities that cannot afford the expense of international schools. It also suggests further options for collaborative work between schools. These avenues need to be explored thoroughly.

Conclusion

The value of global connectedness is particularly appealing for 'internationally-minded' schools that do not have vast cultural diversity on their premises, and it is with internationally-minded schools that I want to end. If international schools wish to preserve their mission of developing tolerance and understanding, they might be well advised to invest heavily in *local* connectedness. They will always continue to serve the global nomads but, by connecting with the 'holes' in the globalization net, they can make a real difference. In helping local schools to become more 'internationally-minded', they can further their mission of internationalism. By bridging the gap between 'haves' and 'have-nots', they can play a part of bringing both an understanding of the nature and significance of culture to the international community and an opportunity for the 'have-nots' to benefit from some aspects of globalization. And, for those international schools in the 'rich', connected world, we can always point out that, if they use the forces of globalization, they can reach out to the 'poor' even if they are some geographical distance from themselves. If we need a model, we can look to another 'virtual education' provider, the Indira Gandhi National Open University, which has, as one of its basic aims, to reach out to disadvantaged groups. That is a lesson for all of us.

The words of Dr Karan Singh, although written several years ago in association with the Delors Report, are as valid today as they were then:

We must have the courage to think globally, to break away from traditional paradigms and plunge boldly into the unknown. We must so mobilize our inner and outer resources that we begin consciously to build a new world based on mutually assured welfare rather than mutually assured destruction. As global citizens committed to human survival and welfare, we must use the latest array of innovative and interactive pedagogic methodologies to structure a worldwide programme of education – for children and adults alike – that would open their eyes to the reality of the dawning global age and their hearts to the cry of the oppressed and the suffering. And there is no time to be lost for, along with the emergence of the global society, the sinister forces of fundamentalism and fanaticism, of exploitation and intimidation are also active. Let us, then, with utmost speed, pioneer and propagate a holistic educational philosophy for the twenty-first century…' (Singh, 1996)

References

African Virtual University (2002) [Online] http://www.avu.org

Al Farra, S (2000) Images of international education in national and international schools: a view from Jordan, in *International Schools and International Education*, eds M C Hayden and J J Thompson, Kogan Page, London

Alice Springs School of the Air (2002) [Online] http://www.assoa.nt.edu.au

Allen, G, Bastiani, J, Martin, I and Richards, J K (eds) (1987) *Community Education: An agenda for educational reform*, Open University Press, Milton Keynes

Allen, K (2000) The international school and its community: think globally, interact locally, in *International Schools and International Education*, eds M C Hayden and J J Thompson, Kogan Page, London

Anderson, B (1993) The new world disorder, *New Left Review*, **193**, May/June: pp 3–14

Avruch, K and Black, P (1993) The Role of Cultural Anthropology in an Institute for Conflict Analysis and Resolution, *Political and Legal Anthropology Review*, **16** (3) pp 29–38

Bell, L A (1988) The school as an organisation: a reappraisal, in *Culture and Power in Educational Organisations*, ed A Westoby, Open University Press, Milton Keynes

Brown, R (2000) Local cultures should be the most important consideration in the design of mathematics education programmes, paper delivered to the CEIC/BAICE conference, Bath, October 2000

Cambridge, J C and Thompson, J J (2001) Internationalism, international-mindedness, multiculturalism and globalisation as concepts defining international schools, CEIC, Bath [Online] http://www.bath.ac.uk/~edsjcc/intmindedness.html

Castles, S (2000) *Ethnicity and Globalization: From migrant worker to transnational citizen*, Sage, London

Cooray, L J M (1996) Multiculturalism in Australia: who needs it?, *Quadrant*, April 1986, pp 27–29 [Online] http://www.users.bigpond.com/smartboard/multcult/index.htm

Dewey, J (1916) *Democracy and Education*, Macmillan, Basingstoke

Eggleston, S J (1967) *The Social Context of the School*, Routledge, London

Farnham, B (1997) comments made at EARCOS Conference, Kuala Lumpur, November 1997

Giddens, A (1990) *The Consequences of Modernity*, Polity Press, Cambridge

Hall, V (1999) Partnerships, alliances and competition: defining the field, in *Managing External Relations in Schools and Colleges*, eds J Lumby and N Foskett, Sage Publications, Thousand Oaks, CA

Hayden, M C and Thompson, J J (2000) Quality in diversity, in *International Schools and International Education*, eds M C Hayden and J J Thompson, Kogan Page, London

Held, D, McGrew, A, Goldblatt, D and Perraton, J (1999) *Global Transformations: Politics, economics and culture*, Polity Press, Cambridge

Hofstede, G (1986) Cultural differences in teaching and learning, *International Journal of Intercultural Relations*, **10** (3) pp 301–20

Hornby, G (1999) *Improving Parental Involvement*, Cassell, London

Indira Gandhi National Open University (2002) [Online] http://www.ignou.edu

Islamic Virtual School (2002) [Online] http://www.islamicschool.net

Jones, P (1998) Globalisation and Internationalism: democratic prospects for world education, *Comparative Education*, **34** (2), pp 143–55

Kennedy, P and Roudometof, V (2001) Communities Across Borders under Globalising Conditions: New Immigrants and Transnational Cultures, *Working Paper 01–17*, Transnational Communities Programme, Oxford [Online] http://www.transcomm.ox.ac.uk/working%20papers/WPTC-01-17%20Kennedy.pdf

Langford, M E (2000) Transition between International Education and National Systems – the Perspective of International Schools, paper delivered to the CEIC/BAICE conference, Bath, October 2000

Lowe, J (2000), Issues in Educational Assessment in a Globalising World, paper delivered to the CEIC/BAICE conference, Bath, October 2000

McLean, M (1995) *Educational Traditions Compared*, David Fulton, London

Pollock, D C and Van Reken, R E (2001) *Third Culture Kids: The experience of growing up among worlds*, Nicholas Brealey Publishing, London

Rikowski, G (2001a) *'The Battle in Seattle': Its significance for education*, Tufnell Press, London

Rikowski, G (2001b) Schools: building for business, *Post-16 Educator*, **3**, pp 14–15

Ryan, K (1997) Character Education: The Schools' Latest Fad or Oldest Mission?, Lecture to EARCOS Conference, Kuala Lumpur, November 1997

Sen, G (2001) Nationalizing the International Baccalaureate Diploma Programme, *IB Research Notes*, **1** (3), pp 3–9

Singh, K (1996) Education for the global society, in *Learning: The treasure within*, Report to UNESCO of the International Commission on Education for the 21st Century, UNESCO Publishing, Paris

Sudarshan, R (1998) *Globalisation and Gandhi at the Dawn of the Millennium*, UNDP, New Delhi [Online] http://rrmeet.undp.org.in/_disc8/00000002.htm

Trompenaars, F and Hampden-Turner, C (1997) *Riding the Waves of Culture: Understanding cultural diversity in business*, Nicholas Brealey, London

University of the South Pacific (2002) [Online] http://www.usp.ac.fj

Vertovec, S (2002) Transnational Challenges to the 'New' Multiculturalism, *Working Paper 01–06*, Transnational Communities Programme, Oxford [Online] http://www.transcomm.ox.ac.uk/working%20papers/WPTC-2k-06%20Vertovec.pdf

Walker, G (1999) Our Shared Values, address to the IB Coordinators' Conference, Muscat, Oman, October 1999

Walker, G (2000a) International Education and National Systems, paper delivered to the CEIC/BAICE conference, Bath, October 2000

Walker, G (2000b) International education: connecting the national to the global, in *International Schools and International Education*, eds M C Hayden and J J Thompson, Kogan Page, London

Walker, G (2001) comments made at an open evening held at St Clare's, Oxford, March 2001

Willis, D B, Enloe, W W and Minoura, Y (1994) Transculturals, Transnationals: The New Diaspora, *International Schools Journal*, **XIV** (1) pp 29–42

Zaw, S K (1996) Locke and multiculturalism: toleration, relativism and reason, in *Public Education in a Multicultural Society*, ed R K Fullwider, Cambridge University Press, Cambridge

Zhou, N (1996) Interactions of education and culture for economic and human development: an Asian perspective, in *Learning: The treasure within*, Report to UNESCO of the International Commission on Education for the 21st Century, UNESCO Publishing, Paris

Chapter 11

International schools and their wider community: the location factor

Brian Garton

Introduction

Although there is still no widely agreed precise definition of 'international schools', there are a number of *de facto* assumptions that make it possible to use the term meaningfully for discussion purposes. Richards has recorded a powerful warning against the dangers of relying too much on what may well be very superficial assumptions about international schools and international education (Richards, 1998). Nonetheless this chapter will proceed on the basis that, although definitions based on such assumptions have serious limitations, yet, in the absence of agreed definitions, the ongoing debate may still be usefully enhanced.

The touchstone assumptions that can most frequently be perceived relate to mission statements, diversity of student enrolment, diversity of board membership, diversity of administrator and faculty appointments, and to curriculum in both its formal and informal contexts (Sylvester, 1998; Thompson, 1998 and Drake, 1998). Of these five touchstones it would appear that literature has placed the greatest emphasis on curriculum. As long ago as 1981 Gellar wrote that 'the concept of international education demands a curriculum which is both concrete and specific, aimed at giving the student the skills that he needs to achieve the goal he has chosen and broad enough to include those subjects that enable him to see the world from a much wider perspective than is generally required in national systems' (Gellar, 1981). The importance of the formal curriculum hardly needs a defence, and in current literature the role of the International Baccalaureate Organization (IBO) justly dominates the field, as it now provides curricula for the whole age range, and its 'international' credentials are essentially unchallenged, however much they may be open to discussion (McKenzie, 1998). The IBO programmes, however, are not confined to international schools, and so offering an IB programme is not in itself sufficient as a definition of an international school, though the IBO is undoubtedly very influential in the context of international education.

The influence of an informal curriculum is, on the other hand, much less well documented, but this should not lead us to discount its importance. Thompson (1998), for instance, places significant emphasis on the importance of the informal aspects of exposure of students to other students and local culture for the 'international' qualities of their educational experience. The results of the structured research into such informal influences conducted by Mary Hayden and Jeff Thompson were recently vividly reinforced for me, albeit in highly anecdotal form. This was in August 2001 on a Finnish lakeshore complete with sauna, beer, and sausages being grilled on an open fire, when I met with 11 young people from four different countries who had been former students of mine at the International School Moshi in Tanzania, which I left in December 1988. It was their personal memories of the situation created for them by their being together in school, and a school that was uniquely the result of particular conditions in northern Tanzania, that appeared to be more important than their reflections on the sophisticated IB Diploma Programme that they had followed.

The specific impact of this personal interaction seemed to have been significantly enhanced by the fact that the school was located in northern Tanzania, and was a boarding school with a substantial enrolment of Scandinavians from missionary and aid worker backgrounds. The peculiar circumstances that led to the creation of that school are unlikely to be replicated. As yet international schools themselves are so recent that they do not yet have a comprehensive and scholarly general history, let alone a range of properly researched individual histories. Many practitioners writing of international schools have therefore emphasized the importance of the specific local context, such as Machabeng College Lesotho (Wilkinson, 1998) or Maru a Pula School Botswana (McKenzie, 1998), but Allen's comment that 'Research indicates that links with the local community have not been seen as important for either international school students or teachers' (Allen, 2000), would still seem to represent a widely held view.

When Alec Peterson wrote his classic *Schools Across Frontiers* (Peterson, 1987), the 'transferability' of the key elements in an 'international education' was still perceived as fundamental. The rapid growth of schools seeking to offer such an education over the past three decades has perhaps, somewhat ironically, led to a greater diversity, as such schools seek to align themselves more comfortably with their specific geographical locations. As Hayden and Thompson point out, 'Many such international schools have grown up in response to local circumstances on a relatively *ad hoc* basis' (Hayden & Thompson, 1995). The same point is made even more cogently by Jim Cambridge when he writes: 'The international school can be viewed as an open system that is influenced by the environment of its host country, whether it embraces or isolates itself from it' (Cambridge, 1998). In exploring issues relating to the wider community and international education in the specific context of international schools, it is the purpose of this contribution to focus on this location factor, as the author perceives this as being of perhaps greater significance than has generally been emphasized in the literature.

In identifying location groups, it is, however, recognized that there is a real problem as there are currently no effective and universally recognized criteria for categorizing the different countries of the world. The historic (but were they ever historical?) divisions between First, Second and Third World countries have long since been abandoned, and 'democracy' and 'market economy' are expressions more appropriately used for discussion than for description. No attempt will, therefore, be made to categorize locations by groups of countries, which indeed could be unproductive, as a school in a capital city may well have significantly different relationships with the local community from those shared by the community with another school in a different location in the same country.

Instead of a survey based on distinctive geographical characteristics, therefore, this chapter will seek to investigate some of the contexts in which the international status of schools can be assessed with reference to their relationship to the wider community in the host country. For this purpose we need a different set of criteria from those noted earlier, and the contexts to be considered will be as follows:

- national and local government factors: registration, work permits, taxation and the Ministry of Education;
- school employment policies;
- awareness of the political situation in the host country;
- the annual school calendar;

- links with local schools;
- community service.

National and local government factors

Registration

Surprising though it may seem, it is nevertheless the case that in a number of instances well established and recognized international schools exist at the present time without any formal recognition from the government of the country in which they are located. Such schools are usually to be found in those parts of the world that were formerly part of, or satellite states of, the USSR. They are not, of course, covert institutions in the sense of being 'underground' and unknown to the authorities, and it is likely that they all have 'recognition' as an important objective.

Even more surprising may be the fact that it is often the 'government' that appears reluctant to change the situation. There are, however, good reasons for this. As such governments grapple with the myriad problems of the post-Soviet period, not least in adjusting national educational structures, the sheer extra effort required to identify a role within the country for 'international schools' may seem daunting. On the other hand the value of such schools is readily perceived for the diplomatic and multinational company expatriate communities, let alone for the education of the children of local elites. This 'limbo' status, however workable in practice, must always have some implications for the truly 'international' status of the schools, as acceptance of the need for legality would appear to be fundamental in defining international objectives.

Most such schools exist because they have the 'sponsorship' of one or more foreign embassies located within that country. The political implications of such sponsorship are, however, far from clear in most cases, and may in themselves appear to invalidate the 'international' status of the school. The largest sponsor of international schools is the US State Department, and the nature of this sponsorship is clearly stated in the formal documentation of the Office of Overseas Schools:

> During the 2000–2001 school year, the Office of Overseas Schools is assisting 181 schools in 129 countries. The purposes of the assistance programme are to help the schools provide adequate education for American government dependants and to demonstrate to foreign nationals the philosophy and methods of American education. The schools are open to nationals of all

countries, and their teaching staffs are multinational. (Office of Overseas Schools, 2001)

Such schools have a total enrolment of around 100,000 and employ over 11,000 teachers and administrators. A rigorous interpretation of the second sentence in the above paragraph would seem to cast doubt on the appropriateness of including such schools within the parameters of a consideration of 'international' schools and 'international' education, since they are focused on only one country. In practice, however, many of these schools actually do play a very important role in current developments in truly international education. Many of them are, for example, very positively committed to the programmes administered by the IBO. Any research in this field at the present time is affected by such an apparently poor correlation between principles and philosophy as delineated in promotional literature, and actual practice.

Where the US State Department is the sponsor, there are clearly important implications for the relationship between the individual school and the particular government, and these often reflect the political relationship of the world's remaining superpower to that particular government. Could this be perceived to affect the 'international' status of the school? Cambridge (1998) wisely notes from observable practice that 'Certain international schools have been founded by government or religious institutions but they are frequently independent of, or "at arm's length" from, the direct influence of government'.

'Non-registered' schools themselves are, of course, only a small minority. On the other hand, the way in which any international school is 'registered' by the government of the country in which it is located is very important in terms of the ways in which this relates to its ability to provide a programme of international education, and, as implied above, sponsorship by the US government, or indeed any foreign government, can be a factor of importance here.

For all the great diversity of details in practice it is, at the present time, reasonable to generalize that almost all international schools have an overall relationship with their host government which, if not always precisely cordial, is usually not negative. The actual details of that relationship, however, can be of great significance in terms of the basis on which the school operates.

Work and student permits

In almost all instances an international school will have to make arrangements with the host country government so it can recruit teachers on a basis consistent with its international education objectives. This can be a major problem in that the regulations may actually prevent such freedom in employment, but also can be a factor leading to high, and undesirable, staff turnover as the difficulties associated with obtaining work permits for non-nationals can have negative consequences on staff morale. Work permits can also be a significant budget expense, and this in itself may be a restriction on the school's objectives in offering international education, as it will tend either to limit the programme offered or increase the fees, or both. In a similar way a number of governments place restrictions on the numbers of host country national students who may be recruited by the school, which may impact on the international balance of the student body directly, and also indirectly, through the budget.

Taxation

The nature of the taxation relationship between a school and the host government can be of major importance for the international education status of that school. If a school is perceived to be operating on the basis of normal commercial principles, ie to make a profit, the freedom of that school to recruit staff and students and to offer an international programme will obviously be affected by the extent of the provision for tax payments (and also for 'profit') in the operating budget. Taxation issues also, however, affect the majority of international schools even where they have a not-for-profit 'foundation' status.

Leaving aside the issues of taxes on the school itself, there is the crucial issue of personal taxation for expatriate employees. Most international schools seek to recruit teachers from outside the host country, and in many cases this can only be done by offering relatively high salary and benefits packages. The value of such packages is perceived to be one of the major factors in successful recruiting, and it is net value that is likely to be the determining factor. Some governments allow personal tax-free status indefinitely or for a specified number of years to expatriate teachers. This enables the schools to recruit appropriate numbers of, presumably, appropriately qualified teachers at a lower cost than would be normal for private schools in that country. If they cannot do this, the schools then have to modify their recruitment criteria or charge significantly higher fees.

It should be noted that the high cost, especially of smaller international schools, can itself affect the international balance of student enrolment as the children of employees of embassies and international organizations that do not provide generous education allowances are excluded even though they may be an important part of the local expatriate community. In either situation, the impact of a significant level of personal taxation for expatriate teachers can markedly affect the international education objectives of the school. The apparent decline in the numbers of missionary children attending international schools in recent years, for instance, would be an interesting area for research.

The Ministry of Education

The Ministry of Education is the most obvious of the various national and local government agencies that currently affect the ability of a school to offer the programme of international education that it would wish. It can be a major factor where, for instance, it insists on a school using a national curriculum in tandem with its international programme, or where it requires very specific teacher qualifications, such as in those countries where a teacher may only teach a subject if she or he has a university degree in that subject discipline. Other countries may require 'local studies' and/or the host country language to be part of the curriculum. The school may be subject to local 'inspection' in addition to any international accreditation requirements. In a number of countries, however, the Ministry of Education is willing not to become involved, and becomes then less of a factor than the three factors discussed above, however paradoxical this may seem.

School employment policies

Few would disagree in principle with Blaney when he wrote, in relation to international schools, that 'Staff should be carefully recruited so as to represent, without any unreasonable financial burden being placed upon the schools, the major culture areas of the world, and as many nationalities as feasible. This... will also provide the students with a variety of racial, ethnic, and national role models' (Blaney, 1991). This objective can be significantly affected by the policies of the government in which the school is located, as regards both work permit requirements and the potential personal taxation liabilities for such employees.

It is not only, however, with teaching faculty employment that the precise geographical location of a school is important for establishing and maintaining its international credentials. The role of support staff in a school is important for establishing the general ethos of the school. Host country nationals are often the largest national group of employees overall, and their position in the school, both as regards positions of responsibility and in the related area of salary, can make a significant difference to the international 'feel' of the school. This is most obviously of importance in locations where the economic situation in the country is relatively low in terms of GNP, and where social relationships can be realistically described as 'post-colonial' or 'post-Soviet'. Such nationals do, however, have a very significant influence on expatriates, both staff and students, as they provide high levels of contact with the host country in terms of non-formal familiarization and are therefore influential in determining staff and student 'attitudes'.

An area where there is considerable potential for tension, and for undermining of a truly international ethos, is that of appointing the Business or Financial Manager. This is particularly so as regards the opportunities for a host country national to be employed in a senior decision-making capacity rather than as a subordinate whose contacts within the local community are valued. It may be the case that the person with the most appropriate skills and experience for the post is not always available locally, yet this is an area in which the school's claims to be truly international in all that it seeks to do should be subject to rigorous examination. It is perhaps not surprising then that the major international accreditation instruments insist on a careful analysis of the role and status of support staff.

Awareness of the political situation in the host country

Many national school curricula have a requirement to offer programmes in citizenship or civics, which in order to achieve any realism must seek, amongst other things, to engage student interest in current political issues in that country. International schools have historically tended to avoid such engagement. Many, through such simulation devices as a Model United Nations (MUN), and/or a celebration of United Nations Day around 24 October, have sought positively to inform and engage students about the United Nations instead. Many would also seek to promote Peace Studies, and such courses are often conceived in non-national or even anti-nationalist terms. Such disengagement from the affairs of the host country may be reinforced by the attitudes of expatriate parents, which are often identified in terms of a negative 'neutrality' or even a fully negative attitude towards political structures and personalities in the host country.

In a number of countries it would not be expedient to attempt to achieve a high level of student engagement with the local political situation. Unfortunately there have been a number of instances where political events in the host country have immediately affected the nature of international schools located there, primarily on security grounds. International schools will generally not have any clearly articulated policies as regards the 'politics' of the host country, although they may well have discreetly formulated contingency plans. International schools do not, and cannot, exist in a political vacuum. The influence of political events is also not just a curriculum matter – it can be much more deeprooted than that. Where schools have been closed for security reasons, there is often considerable pressure to reopen at the earliest opportunity 'for the sake of the students'. The school may indeed reopen, but there may be a question as to whether it is still as 'international' a school as it was before.

The annual school calendar

The construction of the annual school calendar always raises a number of issues of sensitivity as regards international status. Most international schools operate a calendar derived from the North European agricultural cycle, although the numbers following a so-called Southern Hemisphere year are now substantial. The traditional cycle usually requires 180–190 'teaching days', but the starting point can range from early August to mid-September and the finishing point from late May to mid-July. The particular arrangement may often be made in order to accommodate particularly articulate nationality groups in the parent body and/or on the board. Many schools do not attempt to synchronize their 'year' with that of the host country, and this can lead to problems.

It is, however, the incidental holidays that raise most issues. Observing Christmas and Easter is not straightforward as a number of countries still retain the Julian calendar for religious purposes, but the status of other major religious and cultural festivals is even more important. International schools in Islamic countries usually adapt to the Islamic calendar but there are also, in many schools, necessary adaptations for, amongst others, Diwali, Hanukkah, Chinese New Year and US Thanksgiving. It is impractical to give equal recognition to all the major cultural and religious holidays recognized throughout the world, but ignoring the challenge this presents would certainly cast doubts on the 'international status' of a school.

Many 'Western' international school administrators and teachers find it difficult to adjust their schedules to public holidays that do not fall on a Monday or Friday, and even more difficult to adjust to holidays that are only announced the day before or even on the morning of the day in question. There may be good rational arguments for designing a school year, complete with all holidays, on a purely educational basis, but it is difficult to avoid accusations of 'Western arrogance' with regard to holidays that do not fit conveniently into such a structure.

The most significant practical problem, however, lies in the status given to holidays designated as such by the host country, especially if the timing of these is such that they are perceived to disrupt the learning cycle of the students. It is reasonable for an international school, which is by definition not a national school, not to follow them all, but this may create problems for host country national employees and also for parents who will themselves be on holiday that day, and would, understandably, wish to share it with their children.

There can be no universally applicable model for an international school annual calendar. Planning the calendar will always be a compromise between what is perceived to be best for the learning situation and showing respect and sensitivity both for the practices of the host country and for those students and families whose cultural and religious backgrounds are different from the host country or the majority of the student body. The policy of the school towards holidays could, however ironic it may seem, be regarded as an important touchstone for its international credentials.

Links with local schools

By definition international schools are different from local national schools. In a number of countries this has led, in the area of sports and cultural activities, to such schools forging strong links with other international schools both within and outside the country in question. The major regional associations of international schools have played, and continue to play, an important part here. In terms of promoting international understanding and awareness, such contacts are indeed of great value for the students, and their overall importance in the spread of international education has perhaps not been fully recognized.

There are, however, at least two significant concerns as regards these connections. The logistical expenses relating to international travel may exclude a number of students from participation. Whereas differences in availability of disposable income are indeed a reality, and so it can be argued that differences in the ability to fund such travel are only a manifestation of that reality and therefore an acceptable element in an international education, such a discrepancy remains at variance with the idealism that has always been a factor in such an education. A number of schools overcome this problem by discreetly awarding bursaries to eligible students, from Parent-Teacher Organizations or other funds, for the purpose of such travel.

A more significant concern, perhaps, is that these 'international' links exist in a context in which there appears to be no real place for links of this nature with local schools. Where this is true, it can only reinforce the perception that international schools are elitist schools operating in isolation from the society in which they are located. Such a perception would rarely be fully compatible with published mission statements. There are, of course, many practical issues to be resolved – do the schools play the same sports at the same time of the year; does the ethos of the international school with respect to 'competitiveness' in sports match that of the local schools; are the facilities of a comparable standard; will there be 'behaviour' problems? In all the schools claiming to be international schools with which I have been involved, these have been real issues. It is, however, my opinion that a school content to remain isolated from local national schools in all those areas of activity not essentially governed by curriculum or the language of instruction, would need to review its international credentials seriously.

Community service

Whether it falls under the brief of Creativity, Action, Service (CAS) activities for the IB Diploma Programme or otherwise, community service provides a very important link with the 'wider community'. Although it may be argued that the primary objective of all community service opportunities should be the 'education' of the students, there are inevitably a number of wider results, so that such programmes can sometimes be characterized as informal 'aid'. For a number of years now there has been an extended debate as to whether 'aid' as such is compatible with a vision that is truly 'international'. A community service programme that is perceived by the students involved, or by the recipients, as essentially paternalistic would seem to be in conflict with such a vision.

The location factor is, however, of much greater specific importance in the practicalities of such a programme. Do the laws and/or the insurance requirements of a particular host country allow for the universal implementation of those very successful programmes that have been movingly recorded in the pages of publications such as the International Baccalaureate Organization magazine, *IB World*? The majority of the fine examples found in the literature of the past 30 years have been implemented in locations that are different from the sophisticated and economically advanced countries in which a number of international schools are currently located.

Service to the community is undoubtedly a concept that almost all who have been involved in international education and international schools would seek to bring to the conscious awareness of young people, but the way in which such service can be expressed will be significantly affected by the precise geographical location of the school.

Conclusion

Anecdotal evidence from international school administrators and teachers tends to emphasize the common characteristics of international schools, and this is indeed often very striking. Recent curriculum developments, and especially the current major expansion of the influence of IBO, reinforce this. Ongoing contacts through the expansion of services provided by the European Council of International Schools (ECIS) and to a lesser, and more specialized extent, International Schools Services (ISS), Search Associates, The International Educator (TIE), the US State Department Office of Overseas Schools and the major regional associations it supports, also contribute to this sense of oneness. The role of the Internet in encouraging international insights and understanding in international schools seems likely also to become increasingly important. Yet international schools continue to be very different from each other and, as each develops its individual characteristics – and with the observed brevity of institutional memory in many schools, this happens unusually quickly – this is a trend that seems likely to continue. At the present time it would appear that the seeds of a corporate international school structure have fallen on stony ground.

It is the thesis of this chapter that it is in the relationships of each school with the wider community of contacts in each individual country, or part of a country, that there are to be found really important differences that will affect the truly international status of each school. The United Nations itself has succeeded because it recognizes the right to individuality of each member state. Some would argue it is most successful internationally when it does not follow the lead of the Security Council. In a world in which the forces of globalization appear to be promoting ever greater uniformity in economic, political and cultural structures, it may seem both radical and naïve to suggest that an international outlook is something different.

Leaving aside mission statements and the curriculum, which, increasingly, are becoming based on a common model, the international characteristics of a school will need to be judged on the national backgrounds and political and cultural assumptions of the students and staff. There are good grounds for suggesting that these are significantly affected by the wider community in which each school is located.

References

Allen, K (2000) The international school and its community: think globally, interact locally, in *International Schools and International Education*, eds M C Hayden and J J Thompson, Kogan Page, London

Blaney, J J (1991) The International Schools System, in *International Schools and International Education*, eds P Jonietz and D Harris, Kogan Page, London

Cambridge, J (1998) Investigating national and organizational cultures in the context of the international school, in *International Education: Principles and practice*, eds M C Hayden and J J Thompson, Kogan Page, London

Drake, B (1998) Pastoral Care: The Challenge for International Schools, in *International Education: Principles and practice*, eds M C Hayden and J J Thompson, Kogan Page, London

Gellar, C (1981) International education: some thoughts on what it is and what it might be, *International Schools Journal*, 1, pp 21–26

Hayden, M C and Thompson, J J (1995) International schools and international education: a relationship reviewed, *Oxford Review of Education*, 21(3), pp 327–44

McKenzie, M (1998) Going, going, gone... global, in *International Education: Principles and practice*, eds M C Hayden and J J Thompson, Kogan Page, London

Office of Overseas Schools (2001) Overseas Schools Advisory Council Worldwide Fact Sheet, 2000–2001 [Online] http://www.state.gov/www/about_state/schools/wide.html

Peterson, A D C (1987) *Schools Across Frontiers: The story of the International Baccalaureate and the United World Colleges*, Open Court Publishing, La Salle, Illinois

Richards, N (1998) The Emperor's New Clothes? The issue of staffing in International Schools, in *International Education: Principles and practice*, eds M C Hayden and J J Thompson, Kogan Page, London

Sylvester, R (1998) Through the lens of diversity: inclusive and encapsulated school mission statements, in *International Education: Principles and practice*, eds M C Hayden and J J Thompson, Kogan Page, London

Thompson, J J (1998) Towards a Model for International Education, in *International Education: Principles and practice*, eds M C Hayden and J J Thompson, Kogan Page, London

Wilkinson, D (1998) International Education: a question of access, in *International Education: Principles and practice*, eds M C Hayden and J J Thompson, Kogan Page, London

Chapter 12

Recruitment and deployment of staff: a dimension of international school organization

James Cambridge

Introduction

It is evident that international schools and international education are intimately linked with the processes of globalization. It may be argued that not only are international schools influenced by globalization, by operating in a global market, but they also facilitate its propagation and spread by easing the mobility of expatriate families involved with globalizing institutions such as multinational businesses, financial institutions, development agencies and non-governmental and parastatal organizations. Many international schools also allow the participation of those sectors of their host country populations whose social and economic interests coincide with the 'transnational capitalist class' (Sklair, 2001). Furthermore, as employers of locally recruited professional, clerical and manual workers, international schools may exert an important local economic influence in some countries by reproducing business practices derived from elsewhere in the world.

Globalizing business practices include the marketization of social institutions such as education and health and the application of quality standards to these services, which lead to changes in employment practices. International schools are not immune from the influence of such practices; as independent institutions with influential patrons, operating in a competitive market, they are likely to be found among the vanguard of innovative organizations in some countries. International schools mix the global with the local in their recruitment policies because many employ both expatriate and locally hired staff. For the expatriates especially, there is no 'job for life' and there appears to be a widespread expectation that they will change employers several times during their professional careers. In return for their flexibility and mobility, and since they have cut themselves off from occupational pension schemes and welfare services in their home countries, expatriate teachers may be amply rewarded, particularly in contrast with the pay and conditions of their locally recruited colleagues. It is proposed that a tripartite organizational structure has developed in many international schools, consisting of a long-term administrative core, often, though not always, including the head or principal (who may be a business manager) and deputies, a fringe of relatively highly paid professional expatriates (who may be curriculum leaders) on shorter-term contracts, and local staff hired at lower rates of remuneration who are likely to be longer term. This model shares some resemblance with the 'shamrock organization' proposed by Handy (1991).

Internationalist and globalizing trends in international schools

International education has been described as a contested field of educational practice involving the reconciliation of economic, political and cultural-ideological dilemmas, which may be identified as competing 'internationalist' and 'globalizing' perspectives (Cambridge and Thompson, 2001). The internationalist current in international education may be identified with a positive orientation towards international relations, with aspirations for the promotion of peace and understanding between nations. This is a view of international education as 'a transformative discourse, which locates all fields of enquiry in a supranational frame of reference and upholds the cause of peace' (Rawlings, 2000). It embraces an existential, experiential philosophy of education that values the moral development of the individual and recognizes the importance of service to the community and the development of a sense of responsible citizenship. Such an educational philosophy was promoted by Kurt Hahn, the inspiration for the United World Colleges movement (Röhrs, 1970; Sutcliffe, 1991). It may be argued that internationalist international education celebrates cultural diversity and promotes international cooperation and an internationally-minded outlook.

The globalizing current in international education is influenced by and contributes to the global diffusion of the values of free market capitalism. These values are expressed in international education in terms of increasing competition with national systems of education, accompanied by quality assurance through international accreditation and the spread of global quality standards that facilitate educational continuity for the children of the globally mobile clientele. Globalizing international education serves a market that requires the global certification of educational qualifications, thus facilitating educational continuity for the children of the host country clientele who have aspirations towards upward social mobility in a global context. It may be argued that an outcome of globalizing international education is cultural convergence with the values of the transnational capitalist class that is 'domiciled in and identified with no particular country but, on the contrary, is identified with the global capitalist system' and that comprises people 'who may have more interests in common with each other than they have with their noncapitalist fellow citizens' (Sklair, 2001).

As Bob Sylvester demonstrates elsewhere in this book, the dual aspirations for internationalism and free trade appear to have been part of the ideology of international education from its inception. However, the internationalist and globalizing approaches to international education are rarely seen in their pure forms. International schools reconcile these contrasting approaches in their practice of international education. The community of schools offering international education appears to be heterogeneous because each reconciliation is unique to the historical, geographical and economic circumstances of that institution.

Globalization and international schools

Globalization has been described in terms of 'a process (or set of processes), which embodies a transformation in the spatial organization of social relations and transactions – assessed in terms of their extensity, intensity, velocity and impact – generating transcontinental or interregional flows and networks of activity, interaction, and the exercise of power' (Held et al, 1999). The goals to which the processes of globalization are leading include 'the establishment of a borderless global economy, the complete denationalization of all corporate procedures and activities, and the eradication of economic nationalism' (Sklair, 2001). This is a perspective that may be identified with hyperglobalism.

It is a paradox that the majority of international schools tend to operate in a variety of local markets. Usually students do not travel very far to attend an international school; many of them reside with their parents, who are expatriates working in a country that is not their home, and attend an international school in their locality or in a nearby city. In the case of a small state an international school might serve a whole country. It may be argued that the only schools offering an international education that really operates in a global market are some of the United World Colleges, particularly those institutions that are wholly residential. These colleges have a policy of student recruitment from all countries in the world, and the students are often funded by scholarships raised from charitable donations to national committees (Sutcliffe, 1991; Wilkinson, 1998). In this case, the students do not attend a school because they happen to reside in that particular country with their parents but, instead, they leave home and move to another country specifically to attend a college offering an international education. These institutions have a global catchment area for student recruitment. While the market for most international schools is confined to the locality of each, however, it may be argued that the curricula they offer are global because they are also available to students of many nationalities in other schools in different countries.

The logic of economic globalization has important implications for the management and organization of education. As Sklair (2001) points out, 'global capitalism succeeds by turning most spheres of social life into businesses, by making social institutions – such as schools, universities, prisons, hospitals, welfare systems – more business-like'. The business-like attributes of such institutions are likely to include a more aggressive approach to efficiency (the optimum method for getting from one point to another), calculability (an emphasis on the quantitative aspects of products supplied and services offered), predictability (the assurance that products and services will be the same over time and in all locales) and control through the application of technology (Ritzer, 2000).

The process of accreditation by external agencies has become an increasingly widespread practice among schools offering an international education, to the extent that Murphy (1998) proposes that 'more and more peripatetic parents are becoming familiar with the process of accreditation and are beginning to feel that placing their children in an unexamined school is a risk they do not wish to take'. Such approaches require a shift in the institutional culture-ideology of schools away from exclusively pedagogical issues towards the espousal of market-oriented values. This is a development that is not peculiar to international schools alone; it is also to be found in the national education systems of several countries (Lauder, 1991). It may even be argued that these values may be identified with the attributes of branded products, and that the development of the globalizing current of international education may be viewed in terms of the transformation of international education into a globally branded product. It has been asserted that international education 'may be compared with other globally marketed goods and services such as soft drinks and hamburgers; a reliable product conforming to consistent quality standards throughout the world' (Cambridge, 2000). Thus international schools may be considered to be the retailers of a globally branded service.

Implications for management and organization

It follows that the need exists for a globally mobile workforce of teachers who are experienced and qualified to provide the globally branded service offered by international schools. Many international schools in various parts of the world recruit expatriate teachers in addition to those staff who are recruited locally. Hardman (2001) identifies three categories of overseas teachers applying for posts at international schools: childless career professionals, career professionals with their families, and mavericks. There are some limitations to this typology, particularly in the way that it avoids discussing how the motives of people might change over time, but it provides a group of illuminating metaphors for conceptualizing the international teacher employment market.

For many international schools, childless career professionals constitute the ideal employees on the grounds that they are cheaper to recruit, transport and house than career professionals with families. The childless career professionals may be motivated by a happy working climate and feeling valued, they welcome new teaching opportunities and they value involvement with students. In contrast with these are the so-called maverick teachers, who are motivated by the prospect of global travel, the challenges of a new country to explore and a possible escape route from their own national system. Such maverick teachers are enthusiastic and creative but for them teaching is a means to an end, and not an end in itself. Consequently they may be viewed as unreliable by school administrators as they may not wish to extend their employment contracts beyond the initial term. On the other hand, Hardman argues that certain career professionals – the 'Penelopes' who become faithful to their adopted country – can over-extend their contracts beyond their useful value. In addition to the expatriate teachers, international schools may also recruit staff locally, often at differential salary rates. Hardman observes that such inequalities in pay and conditions of service between expatriates and locally hired staff can lead to feelings of resentment, an issue that has also been discussed elsewhere (Cambridge, 1998; Richards, 1998; Wilkinson, 1998).

This arrangement for the organization of international schools bears a resemblance to the shamrock organization discussed by Handy (1991). The employees of shamrock organizations can be identified with three groups: the administrative core, the professional contractual fringe and the flexible labour force. Such a model acknowledges the mobility and short-term orientation of at least part of the workforce, takes a pragmatic view of the salary inequalities that exist between labour markets in different geographical locations, and represents an adaptation to the current employment dogma that there are no 'jobs for life'. In its original conception, the three 'leaves' of the shamrock organization have distinctive functional attributes. The core is composed of qualified professionals who manage the organization. Handy (1991) points out that 'they get most of their identity and purpose from their work. They *are* the organization and are likely to be both committed to it and dependent on it'. Members of the core are few in number and have a flat organization with little hierarchical differentiation between them. Increasingly, a large proportion of the income of core workers is made up of performance-related bonuses; this is because they are more like partners in the organization than employees of it.

The contractual fringe is 'made up of both individuals and organizations... the individuals will be self-employed professionals or technicians, many of them past employees of the central organization who ran out of roles in the core or who preferred the freedom of self-employment' (Handy, 1991). The innovative point about the contractual fringe is that it is composed of workers who are not waged but who work for fees; they are paid in terms of results, not in terms of how much time they spend at work. Contractual fringe workers are effectively self-employed and may take fees from a variety of employers. As well-qualified professionals, their skills are in demand; they are not tied to a particular employer and are free to move on if they are attracted by better pay and conditions elsewhere. As self-employed workers, they take responsibility for organizing their own pension and taxation arrangements. The flexible labour force may be seen in terms of being the 'hired help division' of the organization but, as Handy emphasizes, they:

> are not all pining for core jobs, marking time on the fringe, having to eke out an existence from part-time earnings until something better turns up. A lot of them are women who do not always want a demanding full-time job, but do want access to money and people, a job to supplement and to complement their other work. Many others have two or more part-time jobs, officially declared, and are therefore more properly described as full-time

self-employed with a portfolio of jobs. Some of them are young, who see work as a series of apprenticeships or as pocket money opportunities.

To what extent then can Handy's shamrock model of organization be applied to the context of the international school? It may be argued that this model is more suited to companies involved in selling sophisticated technological services. Many critics would object to the introduction into the educational context of performance-related bonuses and payment by fees. However, attempts have been made to introduce such features into national systems of education (Storey, 2000), and it is reported that some international schools already have in place systems of performance-related payment linked to appraisal of teaching staff (Blandford and Shaw, 2001). Many expatriate teachers on short-term contracts share certain attributes with self-employed professionals. As has already been pointed out, they are frequently responsible for their own pension and welfare arrangements. Many have to bear personally the expense of long haul travel to attend recruitment fairs if they wish to change jobs.

It may be argued that the existence of the small administrative core ensures the long-term survival of the international school, but the most serious objection to the application of Handy's shamrock model to international schools could be associated with the high turnover of staff, in particular the high turnover of head teachers and principals. Fink (2001) observes that 'with constant staff turnover, different wage scales between expatriates and indigenous staff, and continually changing formal leaders and governors [the] dilemma of sustainability is particularly appropriate for international schools'. Hawley (1994, 1995) reports high turnover among head teachers of American international schools; this is a frequently cited source but, since it is based upon a sample comprising 81 American international schools and has not yet been followed by other studies, it is difficult to evaluate the extent to which it describes a more widespread phenomenon. It may, however, be interpreted as indicating that, in many international schools, principals and heads may also be considered part of the contractual fringe.

The contractual fringe group of education professionals recruited from abroad on short fixed-term contracts may be recognized and rewarded as globally mobile curriculum leaders and middle managers, such as heads of departments. These teachers are recruited because they have particular skills and experience; they may be native English speakers, subject specialists in key areas of the curriculum and experienced with working in a particular assessment framework. Most importantly perhaps, they may share the same nationality as many of the students at the school. The challenge for the locally recruited teachers is to win recognition as members of the contractual fringe, with equal status to their expatriate colleagues, and to avoid being stereotyped as part of the flexible labour force. Some expatriate teachers may also be found amongst the members of the flexible labour force: those who are often identified as the 'trailing spouses' of partners employed other than by the international school. Such teachers may be involved with a school over a long period of time, but if their partner is required by the employer to move at short notice, or during the middle of an academic year, then the 'trailing spouse' is most likely to leave too.

The locally recruited staff constitute the flexible labour force that may comprise some education professionals but also consists of non-teaching support staff. The personal experience of the author in less developed countries is that many of the non-teaching support staff have subsidiary jobs, for example as taxi-drivers, caterers or domestic staff. However, in many situations even these workers have been transformed into members of the contractual fringe as schools have stopped directly employing support staff and, instead, have out-sourced their provision for cooks, cleaners and security staff to small external service companies. Thus free market capitalism, with its agenda of privatization, marketization, deregulation and introduction of flexible employment practices, reproduces itself globally.

Multinational teams

International schools are working environments in which there is frequently great cultural diversity. Hambrick *et al* (1998) speculate on the influence of cultural diversity on the 'organizational effectiveness' (however that is defined) of multinational groups (MNGs). They propose that cultural diversity of multinational groups may be described in terms of the following dimensions:

- diversity of values, comprising differences in fundamental preferences for some states of affairs over others among different cultures;
- diversity of cognitive schema, comprising different knowledge, assumptions and perspectives among different cultures;
- diversity of demeanour, comprising various kinds of surface behaviour involving punctuality, conversational style and body language among different cultures; and
- relative facility with the working language of the group.

A typology of group tasks, comprising three categories, is also proposed:

- open-ended creative activities;
- closed computational activities; and
- activities that require high levels of coordination between members of the group.

Hambrick *et al* form hypotheses about how diversity of multinational groups in each of the four dimensions described may be expected to influence the three types of group tasks. They predict that, whereas increasing diversity of cultural values is unrelated to the effectiveness of the group in performing computational tasks with closed outcomes, it may be expected to inhibit the effectiveness of the performance of co-ordinative tasks, and enhance the effectiveness of groups working on open-ended creative tasks in a multinational group context. They explain that 'when the group is engaged in a creative task, diversity of values can be expected to be beneficial for group effectiveness. The varied perspectives and enriched debate that comes from increased diversity will be helpful in generating and refining alternatives' (Hambrick *et al*, 1998). On the other hand:

> when the task is coordinative, involving elaborate interaction among group members, diversity of values will tend to be negatively related to group effectiveness. In such a task situation, fluid and reliable coordination is required: debates and tensions over why or how the group is approaching the task – which will tend to occur when values vary – will be counterproductive. In addition, disparate values create interpersonal strains and mistrust, which become damaging when the group is charged with a coordinative task. (Hambrick *et al*, 1998)

In the context of the international school, it may be expected that some of the tasks described above will be performed more effectively than others by groups of culturally diverse teachers. For example, interactions between teachers and students, as well as between teachers and other teachers, may be expected to be influenced by diversity of demeanour and cognitive schema although, in an English-medium school, one might expect the facility of teachers using the working language of the organization to be relatively good. In certain schools, however, there are separate language streams in the same institution, and anecdotal evidence from conversations with practising teachers suggests that this contrast might contribute to the reinforcement of a sense of difference between sectional groupings of teaching staff based around language. Furthermore, teachers from different cultural backgrounds may have contrasting values with respect to education. These differences might take various forms, including contrasting views about the relations between adults and young people, the nature and purposes of education, and the use of questions in the context of the classroom. In addition, there may be profound sociological and economic differences between expatriate teachers and their colleagues recruited locally. Numerous theorists (including Hofstede, 1986, 1991, 2001; and Trompenaars and Hampden-Turner, 1997) have discussed frameworks for the description and analysis of contrasting national cultures. These frameworks have been applied to the study of organizations in general (Tayeb, 1996; Schneider and Barsoux, 1997) and international schools in particular (Cambridge, 1998, 2000; Shaw 2001).

Conclusion

A distinction needs to be drawn between the 'internationalist' and 'globalizing' aspects of international schools and international education. An outcome of the internationalist perspective is the encouragement of international understanding and 'international-mindedness' contributing to the maintenance of good bilateral relations between nation states based on principles of equity and human rights. Critics of globalization, on the other hand, argue that it is a process leading to cultural homogenization (Klein, 2000). Multiculturalism in education has been described in terms of 'a substantial monoculturalism as to values, mitigated by tolerance of exotic detail' (Zaw, 1996), which is to say that it has led to cultural homogenization through convergence with the normative values of the organization.

It may be argued that an outcome of economic globalization is the growth and intensification of economic inequality as corporations attempt to drive down employment costs by relocating global manufacturing operations in low wage economies (Klein, 2000). While it is absurd to compare directly the activities of international schools and multinational corporations, it is also evident that, in particular situations, their employment practices may exploit and perpetuate economic inequality between teachers recruited from rich and poor countries. This practice may be difficult to reconcile with claims that international schools should have 'a management regime value-consistent with an institutional philosophy' of internationalism (Hayden and Thompson, 1996). It may be concluded that the institutional philosophy of an international school should address the issues of multiculturalism, pluralism and cultural hegemony since it has been argued that human rights, cultural diversity, social justice and sustainable development are global issues that contribute to the essential learning of the active world citizen (Thomas, 1998). Handy's shamrock model demonstrates how contrasting categories of employees in the same organization can develop out of different contractual arrangements.

References

Blandford, S and Shaw, M (2001) The Nature of International School Leadership, in *Managing International Schools*, eds S Blandford and M Shaw, Routledge Falmer, London

Cambridge, J C (1998) Investigating National and Organisational Cultures in the Context of the International School, in *International Education: Principles and practice*, eds M C Hayden and J J Thompson, Kogan Page, London

Cambridge, J C (2000) International Schools, Globalization and the Seven Cultures of Capitalism, in *International Schools and International Education*, eds M C Hayden and J J Thompson, Kogan Page, London

Cambridge, J C and Thompson, J J (2001) 'A Big Mac and a Coke?' Internationalism and Globalisation as Contexts for International Education, unpublished paper, University of Bath

Fink, D (2001) Learning to change and changing to learn, in *Managing International Schools*, eds S Blandford and M Shaw, Routledge Falmer, London

Hambrick, D, Davison, S, Snell, S and Snow, C (1998) When groups consist of multiple nationalities: towards a new understanding of the implications, *Organization Studies*, **19** (2), pp 181–205

Handy, C (1991) *The Age of Unreason*, Arrow, London

Hardman, J (2001) Improving Recruitment and Retention of Quality Overseas Teachers, in *Managing International Schools*, eds S Blandford and M Shaw, Routledge Falmer, London

Hawley, D (1994) How long do international school heads survive? A research analysis. Part 1, *International Schools Journal*, **XIV** (1), pp 8–21

Hawley, D (1995) How long do international school heads survive? A research analysis. Part 2, *International Schools Journal*, **XIV** (2), pp 23–36

Hayden, M C and Thompson, J J (1996) Potential difference: the driving force for international education, *International Schools Journal*, **16** (1), pp 46–57

Held, D, McGrew, A, Goldblatt, D and Perraton, J (1999) *Global Transformations*, Polity Press, Cambridge

Hofstede, G (1986) Cultural differences in learning and teaching, *International Journal of Intercultural Relations*, **10** (3), pp 301–20

Hofstede, G (1991) *Cultures and Organizations*, Harper Collins, London

Hofstede, G (2001) *Culture's Consequences: International differences in work-related values*, Sage, Beverley Hills

Klein, N (2000) *No Logo*, Flamingo, London

Lauder, H (1991) Education, Democracy and the Economy, *British Journal of Sociology of Education*, **12**, pp 417–31

Murphy, E (1998) International School Accreditation: Who Needs It?, in *International Education: Principles and practice*, eds M C Hayden and J J Thompson, Kogan Page, London

Rawlings, F (2000) Abstract of Doctoral Thesis: Globalisation, Curriculum and International Communities: A Case Study of the United World College of the Atlantic, *International Journal of Educational Development*, **20**, pp 365–66

Richards, N (1998) The Emperor's New Clothes? The issue of staffing in international schools, in *International Education: Principles and Practice*, eds M C Hayden and J J Thompson, Kogan Page, London

Ritzer, G (2000) *The McDonaldization of Society*, Pine Forge, Thousand Oaks, Ca

Röhrs, H (1970) *Kurt Hahn*, Routledge and Kegan Paul, London

Schneider, S and Barsoux, J-L (1997) *Managing Across Cultures*, Prentice Hall, London

Shaw, M (2001) Managing mixed-culture teams in international schools, in *Managing International Schools*, eds S Blandford and M Shaw, Routledge Falmer, London

Sklair, L (2001) *The Transnational Capitalist Class*, Blackwell, Oxford

Storey, A (2000) A Leap of Faith? Performance pay for teachers, *Journal of Education Policy*, **15** (5), pp 509–23

Sutcliffe, D (1991) The United World Colleges, in *World Yearbook of Education 1991: International schools and international education*, eds P Jonietz and D Harris, Kogan Page, London

Tayeb, M (1996) *The Management of a Multicultural Workforce*, John Wiley, Chichester

Thomas, P (1998) Education for Peace, in *International Education: Principles and practice*, eds M C Hayden and J J Thompson, Kogan Page, London

Trompenaars, F and Hampden-Turner, C (1997) *Riding the Waves of Culture*, Nicholas Brealey, London

Wilkinson, D (1998) International Education: A question of access, in *International Education: Principles and practice*, eds M C Hayden and J J Thompson, Kogan Page, London

Zaw, S K (1996) Locke and Multiculturalism: Toleration, Relativism and Reason, in *Public Education in a Multicultural Society*, ed R K Fullwider, Cambridge University Press, Cambridge

Chapter 13

An international dimension to management and leadership skills for international education

Terry Haywood

The nature of international education – an inclusive approach

For many years, some of the most inspired exponents of international education have been involved in an ongoing yet inconclusive debate about exactly how this concept should be defined. Numerous articles in the professional literature have contributed reflections, analyses and even the first steps of empirical research to this debate, but the term itself still seems to indicate a galaxy of ideas and experiences rather than a distinctive approach to education. Before addressing the question of where we might find the 'international' in school management, then, it will be useful to clarify where I am going to seek the 'international' in education as a whole.

The origin and durability of this debate can perhaps be traced to the very different kinds of school that have taken this term as their own. Educational institutions that aspire to be 'international' derive their origins and purpose from a range of backgrounds and there are various classifications of these typologies, which are well represented by Hayden and Thompson (2000). In general, however, we can identify two overt strands that characterize the field. These two strands are not necessarily in contrast or opposition but their perceptions derive from different perspectives about the function of the schools themselves. On the one hand we encounter schools with a *pragmatic* rationale that view the community they serve as the defining factor – these schools are 'international' because their enrolment populations are multinational or because their very existence can be traced to the goal of educating expatriate families living temporarily away from their home countries. On the other hand there are schools that derive their 'international' goals from the more *visionary* ideal of offering students an experience that will help to promote a world view based on cross-cultural understanding, leading towards a holistic view of world affairs and ultimately towards more peaceful collaboration between peoples and nations.

The visionary ideal of international education has a long and distinguished history but very few of the successful international schools that exist today can actually trace their origins to the promotion of ideals. Indeed, a number of pioneering institutions that were founded at different times on the purely visionary rationale have not managed to survive, while others have had only marginal influence on the evolution and development of the way that international education exists today. It can hardly be disputed that the growth, expansion and consolidation of this sector since the 1950s has been due almost entirely to schools that were initially founded on the pragmatic rationale to serve the needs of expatriate communities, and I will identify this group as the *mainstream international schools* in the following pages.

As I have already indicated, however, the two typologies need not be in contrast and to a large extent they coexist alongside one another. Indeed, they frequently coexist within the same institution. Pragmatic needs must be met if any school is to succeed and survive but educational goals are enhanced when they are supported by what Postman (1995) has called a 'narrative' that gives a greater sense of mission to the educational project. In this respect, the visionary narrative has always been a strong motivating factor that has inspired educators and families to look beyond their immediate environments and to see themselves and their schools as part of a wider movement that is ideologically driven. This is why mainstream international schools today can be found at all points on the visionary-pragmatic spectrum and it is one of the reasons why observers find it hard to identify essential and common traits in such schools.

While the mainstream group has a clear functional base that has enabled it to underpin the success of international *schooling* as a commodity, it should not be confused with the more profound concept of international *education*, which would lose much of its value if it were limited as an experience uniquely for expatriate populations. Indeed, there would appear to be evidence at the present time that many *national* communities are increasingly interested in the *international* dimension of education for their children. At its simplest level, this can be seen in the way that many international schools are nowadays open to host country nationals. Some 'purists' think that this might affect educational standards and detract from the international experience for students, but this argument can be strongly contested by many schools that recruit substantial numbers of host country nationals who are attracted through a combination of visionary as well as pragmatic goals. The latter are usually provided by the benefits of becoming bilingual in English and the national language but the magnetism of an international mindset also provides a powerful drive for many parents.

More importantly, there is extensive interest in international education from institutions that operate exclusively within national systems and that cater for monocultural, monolingual and relatively stable populations and communities. Some observers, exemplified by Hill (2000), have coined the term 'internationally-minded schools' to describe this group. They often fall outside the scope of research into international education, although they represent fascinating examples of schools that are actively seeking to incorporate international ideals and opportunities into their programme from a predominantly visionary perspective.

They also represent a phenomenon that can be found in many countries, but much of the available literature tends to treat it as a separate sphere of interest from the mainstream international schools and most references still see international schooling almost uniquely in the English-speaking context. After all, in most cities the 'international' school is one with a curriculum taught in English using a curriculum model that owes much to the United States and the United Kingdom. Interestingly, the International Baccalaureate Organization (IBO) has openly begun to seek 'collaboration with state systems of education, because it is obviously there that the major influence for the future lies' (Walker, 2001). This assertion is based on the realization that mainstream international schools are 'a drop in the ocean' (Walker, 2001) and that to exert any influence on significant numbers of the world's youth it will be necessary to go well beyond the 500–600 schools that are currently members of the European Council of International Schools (ECIS, 2002) or the Association for the Advancement of International Education (AAIE, 2002) or the 1,000 or so schools that are currently affiliated with the IBO (IBO, 2002). Inherent in this goal is the recognition that many schools would aspire to become visionary exponents of international education even if they fail to fulfil the pragmatic rationale for inclusion in the mainstream movement as it is currently defined.

The growing recognition of international education's visionary component has brought about a shift in the provision of training and professional development. The mainstream international schools have tended to focus heavily on pragmatic concerns when seeking programmes for development and institutional improvement. There have, of course, been good reasons for this, not least the fact that for many years their very survival required that they find practical solutions to basic problems. Many operate in competitive marketplaces with a high turnover of families, prone to fluctuating enrolment following local and global business trends, while others have faced obstacles in host country regulations or the limitations of running on low budgets entirely financed by income from tuition fees.

Not surprisingly, the primary concern of these schools has been to develop strategies for tackling these pragmatic issues, including their educational implications such as the delivery of a curriculum in the English language to children who speak a different mother tongue at home and perhaps require a third language in the local community. Today, it is possible to access specific strategies for many of these concerns, and international schooling has an established record of successful educational development, supported by sound expertise that has been accumulated through experience and research. With greater confidence in acquired know-how and the pragmatics of managing international schools, the visionary components of international education are now coming to the fore more prominently.

It will be a major contention of this chapter that if the term 'international education' is to have any value beyond the parochial, then its definition must be an inclusive one. It must also be one which all schools that describe themselves in such terms should be able to identify. Consequently, I propose that the real questions of international education are at the visionary end of the spectrum. The defining feature of international education should really be the attempt to construct an experience that provides a distinctive opportunity for children to develop mindsets, values and attitudes that are characteristically international. In what follows I will therefore take a broad view in exploring the issues that educational managers have to encounter in this process.

The 'international' in school management and organization

To what extent does a set of specific skills for the effective management of international education exist? The question is not as rhetorical as it may seem. Indeed, for many years the majority of mainstream international schools would appear to have been managed through a mixture of strategies imported directly from the two major national systems (US and UK) that characterize the sector. This approach is akin to the globalizing effect of international schooling that has been identified by Cambridge (2000) and Lawton (1998). In any case, a great deal has been written and taught about school management in national contexts and it is only natural to ask what other attributes, in addition to the skills that are needed in any location, does international education require of its management.

The question is complicated by the fact that management training is largely concerned with the development of flexible strategic thinking that can be applied in a range of circumstances that the manager will face in the course of any career. The fact that a particular skill is a general requirement for a manager does not mean that it is applied in the same way all the time. For instance, managers in any national system have to deal with a wide variety of school environments and heads who move from school to school in the same country will have to apply the same general skills in different ways that are appropriate to the local circumstances in each new posting. Is the extension of these same processes to international education merely their application to another environment in which they can be interpreted and applied without adaptation to any 'special' needs of this sector?

This question is highlighted if we look at some of the approaches that are used to promote quality in international education. A good example is the accreditation protocol that the European Council of International Schools has developed and which is highly regarded around the world as one of the most valuable tools for school improvement (ECIS, 1997). The section on Organization and Administration in this protocol contains 14 standards and 17 descriptors of effective practice, yet not one of these statements has an overt international dimension. The ECIS instrument is a model of good practice for schools in general but it does not appear to have been structured especially for international education. This would tend to reinforce my previous assertion that mainstream international schools have often been concerned more with providing sound responses to pragmatic concerns of the institutions than with the visionary components of the educational process. My contention that pragmatic responses alone do not provide a satisfactory rationale today is, however, borne out by the fact that the projected seventh edition of the ECIS accreditation protocol will include specific international references for the first time.

In recent years a number of less formal instruments have appeared, which reflect the growing awareness from international educators that their profession does have special characteristics that are identifiable and measurable. For instance, along with material produced for its Primary Years Programme, the International Baccalaureate Organization has included a simple but useful checklist for self-assessment of the international identity of a school (IBO, 2000). At the same time, the International Schools Association (ISA) has been working to develop tools that enable schools to assess and improve their international dimension (Timmermans, 2000). These approaches are less formal than the ECIS accreditation instrument but they do give administrators and leaders an insight as to how they might encourage a greater international consciousness into their own schools.

International education has now come of age in other ways. For instance, there is a growing market in the training of international school managers and several institutions are actively involved in this, ranging from universities to independent trainers and consultants. In its stride this has also led to a growing number of publications, including research journals and books from mainstream publishing companies. Although many mainstream international schools still access national consultants to help them resolve specific management issues, it would appear that many trainers have begun to incorporate international components into their programmes.

Most of all, perhaps, there is at least one piece of strong empirical evidence that would lead us to ascribe a key role to management in the development of international education, and it is confirmed directly by research from many national systems. It is a well-established research finding (see, for instance, Hopkins *et al*, 1994) that leadership (through heads, superintendents or principals) is the single most important contributing factor in creating a school's ethos, identity and, ultimately, its success or failure as an institution. We must therefore seek to identify how successful managers have been able to influence their schools and generate an international ethos in the educational project. We might also learn from some of the successful developments in international education what features are required for effective implementation of an international vision.

The research needed for such an investigation is beyond the scope of this chapter but I suggest that as we pursue this conjectural exercise we will find that, as with the schools themselves, we can divide management skills into pragmatic and visionary components. I will now turn to addressing each of these in turn.

Pragmatic management and learning from experience

By pragmatic management I mean the application of general skills to problem-solving in the local environment. Most of these skills have been clearly identified by research over the years and there are strategies of management training based on experience and 'know-how' that is part of an established pattern. By its very nature, pragmatic management can be analysed in terms of specific issues. On the simplest level, some of the ways that school managers deal with these issues can be phrased in almost exactly the same terms that might be used by their national system counterparts. Any good textbook on school management will give some indication about what these might be, such as:

- timetabling and the identification of staffing needs;
- attention to safety, security, architecture and the design of learning environments;
- provision of services such as food and transport;
- time management;
- financial management.

If this first level of concerns would not seem to pose the need for skills that are necessarily international in character, the same cannot be said of higher-level management functions and those tasks that involve aspects of the affective domain:

- teacher recruitment and retention;
- teacher motivation and the creation of effective teams;
- professional development;
- management of change;
- managing community involvement for stakeholders and the wider society.

Each of these tasks provides scope for an international dimension of management. Most mainstream international schools, for instance, have to be adept at dealing with expatriate concerns among their professional staff, the student body and the community as a whole. Expatriates have to face a range of novel problems that are sometimes underestimated by the organizations for which they work and, since job and career factors still predominate in the selection of which employee will be sent on a foreign posting, this can often mean that 'a foreign assignment can be tougher on the rest of the family than on the working expat' (Hernberg, 2001). This is true even in supposedly 'easy' locations such as Western

Europe, which may not be considered as calling for special adaptation, and dealing with these problems is clearly an issue that will require specific skills from management. Similarly, an expertise and awareness in dealing with third-culture kids is also characteristic of mainstream international school environments.

International school managers often have to deal with multinational groups of teachers and parents, which can create the need to develop new skills in teamwork and communication. It would seem that such situations are recognized throughout the business world as the sort of special challenge for which international organizations need to develop a specific response. Training for *international* management is currently the fastest growth area in business training, a fact that is borne out by the way that MBA programmes are tailored and marketed, and according to the Dean of the London Business School, 'One thing we do really well is cross-cultural teamwork… Our students have the capability to work within international task forces' (Quelch, 2001). International schools may have much to learn from business experience in this respect.

The comments above seem to suggest a distinction between national schools and mainstream international schools, a distinction that has been recognized by the institutions themselves. Awareness of this distinction led to the creation of new networks for professional development and the exchange of skills and know-how through the establishment of regional schools' associations that can now be found in most parts of the world. In a similar context, some governments actively promote their national schools that operate abroad through financial support, staffing and training, so that we find French, German and Swedish schools in many cities functioning in close contact with their home countries but with articulated support systems in place.

If we look closely at the activities that the schools' associations promote then we find a distinct focus on the pragmatic aspects of management. There are very good reasons for this. In the first place, their establishment was related to the real need perceived by the schools themselves for 'services' that they could not easily access, and to provision of an exchange mechanism whereby successful problem-solving in one school could be a learning experience for others. Most mainstream international schools came into the world as a result of local market needs and had to tread pioneering ground – from curriculum issues such as working in English as an academic language for mother-tongue speakers of other tongues, to high-level management concerns such as negotiating with local governments about recognition problems affecting the very existence of the school or adapting employment contracts to host country norms – and a lot more. Pragmatic needs, by definition, have to be tackled in every school and there will continue to be a need for these exchanges of skills and expertise in the future. It is also true that many of the pragmatic concerns are genuinely common across the mainstream international sector, so that even schools with different perspectives on curriculum and national influence can share perspectives and solutions to these issues with mutual benefit.

For the most part, these associations do not exist to support 'international education' as an ideal but their purpose is to provide a host of technical support mechanisms for international schools. This is frequently evident in their mission statements. ECIS, for instance, is 'dedicated to the advancement of internationalism through education by the provision of services to its members' (ECIS, 2002), while ISA states its main aim as the encouragement of 'cooperation among international and internationally-minded schools through consultation on teaching and administrative questions' (ISA, 2002). International school managers generally find that these organizations provide some of the essential components of their professional toolkit. Through their links with other professionals and their accumulated expertise in the field, they contribute to the creative transfer of problem-solving for international schools. In addition, there is a growing base of research experience that can now be drawn upon, thanks to the involvement of universities that actively encourage the involvement of internationally located educators in research projects.

Schools that operate in national settings have, of course, their own networks for access to management and professional support systems. It is also true that many national systems encounter management issues that are parallel to those encountered in the international sector. Dealing with multicultural, multilingual and multinational communities is a common feature for urban schools in all developed countries and it would be erroneous to assert that these do not pose management challenges of a similar type to those faced in international schools.

Pragmatic management is the lifeblood of every school head and without a well-developed range of skills and know-how, institutions will not be run effectively – but the most profound questions about what international education is and how its goals can be promoted are not essential to many of the tasks that this involves. Pragmatic skills can be applied equally in The British School of Ruritania as in the American School of Europa. The focus on international *schooling* has only partly contributed to the debate on international *education*, which essentially needs to go beyond pragmatic issues by seeking to provide a vision of how each school can actively promote an international mindset in young people; providing this vision is more often associated with *leadership* than with *management*.

Visionary leadership to promote international education

We have seen that some of the most influential organizations that service the international schools do not refer to international education in their mission statements, but many of the schools themselves make overt references to this concept in their philosophies. The United World Colleges (UWC), for instance, work to a common statement of mission, which openly commits them, 'through international education, shared experience and community service… (to) encourage young people to become responsible citizens' (UWC, 2002). Similar phrases can be found in the philosophy statements of many other schools. It therefore follows that the role of the head, director or superintendent, as overall manager of the school, is to ensure that the institution develops an ethos that is in tune with these goals and develops an identity that is consistent with them. In the first section of this chapter, I pointed out how difficult it has been (and still is) to arrive at a specific definition of international education in a broad sense but this need not be an obstacle in so far as heads perceive their roles in individual schools. The question they need to pose is 'How can we develop international education for students in the context of our particular school?'. Working from the general to the specific and the global to the local, this has to begin with the school management team developing an agreed understanding of what international education involves and how it intends to promote this feature in the unique school context.

What being 'international' means to the United World Colleges, with a carefully balanced, selected and diverse student population, may not be the same thing that it means to an expatriate school or one that operates in the confines of a national system with a monocultural enrolment. What unites the experiences of these schools, however, is that each one is involved in a conscious commitment to values, and attempts to construct a pedagogical and life experience that will inculcate these values in young people. One of the oldest institutions to have been founded with this goal, the Yokohama International School, has an articulate statement of philosophy, which makes explicit what it believes an international education should work towards (Yokohama International School, 2002):

- develop… a sense of self-esteem and identity, and an awareness of interdependence;
- provide each student with communicative, academic, social and emotional skills;

- foster a respect for, and an appreciation of, the worth of cultural differences;
- foster a commitment to the elimination of poverty, hunger and disease.

This is followed by a reference to four key universal values:

- that we should be mindful of the needs and rights of others;
- that we should be honest in our dealings;
- that we should be peaceful in our intentions;
- that we should be considerate in our actions.

Other schools may word their statements of belief differently, but this example demonstrates well how one school has created a detailed narrative of international education to motivate the learning experience that it will attempt to provide.

Even the visionary voices, however, have sometimes struggled to propose a consciously articulated strategy for internationalism through school management. For instance, there is considerable debate about how to generate a lasting international experience for children. An influential article by Gellar (1993) sums up one approach when he points to the development of positive attitudes and values emerging 'not so much from curriculum, but (from) what takes place in the minds of children as they work and play together with children of other cultures and backgrounds. It is the child experiencing togetherness with different and unique individuals; not just toleration but the enjoyment of differences; differences of colour, dress, belief, perspective'. Such casual interaction between students of different nationalities may be a strong contributor to fostering international values and attitudes but it is hardly an articulated and consciously constructed part of experience. For some schools, moreover, it is not an option. In any case, there is anecdotal evidence that learning that occurs casually through interaction with friends in the playground may lead to strong affective bonds but it does not resist the forces that are at work once the children return to their cultural communities (Walker, 2001).

The chances for successful transmission of values are much enhanced when the school is managed in such a way that a positive international culture pervades the ethos of the community in general. Indeed, the question of whether an international student body (something that may be outside of the school's direct control) is an essential component for international education has received a surprising amount of attention when compared with the way that curriculum and student life are structured (something that is very much the school's responsibility to control and manage). Yet it is surely the role of managers to attempt to provide a conscious articulation of curriculum and organizational inter-action so as to provide a learning experience that can stimulate children to develop international ideals and values. Walker (2001) has made a powerful case for insisting that learning to live together, one of the key features of all educational programmes but that is central to international education, 'is a matter for the head rather than the heart'.

In a powerful call for higher-level leadership in international educa-tion, Lewis (2001) identifies three areas that must be addressed in order for schools consciously to structure a genuinely international learning experience. He refers to these as a universal value system, the formal curriculum and the hidden curriculum. While agreeing with this analy-sis, I would argue, however, that none of these aspects actually has a 'universal' solution but rather that they all have to be interpreted and defined for each specific school. In contrast to the 'problem-solving' approach that is typical of pragmatic management, the visionary role for leaders in international education is better seen as that of 'question-posing'. Such questions might include, perhaps, 'How can we provide an international experience for our students?'; 'How can we incorporate international themes into the curriculum?'; 'How should we handle conflict resolution, especially when it occurs from values that are perceived differently by different cultures?'; 'What extra-curricular and student-life components are going to contribute to developing an inter-national mindset?'; 'How should issues of current affairs and global awareness be dealt with in school?'; 'How can we create opportunities for international interaction where it does not occur naturally?'; 'How can we forge an appreciation of the needs and aspirations of the less privileged?'. It is not necessarily the role of managers to answer all of these questions, but it is their role to raise these and similar concerns and to seek the involvement of the wider community (and especially the professional staff) in developing responses for the specific school context.

Each school operates within a host of inevitable constraints. Restrictions imposed by local environments, enrolment trends, the competitive marketplace, the host country or national constraints on operation and curriculum, are all challenges that do not impede the development of an international conception of education but do mean that the overall concepts and values have to be reconciled with the local forces so as to create a unique approach that reflects local conditions. The leader's role is to ensure that the philosophy statement does not exist just on paper but is explicitly promoted in the community and actively utilized to direct planning so that the curriculum is structured with features that promote international vision and opportunities are made available through curricular and extra-curricular initiatives for transforming the vision into action. This can be further extrapolated into every aspect of the school's operation so that as pragmatic solutions are found to management problems, there is conscious inclusion of a visionary strand to ensure the suitability of these solutions for an international education.

If Walker is right, then the central element in creating an international education is curriculum and the demand for a curriculum that supports international vision has given rise to several significant developments over the past decade. The International Baccalaureate Primary and Middle Years Programmes evolved from attempts by international educators to respond to this demand and more recently the International Primary Curriculum has provided an alternative framework. In each of these cases the schools themselves play the determining part in planning the actual curriculum that students will encounter and this ensures a strong local component. Even so, there is some danger in seeing these programmes as the only legitimate format for international curricula, whereas there is no *a priori* reason to presume that schools cannot identify strategies to develop their own versions of international education if managers and leaders perceive that local circumstances call for a different approach. This may even be a healthy phenomenon and a counter-balance to what some might see as the globalizing influence of British and US curricula and organizational models that may not always be in tune with other cultural interpretations of schooling.

Conclusion

In conclusion, the essential management function in international education is to keep the ultimate vision and values in focus and to steer the school towards these long-term aspirations through the involvement of the community in general (and especially the teachers) in the educational project. The visionary role of the leader complements the technical features of pragmatic management and ensures that the school is not only managed well and successfully but that it has an ethos that can genuinely allow it to aspire to be international in nature as well as in name.

So, where do we go from here? Earlier in this chapter I looked at the implications of pragmatic and visionary aspects of international education, before moving on to associate the pragmatic components with technical aspects of school management and the visionary components with leadership characteristics. Since the schools themselves are often independent organizations operating in their own market environments, I have proposed that the key attribute for managers who wish to promote international education is to be able to balance the pragmatic and the visionary by leading the school community to seek local solutions to the underlying universal themes and goals. This is an inclusive approach, which is not associated with any particular system or model of schooling.

There are currently a number of school membership associations devoted to assisting with the management of pragmatic issues, but there are relatively few opportunities for schools to come together to share their visionary and leadership styles across the boundaries and categories into which the schools inevitably find themselves grouped. It is also true that there are still barriers to effective interaction and exchange and the various school movements (international, multicultural, bilingual, internationally-minded, peace, cross-cultural etc), which could contribute to this exchange rarely have the chance to share their interpretations and approaches in a common forum.

International education now commands a consolidated place in the world of schooling. It is extensive enough to offer a whole career path to young teachers and the prospects are that it will continue to grow for the foreseeable future. There is a growing research base in universities that recognize the distinctive nature of this discipline. It is supported by an extensive range of support services, from consultants to publishers and suppliers. Perhaps the next step will be for the creation of a forum where exponents of international education can develop their visionary expertise in the same way as they have developed their pragmatic skills so as to strengthen their overall capability to be institutional leaders. To rephrase George Walker's assertion quoted earlier: 'international education is a matter for the Head…'.

References

Association for the Advancement of International Education (AAIE) (2002) [Online] http://www.aaie.org

Cambridge, J C (2000) International Schools, Globalization and the Seven Cultures of Capitalism, in *International Schools and International Education*, eds M C Hayden and J J Thompson, Kogan Page, London

European Council of International Schools (1997) *School Improvement Through Accreditation,* 6th edition, ECIS, Petersfield

European Council of International Schools (ECIS) (2002) [Online] http://www.ecis.org

Gellar, C A (1993) How International Are We?, *International Schools Journal*, **26**, pp 5–7

Hayden, M C and Thompson, J J (2000), International Education, Flying Flags or Raising Standards?, *International Schools Journal*, **XIX** (2), pp 48–56

Hernberg, K (2001) The Right (Wo)Man for the Job, *Expat*, **1**, pp 27–29

Hill, I (2000) Internationally-Minded Schools, *International Schools Journal*, **XX** (1), pp 24–37

Hopkins, D, Ainscow, M and West, M (1994) *School Improvement in an Era of Change*, Cassell, London

International Baccalaureate Organization (IBO) (2000) *Making the PYP Happen*, IBO, Geneva

IBO (2002) [Online] http://www.ibo.org

International Schools Association (2002) [Online] http://www.intschoolsasso ciation.com

Lawton, C (1998) Is multiculturalism just a front for cultural oppression?, *IS*, the ECIS magazine, **1** (1), pp 10–11

Lewis, C (2001) Internationalism: towards a higher standard, *International Schools Journal*, **XX** (2), pp 23–38

Postman, N (1995) *The End of Education*, Vintage Books, New York

Quelch, J (2001) in The MBA Goes Global, *Time*, 21 May, pp 75–82

Timmermans, L E (2000) Has the International Schools Association completed its mission?, *International Schools Journal*, **XIX** (2), pp 57–60

United World Colleges (2001) [Online] http://www.uwc.org

Walker, G R (2001) Learning to Live with Others, presentation to the Biennial Conference of Nordic Schools, Herlufsholm, Denmark, 14 September

Yokohama International School (2002) [Online] http://www.yis.ac.jp

Chapter 14

International education and issues of governance

David Wilkinson

Introduction

'Every ten years or so, there arises the urge to define ourselves, to grapple intellectually with the term "international"'. This was the opening of the editorial in the *International Schools Journal* of October 1993. Perhaps the editor, Gellar, overestimated the time frame, for the literature indicates no slackening of interest in this question in the years that have passed. In fact, since then, the questions have surfaced regularly in articles and papers, their frequency mirroring the remarkable growth in numbers and diversity of international schools.

This chapter will examine the role of governance in providing, through long-term planning, a clear sense of purpose and direction for the growing collection of schools bound loosely through the term 'international'. It will consider the relationship between the governance of individual international schools and the governance in international education in its widest sense. The distinction is important. Individual schools serving particular and immediate needs may have a present sense of purpose. In fact, the mission statements of many international schools suggest that this is the case. All too often, however, external circumstances such as local, political or economic changes call these into question. Without a deeper idea of the meaning of the education that the school provides, such changes can, and do, cause disruption and often a feeling of disorientation through the loss of immediate purpose and a break in the continuity of the education provided.

The need for a sense of continuity and the dangers of its absence have been highlighted in a number of recent papers. Hawley (1995) reported on the rapid turnover of international school heads. His research sample of 336 school heads revealed an average time in one post of just 2.8 years. More recently, Littleford (1999) reviewed this work, reporting that almost 80 per cent of international school heads are dismissed. Evans (2000) pointed to some of the problems in his article 'Why a school doesn't run... or change... like a business'. The need for long-term planning is clear, as Nelson (2000) says: 'Without proper planning... the goal of achieving a high-quality standard of education is likely to be ephemeral'. Yet Leggate and Thompson (1997) report that a quarter of the international schools in their survey did not have a development plan in place.

According to Brown (2000) the long-term and strategic planning for a school is the responsibility of the school board. 'No other individual, group or organisation' he says 'is charged with it. Nor can anyone else do it as well as the Board'. If this is so, it places enormous responsibility on the board. More than this, however, it assumes that the board understands clearly the longer-term or deeper issues involved in providing an international education. Strategic planning in such schools is not solely a matter of projecting numbers and income in the light of possible future changes in the school's environment. If the school is to have a sense of continuity despite external changes, strategic or long-term planning must come to terms with its values and its guiding philosophy. It must understand the meaning it has given the school when it has given itself the name 'international'.

All forms of education seek a sense of continuity. Evans (2000) puts it most clearly when he talks of 'the enduring values that have bound people together and that lie at the heart of the school, not simply sold as the latest new idea'. The establishment of traditions, so rapid and so obvious in newly established schools, is a clear example of the need for such continuity. For international schools, the place of the 'international' in establishing such values cannot be taken lightly and ought to be understood explicitly. Yet this is not often the case; the very terms that appear in mission statements or statements of a school's philosophy – terms such as 'international understanding' and 'multiculturalism' – cannot be simply taken for granted. They carry different values in different circumstances and certainly by the very people (board members, school heads, faculty, parents and students) who form the school community.

How then might we seek a coherent sense of what is implied when a school takes on the title of 'international'? It is clear that there is no simple or straightforward solution. The following sections will examine a number of issues, some practical, some of a more philosophical nature, which may shed light on the nature of the problems themselves. When this has been done, we will return to the question of governance and how school boards themselves, although they must play a leading role in determining the ends which international schools seek to achieve, cannot do so as isolated entities, each concerned solely with its own school.

Finding the 'international' in 'international education'

In the first instance it is important to examine, on a school-by-school basis, what the school means when it decides to call itself 'international'. There are the well-known criteria that have been set out clearly by Hayden and Thompson (1998) and by others. However, as Thompson himself noted at a recent research seminar on international education (2001): 'If science education grew out of science and music education grew out of music, out of what did international education grow?'. In doing so, he was referring to the fact that the qualifiers of these forms of education (science, music and so on) all have a clear historical identity. Science education rests on the body of knowledge and processes, albeit a changing one, that makes up science. Science education seeks to introduce young people to this body of knowledge, its methodology and its philosophical assumptions about itself and the world around us. It acknowledges that these are not static but form a dynamic, and hence that science education will itself change in the future as it has done in the past. Nonetheless, it takes its authenticity, its way of knowing, and its values at any time from an accumulated, established and well-tested body of knowledge about the world. 'Science education', said Thompson at the same seminar (Thompson, 2001), 'leads people into science'. In drawing the analogy he went on to ask 'Into what does international education lead?'. What established way of knowing does it draw upon, from what practice does it find the inspiration for the values upon which it rests?

The analogy is a useful one if we look at the variety of meanings attributed to international education, if we examine in what manner or for what purpose international education might 'lead people into international', for a completion of the statement. What is it, that international education should lead people into; an international lifestyle? Work with an international company or organization? Or perhaps the belief in a set of values or attitudes about other peoples, cultures or nationalities?

In this context it is useful to examine, as Sylvester (2001) has suggested, the changes in the names given to international education over the past 150 years, and to note that the names themselves indicate very different perceptions. In the period from around the middle of the 19th century until World War I, the terms 'international educational relations' and 'world education' were in common use. Immediately after World War I, in the founding charter of the League of Nations, the older terms were no longer used. In their place, 'international intellectual cooperation' was coined; whilst the 1930s saw the introduction and promotion of 'worldmindedness education' at several major educational conferences. As with World War I, the aftermath of World War II saw another complete break with the earlier terminology. In 1947, in the framing of the UNESCO charter, 'education for international understanding' was used and still remains in use alongside the more recently coined term 'global education'.

It is clear that, as with any area of human concern from which education has drawn inspiration, the field has not remained constant. To date, however, there has been little study of the relationship between the terminologies used at different periods with respect to international education and the sets of assumptions, attitudes and values that underpin them.

Internationalist and globalizing perspectives

The rapid growth of schools calling themselves 'international' in the past four decades has resulted in widely different types of educational institutions subsumed under this 'banner'. The purpose here is not to examine whether this is a 'good or bad thing'; it is accepted as a fact. It has, however, enabled Cambridge and Thompson (2001) to identify two different perspectives amongst such schools, as described elsewhere in this volume by James Cambridge. Their distinction is useful.

In examining differing sets of values underpinning the meaning attributed to the term 'international' by many of the schools, what they have done is to describe the two perspectives as 'internationalist' and 'globalizing' perspectives. The former they describe as being 'identified with an orientation towards international relations, with aspirations for the promotion of peace and understanding between nations'. The latter, they claim, 'is influenced by and contributes to the global diffusion of the values of free market capitalism. These values are expressed in international education in terms of increasing competition with national systems of education'. Cambridge and Thompson (2001) clearly state that 'the internationalist and globalizing perspectives are rarely seen in their pure form, for even the most fervent idealists are tempered by the material conditions of the market place'. It is important to question the cost of such a reconciliation, particularly when made without making explicit the compromises that are involved in practice and the extent to which any such compromise affects the values of the school.

The local and the global

The practical considerations that impose a forging of the internationalist and the globalizing perspectives include most prominently the community that the school exists to serve. 'It is a paradox', says Cambridge (2001), 'that the majority of international schools tend to operate in a variety of local markets. Usually students do not travel far to attend an international school; they reside with their parents, who are expatriates working in a country which is not their home'. Many of these students are the children of parents who are internationally mobile, residing in a country only for the relatively short period of their contract before they move on to another, similar situation or return to the home country.

Such parents are themselves concerned with continuity; not so much the continuity within one school, but the continuity of their children's education as they are moved from one school to another. Many international schools have responded to this need, recognizing their responsibility in this matter. The very wide-scale development, first of the International Baccalaureate (IB) Diploma Programme, then of internationally recognized programmes for younger children, stands as a testament to their response. The result is that, in terms of curriculum, the three International Baccalaureate programmes (the Diploma, the Middle Years and the Primary Years) have for many schools become the most obvious outward manifestation of their international school status.

The mobility that has in part led to greater coherence within the curriculum of international schools as a whole is often the source of discord within individual schools. Parents, who seek continuity between schools for their children, often look for short-term solutions from the school at which their children are currently enrolled. It is this, along with the rapid turnover of boards and of school heads that disrupts the very continuity that is sought.

In his article on leadership of schools and the longevity of school heads, Littleford (1999) links the length of time served by a head to the length of tenure of the board chairman. He notes the increasing tendency for board chairs to change in the relatively short period of two to three years. He suggests that 'International schools might benefit from more expatriate "locals" who live in the community... but retain a commitment to, and an understanding of, an international education'. Such practical considerations add an important dimension to the development of longer-term strategies, recognizing that short-term goals cannot be ignored but that their solution must be guided by the underlying values and philosophy into which it is embedded and which itself must guide the longer-term strategic planning of the school.

The training of international faculty and administration

The continuity of leadership, the relationship between the head and the board and the clarity of vision for the school are of fundamental importance. In practice, however, the major impact on students is through their interaction with the faculty. Peterson (1987) wrote: 'Much will depend on the teacher rather than the syllabus – and the influence of the teacher can last a lifetime'. In an international school, teachers have a unique and additional responsibility beyond that of their colleagues in national systems. The importance of their understanding of the values implicit in the school's international mission, and their agreement with it, should not be underestimated. Overwhelmingly, teachers are recruited by international schools from a background in a national system of education. The evidence of surveys and feedback from both teachers and school heads suggests that they receive very little induction within international schools concerning the international component of their work.

Hayden (2001) has distinguished two main dimensions in any teacher-training programme: the pragmatic and the professional. These refer to what teachers and administrators want (the pragmatic) and what they need (the professional). This useful classification distinguishes accreditation, qualifications and recognition that lead to likely improvements of career prospects, from the enhancing of one's own understanding and an awareness of the issues implicit in providing an international education. In both respects, the training of teachers, both of those entering international education for the first time and of those currently employed in international education, presents serious challenges. Returning to the science education analogy, science graduates are trained to be science teachers, but there is no similar pool of 'international' graduates to be trained as international teachers. The establishment of post-graduate courses for professional development in international education by a small number of universities recognizes the need for specific teacher training to be provided and for this to be developed further.

Continuity lies also at the heart of faculty contribution and is what can be most effectively provided through training or professional development. When provided outside the school by bringing together teachers from different schools, this can serve to foster a sense of belonging to a greater mission than can be generated within a single school. By having an opportunity to discuss the issues that cut across international education and to understand the foundations from which these arise, teachers gain the impression of belonging to a specialist and identifiable class of educators. When they do, they are likely to carry with them this understanding and the values upon which it rests as they themselves move from school to school within the international network.

Governance of and in international education

Two themes, continuity and meaning, have run through each section of the foregoing discussion. Both concern to the relationship between individual international schools and to the provision of international education as a whole. As has been proposed, the two cannot be dealt with in isolation. International education is not simply the sum of what the whole range of international schools does. This is already evident in the increasing reliance of all such schools on the International Baccalaureate Organization for the provision of their educational programmes.

The two issues concern the continuity of education both within individual schools and between schools, and hence a recognition of the essential features of an international school. It is to these ends that governance of international schools and in international education must direct its attention. There must be a recognition by individual school boards that, although they have a principal responsibility for the well-being of their own schools, they have, by calling themselves 'international', taken upon themselves a commitment to a wider concept that makes of them both practical and philosophical demands. These will need to address practical concerns such as the high mobility of the student body and their teachers, the lack of initial training of teachers, the cultural impact of the host city or country, and the local market forces operating on the school. In addition, they must address the values that are implicit in being an international school rather than a school that serves an internationally mobile student population.

But to what, or where, do they turn for inspiration and guidance in taking on these challenges? There are organizations that are currently used by schools for practical solutions. The International Baccalaureate Organization provides schools with more than a curriculum and assessment. It embodies a philosophy of educational practice and a set of internationalist values. Regional groupings of schools, and in particular the European Council of International Schools (ECIS), provide a range of services, including school accreditation, faculty and administrative recruitment and help for school boards. A small number of universities have departments specializing in international education and increasingly provide research information as well as professional development opportunities for teachers and administrators. All provide an invaluable service to the network of international schools, and all have become integral parts of the provision of international education.

For all of its many and undeniable successes, international education is still searching for an overall and coherent sense of purpose and direction. This must be provided through governance, yet governance in an international context has received less attention than any other aspect of international education. This is perhaps because governance is still seen very much in terms of its relation to individual schools. In providing a sense of direction, governance must concern itself with the ends to which the whole educational experience is directed. Yet no single body exists that pulls together the many constituents of international education, its philosophy and values, assessment and the maintenance of standards, accreditation, training and professional development – to name but a few. Is there a need at this time for the schools, universities and other stakeholders to pull their increasing diaspora together? Is there a need to recognize that governance at the school level requires vision and inspiration beyond that which individual governing boards have either the competence or the time to achieve? Is there a need for a body that can provide the many governing boards with the help they often seek when setting out the plans for the futures of their own schools? Might not the time be right to consider the question of governance in international education as a complement to that of international schools?

Such a body, as proposed by Hayden and Thompson (2000), would have to direct itself to the task of clarifying what it is about governance that is specific to the international context. If such governance is to be effective, what beliefs and values must governors share, if they are to make choices that reflect the international nature of the educational experience that the children in their schools will encounter? This question is crucial, if we accept that within a school only its board of governors has responsibility for long-term and strategic planning. The authority and power vested in a board gives it the capacity to take the decisions that will direct the school.

The boards of international schools are not made up of specialists, nor should they be. However, they do need clear advice about what core features distinguish the aims of international education from those of national education. Before accepting a position on the board of an international school, nominees should be made aware of such features and of the vision that inspired international education. They must know of the major influences upon it: the International Baccalaureate Organization and the United World Colleges, for example. Training for newly elected governors and for those already serving is essential, even when board members have some educational experience. It cannot be assumed that experience and understanding in a national context is sufficient for a governor to make an effective contribution in an international context.

A new model of governance called 'policy governance' by its creators, Carver and Carver (1996), provides a useful framework for both the development of an advisory body for international education as a whole and its relationship to the governance of international schools. In their article on basic principles of policy governance, the authors begin by distinguishing ends and means, governance and management, as follows: 'But governance' they state 'is more than management at large. And it is more than a quality control board of expert managers and technicians running inspections and approvals to maintain order. The secret of modern governance lies in policy-making, but policy-making of a finely crafted sort'.

Policy governance begins with the premise that 'boards exist to own the organization on behalf of some identifiable ownership to which they are answerable' (Carver and Carver, 1996). There are international schools in which ownership is easy to identify; in others it is more difficult. There are certain 'owners' common to all: the major stakeholders in the education that the school serves, for example – the parents and their children; those who fund the school, directly or by providing the employment through which parents are able to pay; the local or national authorities that have approved the opening of the school. The list may be longer or shorter, it may or may not include employees of the school, but at the outset it must be identified. Only then can the authority entrusted to the board be made fully accountable.

It is, however, the manner in which policy governance defines policy decision-making that makes it of particular relevance to international education. This definition is 'the value or perspective that underlies action' (Carver and Carver, 1996). Walker (1999) gave examples of the values that underpin certain key objectives that international schools should consciously seek to inculcate in their students:

1. an in-depth understanding of the issues that transcend nationality;
2. an understanding of the priorities of other cultures or nations; and, above all,
3. the belief that the reality of living in an interdependent world will replace the dangerous illusion of belonging to an independent nation.

By their very nature, objectives such as these rest on values that cannot be central to a national education, no matter how enlightened it may be.

Policy governance separates very clearly the ends to which the organization is committed from the means by which these are achieved. In doing so, it removes from board responsibility the many immediate obligations: 'budgets, personnel policies, building, equipment, and a host of other matters which traditionally consume board time' (Carver and Carver, 1996). These are the very issues that, at present, the boards of international schools share in common with those of national schools. By freeing boards from such direct responsibilities and making their staff of professional educators accountable, governance becomes more clearly focused on matters that, if the school claims to provide an international education, are surely its overwhelming concern. These are (Carver and Carver, 1996):

1. Ends. The board defines which consumer results are to be achieved, for whom, and at what cost. Written with a long-term perspective, these mission-related policies embody most of the board's part of long-range planning.
2. Executive limitations. The board establishes the boundaries of acceptability within which staff methods and activities can responsibly be left to staff. These limiting policies, therefore, apply to staff means rather than to ends.
3. Board-staff linkage. The board clarifies the manner in which it delegates authority to staff as well as how it evaluates staff performance on provisions of the ends and executive limitations policies.
4. Governance process. The board determines its philosophy, its accountability, and the specifics of its own job.

Conclusion

As international education comes of age, its aims, its beliefs and its value systems are becoming increasingly more clearly articulated. A wealth of research evidence is accumulating that provides support to its impact on the values of students who have experienced such an education. To be most effective and to sustain its effectiveness, however, an international school needs enlightened leadership, vision supported by an understanding of the pillars of belief and value on which this form of education rests.

Such a combination cannot be assumed of the many men and women who give freely of their time to provide leadership through the membership of the governing boards of international schools. Just as they provide support and direction, they, in turn, require help to make their contribution an effective one. It is clearly time for a formal body concerned with the governance of international education to be established so that the governing bodies of international schools might be provided with the support they deserve fully to meet the challenge that their role as strategic leaders demands.

References

Brown, G C (2000) Long Range and Strategic Planning, a Memo to the Board, A development Program for American/International Overseas School Board Members, Association for the Advancement of International Education, New Wilmington, PA

Cambridge, J (2001) Paper presented at an international education research seminar, University of Bath, June

Cambridge, J C and Thompson, J J (2001) 'A Big Mac and a Coke' Internationalism and Globalization as Contexts for International Education, unpublished paper, University of Bath

Carver, J and Carver, M M (1996) Basic Principles of Policy Governance, Jossey-Bass, San Francisco

Evans, R (2000) Why a School Doesn't Run... or Change... Like a Business, Independent School Magazine, Spring

Gellar, C (1993) How international are we?, International Schools Journal, 26, pp 5–7

Hawley, D B (1995) How long do international school heads survive? A research analysis (Part II) International Schools Journal, XIV (2), pp 25–36

Hayden, M C and Thompson, J J (1998) International Education: Principles and practice, Kogan Page, London

Hayden, M C and Thompson, J J (2000) International education: flying flags or raising standards?, International Schools Journal, XIX (2), pp 48–56

Hayden, M C (2001) Paper presented at an international education research seminar, University of Bath, June

Leggate, P M C and Thompson, J J (1997) The Management of Development Planning in International Schools, International Journal of Educational Management, 11 (6), pp 268–73

Littleford, J (1999) Leadership of schools and the longevity of School Heads, International Schools Journal, XIX (1), pp 23–34

Nelson, N (2000) Strategic planning for international schools: a roadmap to excellence, in *International Schools and International Education: Improving teaching, management and quality*, eds M C Hayden and J J Thompson, Kogan Page, London

Peterson, A D C (1987) *Schools Across Frontiers*, Open Court, La Salle, Illinois

Sylvester, R (2001) Paper presented at an international education research seminar, University of Bath, June

Thompson, J J (2001) Presentation to an international education research seminar, University of Bath, June

Walker, G R (1999), Keynote address to the meeting of heads of International Baccalaureate schools held in Accra, Ghana, March

Chapter 15

International school governance: board renewal and the pathway to bold vision

Richard McDonald

Introduction

In the future it may become increasingly absurd to talk about 'international' schools. We can and do expend great quantities of ink or breath attempting to define what we mean by international. But we may forget that we are heading in all likelihood towards a future where global issues are an inescapable part of all educative process. The internationalization of curriculum content is merely an awakening to the fact that all mankind has, at a reductionist level, two common concerns: survival now, and survival in the future. This analysis may appear stark or sterile. Bundled within it there is, of course, a range of other core priorities: growth, renewal, adaptability, well-being. Each of these in turn can be subdivided into increasingly sophisticated sub-sets of learning priorities. But how much time do we devote to asking bold questions about which of these priorities are core subsistence issues, and which are 'higher level' areas? What is the place of thought, or logic, or spirituality, or philanthropy, or ecology? Or indeed numeracy, literacy or communication? Or love and hate? And which of these issues are anything other than international?

Let us begin with the issue of how much time we devote to bold questions. To whom does 'we' refer? Away with the woolly answer 'all of us who are concerned with education'. If we are to be pragmatic and purposeful, the 'we' refers to those who have the will and determination to be the active architects of educational evolution, or revolution. It will include many teachers. But how many have the time and energy to step out of their busy routines to become 'architects of educational evolution'? It will include many heads and administrators in schools. These too are besieged by the compelling management demands of today. It will include a number of governors or trustees, but for how many of these is education truly their central focus? It will include many parents, fired in varying degrees by idealism and ambition. Indeed there will be many who are not directly involved in the formal education process, but for whom education figures as a fundamental pillar of civilization. And what of the biggest component of the educational pie-chart, the 'learner'? It is less paradoxical than we might think to accept that the richest vein of evolutionary thinking in education may come from pupils, students, or whatever we may choose to label those who are ostensibly the beneficiaries of formalized education.

Each of these constituencies deserves a chapter in its own right, but here I shall confine myself to addressing one sector in particular: the governor (a generic term that I will use also to encompass the concepts of 'trustee' and 'board member'). My comments will be directed in particular at governors in 'international' schools; but it should be clear from my opening comments that any governor who fails to see an international dimension to their brief will have consciously or unconsciously overlooked the ineluctable impact of global issues on every single learner.

The role and qualities of the governor in international education

It is as hard to define the function of a governor as it is to do the same for a teacher. It is conversely as easy to define a really good governor as it is to define a really good teacher: that person will be inspiring, and will leave a beneficial legacy of lasting value. By this definition, how widespread are really good governors? In an attempt to answer this question, it might be useful to reflect on the qualities that arguably are essential in the effective international school governor:

- *The active and philanthropic will to govern.* This does not necessarily equate with wanting the kudos of being a governor. It is still common, in some contexts, for certain school board positions to be allotted (to universities, multinational companies, churches) on an allocation process fossilized in founding statutes. This can often result in places being taken by people without the interest, personal skills, will or humility to serve actively and positively.

- *A recognition that strategy, leadership and management, for all their overlaps, are far from synonymous.* Governance must distinguish itself from management, or face the confusion or conflict that is the most common failing of boards.
- *Loyalty of purpose.* This purpose should be the one spelled out in the school's mission statement. Loyalty of purpose presupposes the determination and courage to strive to fulfil the mission in actions, rather than in words or principles that evaporate when there is a call to action.
- *The will to learn.* Commonly governors are appointed on the strength of their professional status, their social status or their pocketbooks: sometimes all of these. It is a wholesome and humbling rule of thumb that each governor should be ready to learn double what they are ready to 'teach' to a board.

None of these suggestions is particularly new or surprising. What is therefore surprising is how difficult it can sometimes be to assemble all these qualities in every member of a board, and most critically in the board chair.

I have consciously excluded one imperative from this list. Not because it is the least important – it is arguably the most important of all – but because it rarely thrives when these other elements are not in place. It is also perhaps the most elusive of the key qualities: *the capacity, the will and the appetite to envision boldly.*

Again the word 'vision' is scarcely unfamiliar in literature on governance, leadership and management. Yet for all the exhortations to creative thinking for the future, it can often appear that the word is bandied around to satisfy some accreditation yardstick, rather than to catalyse a powerful and energizing process. Recognizing that the need for change exists, and having a supporting rhetoric, falls well short of having a vision. And the apparently immutable constraints of existing systems can stifle radical thinking. Edward de Bono makes a similar point, relating it to the 'locked in' nature of existing institutional education:

There are a lot of very talented and highly motivated people in education – possibly more than in any other sector. Yet they are locked into a system and have to follow that system... schools and teachers are locked in by existing exams and by the needs of universities. The people who run the system have

> grown up with the existing system and have become experts at running it,
> so they see no need for change. In any case, change would be very difficult
> because a change in any one part would put that part out of synchrony with
> all other parts. (de Bono, 2000)

The issue of synchrony – the notion that the current institutionalized structure of education is a balanced eco-system that cannot be upset – is at the root of the greatest paralysis in educational evolution. I shall return to this, and to the issue of vision, later, but let us first return to the list of governance qualities referred to above. It is worth drawing attention to the fact that each one has a significant *affective* content. Will, loyalty, philanthropy and appetite may have an intellectual ingredient, but they are heart-driven rather than head-driven. It is both the luxury and the obligation of a school board that it must bring heart as well as vision to a 'business' where the 'product' is young lives, unfulfilled destinies. I use the inverted commas with conscious irony; yet many business leaders would doubtlessly echo the power of heart as not just an adjunct to vision, but as its vital partner.

The list of desirable qualities for a governor could of course, if we wished, be extended almost indefinitely. Identifying qualities in this way is an increasingly common and, I believe, misleading way of profiling candidates for a position. It has the pernicious effect of trying to isolate qualities that are in fact often woven together, and neglecting the fact that it is the *affective* harmonization of qualities that makes them desirable.

How can such a broad indicator list be of help, particularly when the indicators are so difficult to measure? Let us assume that a school is reviewing the renewal of its board. A common approach to traditional board regeneration is the following: a nominations committee will identify absent skill sets within the existing board structure, and set about finding an appropriate individual to fill the vacancy. All too frequently specious assumptions are made that certain key professions must be represented, such as lawyer, banker, business leader or university academic. In recent years the frequently oligarchic nature of traditional board renewal has triggered an embarrassed swing towards highly democratic processes of board election. This is at its (not uncommon) extreme almost as absurd as selecting new teachers by vote. It has also resulted in a huge (and only partially desirable) rise in parental involvement in governance. It has fostered, too, an obsession with 'equilibrium' – of characteristics such as gender, race, age, creed, political leaning, educational background and wealth. The result is that a complex set of criteria is set in place, none of which guarantees the core qualities postulated above.

The dilemma then is this: how does one avoid a situation where the place on the board to be filled must be allotted to an individual who exhibits a particular set of personal characteristics? (Assuming that a person exhibiting such characteristics exists, that they want to be a governor, know the difference between governance and management, have loyalty of purpose, have the will to learn and the capacity, will and appetite to envision boldly.)

This challenge is exacerbated in a school with a significant diversity of nationality and culture, the kind of institution often labelled (rightly or wrongly) as an international school. The imperative to reflect the broadest possible diversity on a board can seem compelling, and indeed that diversity can provide vital breadth of thinking and creativity. Taken to a logical if somewhat absurd conclusion, however, we should expand our boards to include several hundred people if we see diversity, and proportional representation of that diversity, as the overriding priority in board renewal. This does not happen, for one of two reasons: first, experience of governing boards as strategy-setting and decision-making entities suggests that large groups are less efficient than smaller groups: secondly, our thinking is stuck, and our paradigm of the vital necessity of a school board is unassailable.

Tempting though it is to set off on an exciting exploration of the concept of schools without governing boards (and boards themselves should perhaps explore this very issue), let us examine the logical consequences of having smaller boards. Diversity is necessarily compromised; but if diversity remains the dominant priority in group profiling, it is likely in turn to compromise in some degree the broad indicators I have cited. Of these the most vulnerable is unquestionably the last. The reason for this is that the capacity (let alone the will and the appetite) to envision boldly is rare in manifest form. It is actually remarkably common in its latent form, but typically requires exposure to its manifest form in order to be made explicit. In simplistic terms, it takes a bold visionary to prompt others to shake off their, sometimes very considerable, inhibitions.

The challenge of vision

Let us focus more specifically on this critical issue of vision. Professor Ted Wragg would not wish to claim a prize for originality when he suggests that 'education must incorporate a vision of the future' (Wragg, 1997). The perfectly natural extension of this suggestion is the supposition that various forces will shape the future, and that institutional education has a responsibility to prepare young people for that future world. For example, if retirement ages continue to fall and life expectancy continues to rise, how will we prepare young people now for their extended 'third age', which may actually last longer than their working life?

Such an approach to mapping the trends of the future is sound and healthy. But it has one drawback. History has taught us that man's evolution, indeed the evolution of all life on the planet, ought perhaps to include the health warning carried at the bottom of financial services literature in very small letters: the past is not necessarily a guide to future performance. The chain of events triggered by the terrorist attacks of 11 September 2001 is evidence of how isolated, localized incidents can have a truly global impact in ways that are diabolically predictable if we dare to imagine them.

Vision, therefore, has to be bold if it is to take account of the wide sweep of possibilities before us. It must take account of the best and worst that may befall us, and enable us to test the tenacious paradigms that have come to infuse education with a tired predictability. In 1976 Ivan Illich, *enfant terrible* amongst educational observers, began his essay 'Imprisoned in the Global Classroom' by stating that 'an analysis of the defects of the school system no longer stirs anyone to action' (Illich and Verne, 1976). By action he appears to mean a radical rethinking of what learning is, how it happens most effectively and whether schools are in fact the answer at all. Action there certainly has been, but it has been at the level of curricular tinkering and the creation of a ballooning industry of evaluation, assessment and monitoring. The vision of people such as Illich has tended to be sidelined as fringe eccentricity at best, and institutional terrorism at worst. Yet, as in most bold visionary thinking, there may be some vital messages that must be heeded, and which are grounded in observations that, intuitively, ring true, even if they incite us to challenge them.

Let us take for example the following statement from one of Illich's provocative works on education:

> School is an institution built on the axiom that learning is the result of teaching. And institutional wisdom continues to accept this axiom, despite overwhelming evidence to the contrary. We have all learned most of what we know outside school. People do most of their learning without, or in spite of, their teacher... we learn to speak, to think, to love, to feel, to play, to curse, to politick and to work without interference from a teacher. (Illich, 1978)

This statement begs debate and contention, which is precisely what makes it fertile visionary soil. If we do not instantly retreat into a position of outright rejection, we are forced to confront our lingering doubts about conventional models of formalized teaching and learning. And since most school boards will consider that their key function is to provide security, stability and certainty, the norm is to shy away from bold vision.

So the challenge of vision in institutional education is not simply one of anticipating future trends and remodelling the curriculum to prepare people for a changed world. It must look at the very essence of schools themselves, and the matrix of parameters that dictate – and often gridlock – their structures and habits. What are these parameters? I would categorize them in the following way: parameters of place, time, content, peer context, expectation and resources, as follows:

Parameters of place:

- the specific location of a centre of formalized learning (local setting);
- the general location (global setting);
- the physical entity (buildings, facilities, classrooms, outdoor features).

Parameters of time:

- the age at which a person, child or adult, is put voluntarily or compulsorily in contact with institutionalized education;
- the units of time into which formalized learning situations are divided (academic years, terms, lessons);
- the duration, intensity and distribution of learning activities.

Parameters of content:

- curriculum (What must be learned? What can be learned? What can be taught? Who decides what matters?).

Parameters of peer context:

- the group of people with whom we learn;
- the group of people from whom we learn;
- the group of people upon whom we try out our learning;
- the group of people who demand that we know, or can do, certain things.

Parameters of expectation:

- parental expectation;
- professional expectation;
- societal expectation.

Parameters of resources:

- educators;

- carers;
- materials;
- information infrastructure.

Each and every one of these elements represents a paradigm that can and must be challenged. Here we can return to the concept of synchrony. As is the case with most paradigms, we find it hard to contemplate creating any significant shift because we see how apparently tightly locked in one paradigm is with another.

A good illustration of this is the question of curriculum review. Imagine we are sitting on the board of a school. We are keen to launch a really creative curriculum overhaul. There are obstacles. There may, for instance, be a national curriculum that creates a perimeter outside which we cannot stray; there may be examinations to be passed; parental, university or professional expectations (frequently of examinations to be passed, diplomas achieved) leave little room to stray from a conventional path; new subjects or shifts in emphasis require major reallocation of teachers, and perhaps space; the school is already burdened with other costs, initiatives or imperatives.

These are real, not imagined, difficulties. Yet there may be a sense in which the balance between the 'visible' curriculum and the 'hidden' curriculum is awry. A lead has to be taken. And it can only be taken by people who are willing, to use an earlier phrase, to be active architects of educational evolution. This requires challenging these paradigms whole-sale, and searching for a new kind of synchrony. We need to design new possibilities. In order to confront such a bold undertaking we must challenge the ways in which we ourselves have been taught to think. In most cases we begin from a framework of analysis, judgement and logic, which has become the dominant thought-processing style in the afflu-ent world. De Bono (2000) has coined the phrase 'design thinking' for a substantively different approach to problems and possibilities:

> Our traditional methods are concerned with 'what-is' thinking. What is this thing? What is this situation? What is the truth? This identification process allows us to use our experience and learning, and that of others, to apply standard solutions to standard situations. We have not been concerned with, nor have we put sufficient emphasis on, the other aspect of thinking, which is the 'what-can-be' type of thinking. This is the thinking that is concerned with creativity, new ideas, new approaches and 'designing' the way forward. Excellent search methods will allow you to find a particular book in a library but such methods do not help you to write a new book.

We need therefore to generate hypotheses, and instead of trying to extrapolate logically forward from the point where we are now, we should try to identify where it is that we wish to be, and design a road back from that point to our current situation. This is the essence of bold vision. The boldness does not presuppose that our ultimate vision is reckless or extravagant, but rather that we are willing to cast off the paralysing presumptions of the present and reassemble the pieces of the puzzle in different order. Why go to all this trouble? The answer is that we should only do so if we feel it is important, if we feel that it will add richness, value and purpose to lives. I use the word 'feel' to re-emphasize the critical link between heart and vision.

The governor of an international school is in a particularly privileged position as an architect of evolution. International education is a sector in which new schools are being created more quickly than in any single national system. Demand for 'international' education (let us here avoid the issue of defining what that means) is burgeoning. Educational barriers between many countries are crumbling. International curriculum models are rapidly becoming more widespread. Many new schools have sprung up opportunistically in places where demand has substantially outstripped supply. This is a climate in which it must certainly be easier to break the stranglehold of traditional paradigms and ask simple yet resonant questions: Why do we have classrooms? Why do we group children together in age groups? Why do we have lessons? Why are literacy and numeracy emphasized in the curriculum rather than survival and kindness? Do we even need schools at all?. Let us not forget that to question is not to condemn; it may indeed lead to reaffirmation of certain existing priorities.

These questions may seem naïve – like the questions of a child – yet they open our thinking to other possibilities, which are arguably nearer to the heart of the one great question anyone concerned with the educative process must ask: What kind of person am I hoping will emerge from this learning process?. Too often the question seems to be: What do I want this person to know as a result of this learning process?. The mission of a school must implicitly or explicitly answer this first paramount question.

As for the most radical of the questions above, challenging whether we need schools at all, let us turn again to Illich:

> I believe that no more than four – possibly even three – distinct 'channels' or learning exchanges could contain all the resources needed for real learning. The child grows up in a world of things, surrounded by people who serve as models for skills and values. He finds peers who challenge him to argue, to compete, to cooperate, and to understand; and if the child is lucky, he is

exposed to confrontation or criticism by an experienced elder who really cares. Things, models, peers and elders… (Illich, 1978)

Illich goes on to describe what he terms an 'educational web', which would depend on 'new networks, readily available to the public and designed to spread equal opportunity for learning and teaching'. Is the Internet not precisely such a tool? Sometimes the bold vision of one generation can come to maturity when it is given wings by the technology of the next.

My point here is not to argue that schools are currently redundant or outmoded, but to suggest that they may one day become so. And if that is the case, they will have been superseded by frameworks for learning that are perceived as more efficient. Those frameworks will be the result of 'design thinking' on the part of people who have the capacity, the will and the appetite to envision boldly. Fortunate indeed are the schools that can find such people to serve as board members.

Conclusion

Let me attempt to draw all these threads together. Core issues of curriculum transcend national considerations and become matters of common humanity. Amongst the different constituencies of teaching and learning communities, school governors hold a potentially influential place as architects of educational evolution. The key qualities for good governance are heart-driven as well as head-driven. International school boards have a duty and an opportunity to play a formative part in the evolution of innovative and responsive educational models. To do this effectively they must be prepared to prioritize the capacity, will and appetite to envision boldly as criteria for board membership. They must recognize that the role of governance is not merely custodial, but dynamic. The issues of vision relate not merely to imagining the world of the future for which people are to be prepared, but also to examining the very entities, institutional or otherwise, that we set up in order to 'educate'. This requires 'design thinking' and fearless questioning.

Yet above all these we must embrace the challenge of the future with passion, generous hearts and a spirit of adventure. Let us make sure that these qualities are at the core of the global curriculum of generations to come. There is much to be done.

References

de Bono, E (2000) *New Thinking for the New Millennium*, Penguin, London
Illich, I and Verne, E (1976) *Imprisoned in the Global Classroom*, Writers' and Readers' Publishing Cooperative, London
Illich, I (1978) *Deschooling Society*, Marion Boyars, London
Wragg, E C (1997) *The Cubic Curriculum*, Routledge, London

Chapter 16

The language of international education

George Walker

Introduction

In May 1859 the English poet and critic, Matthew Arnold, set off to visit schools in France, Holland and Switzerland. Britain's economic supremacy, celebrated at the Great Exhibition in London in 1851, was already in discernible decline and Arnold was despatched by a Royal Commission to see if the education systems of continental Europe offered any solutions. In what he later described as his finest essay (Arnold, 1864), he reported that he had seen the '... spreading ferment of mind... liberalised by an ampler culture, admitted to a wider sphere of thought, living by larger ideas, with its provincialism dissipated, its intolerance cured, its pettiness purged away. The truth is', wrote Arnold, 'the English spirit has to accomplish an immense evolution'.

Arnold was a man of vision, but in his daytime job he was one of Her Majesty's Inspectors of Schools and for 35 years he travelled the length and breadth of the country listening to the responses of children and teachers to his routine tests. It brought him neither wealth nor satisfaction but it did give him a powerful sense of pragmatism to temper his vision. He knew that ideas are translated only with difficulty into reality and then with even greater difficulty into a system that lasts, that influences, that changes the landscape.

Globally, there is again today a desire for change, arising from a widely shared perception that things simply cannot go on as they are. Rather suddenly, and rather unusually, the status quo has become very unattractive. In a world that is nervously looking in on itself, the tectonic plates of different cultures and different religions, driven by unsustainably wide differences in the quality of life, are grinding noisily together. The visible but superficial impression of a new global unity conveyed by fast food, branded sports trainers and pop culture, conceals deep cultural differences that are being forced up into mountain ranges of separation. Little seems to have changed since Arnold (1877), aware of the latest geological speculation about the origins of the continents, wrote the lines:

> For surely once, they feel, we were
> Parts of a single continent!
> Now round us spreads the watery plain –
> Oh might our marges meet again!

Against our contemporary background of a renewed sense of precarious isolation, the vocabulary of international education – responsible citizenship, compassionate thinking, tolerance, diversity within a shared humanity, cultural understanding – no longer sounds like high-flown idealism but seems, on the contrary, to offer the only practical hope for the future of humankind. Others have already seen this and Peel (1998), for example, has written of the 'coming of age' of international education. He was strongly influenced by the 1994 International Conference of Education in Geneva, which reaffirmed an earlier commitment (UNESCO, 1974) by the governments of the member states of UNESCO to the introduction of an 'international education' into their national systems.

But as we look across the globe at the reality of international education at the beginning of the 21st century, we see the same tantalizing glimpses of 'what might be' that Matthew Arnold saw during his continental visit more than 150 years ago. We can see it taking place in many schools (some of which do not use the word 'international' in their title), we can hear about it at conferences and we can read about it in journals. The challenge that now faces us is to build these different pockets of experience into a worldwide system that begins to change the educational landscape, to convert the micro into the macro, to turn the vocabulary into a language of international education.

This kind of a challenge is not new; indeed it is familiar to any group of people who have had a good idea that catches on and spreads. It soon becomes clear that others have already had a similar idea, so organizations are established to bring like-minded people together to consolidate, to stimulate and to sustain. The new concept then begins to seep into national institutions; research is commissioned and governments express an interest; then mechanisms for establishing standards are put in place. But at this point, international education has already hit a barrier because every government in the world has in place its own national system of education, which sustains its own cultural identity, often in an attempt to maintain the mythology of nation-state self sufficiency.

So if further progress is to be made the torch must be passed to intergovernmental organizations (IGOs) like UNESCO and to non-governmental organizations (NGOs) like the International Baccalaureate Organization (IBO), which are better placed to surmount the intellectual barriers still erected at national frontiers. International education is certainly moving forward. We can point to more examples; we can belong to more organizations; we can attend more conferences and we can read more articles. But there is, so far, little evidence that we are changing the appearance of the educational landscape.

International cooperation

The huge stumbling block of national education identity was apparent in 1921 when the League of Nations voted against setting up either an International Office of Education, or even a committee to examine international questions regarding education. Too many member states were worried that the League wanted to map out a scheme of education and impose it on the different nations (Rossello, 1944). But a generation and another World War later, attitudes were beginning to change and the fundamental act of faith that links world peace to education was formally acknowledged in the memorable words, attributed to the US poet Archibald Macleish (*The Courier*, 2001), of the opening to the preamble to UNESCO's constitution: 'Since wars begin in the minds of men, it is in the minds of men that the defences of peace must be constructed' and today we can point to many examples of international cooperation in the field of education, usually supported by IGOs. For example, if the education ministries of developed countries want to know where they stand relative to their economic competitors, they can turn to the international league tables published by the Organization for Economic Cooperation and Development (2002). Less favoured countries must put their faith in the Education For All initiative, the responsibility of UNESCO (2000) and largely funded by the World Bank, which has published its own influential global Education Sector Strategy (1999).

But, important though they are, none of these initiatives is concerned with international education as such. They are rather aimed at international support and comparison and the exchange of effective practice. Blaney (1991), on the other hand, suggested more than a decade ago that there was a powerful case for constructing a system of international schools. National systems of education are becoming obsolete, argued Blaney, yet there are no models of international systems to guide them towards what they could become. By the time the International Schools Association had set up a pilot project in 1996 to test Blaney's proposals, the goal had changed from a system of international schools to a system of international education (Thomas, 1995). However, though the project sample did contain some national schools, it was heavily weighted towards independent, international schools.

The International Education System Pilot Project, as it was titled, achieved mixed success. On the one hand it produced some valuable curriculum developments in the fields of peace education and sustainable development (International Bureau of Education, 1999). It also revealed the untapped potential of electronic communication as a means of bringing together a group of like-minded schools across the world into a collaborative relationship. On the other hand, it never showed convincingly how the curriculum, staffing and qualifications appropriate to the phrase 'international-mindedness' could be accommodated comfortably within a variety of different national systems.

The project helped us to define the task, and it identified the school's value system, its curriculum, staff development and information and communication technology (ICT) as key elements in the encouragement of international-mindedness: a predictable mixture of the idealistic and the pragmatic. However, by starting with a core group of experienced international schools and inviting others to join them, it was clear from the start where the initiative was coming from, and it was probably coming from the wrong direction. Powerful systems of education already exist within nation states, and instead of trying to reshape them to a model that was developed in response to very different circumstances (notably those of the globally mobile student) it is surely more appropriate to ask 'What factors are open to modification and change within national systems of education as governments become persuaded of the need to make them more internationally-minded?'. Instead of a template of international education to impose, can the international schools offer a language of international education to share? We have already identified some of the vocabulary; what do we need in order to develop this into a language?

Values in international education

Before we can progress far we need to seek agreement on what might be called the 'deep structure' of international education. What values must we all share if we are to have any chance of understanding what each other is saying? As Charles A Gellar has noted (Chapter 3), 'this issue has become a matter not of evidence, but of the survival of human kind' and Mattern (1991), another pioneer of international education, has insisted that without a sense of values young people: 'may be clever, knowledgeable, even wondrously creative, but they will never become citizens of the world nor give it their gifts as should those who have known a true international education'.

Surely the time has come for a renewed commitment to the Universal Declaration of Human Rights, signed by every member state of the United Nations (1998). The world has nothing else like it and, although many nations have good reason to feel guilty about their interpretation of some of its 30 articles, this is no reason for ignoring it. When was there last a serious discussion on the implications of Article 5 (torture and degrading treatment), Article 18 (freedom of thought, conscience and religion) or Article 25 (a universal right to education)? This document touches every aspect of the world's current crises and it would be a serious error to imagine that the much-abused term 'democracy' implies a guarantee of human rights. The Universal Declaration should be taken down from the shelf, the dust blown off and a new debate launched to bring it back into the public consciousness.

Our next step must be to seek a structure that will encourage us to build our values into a balanced educational experience that is appropriate to the challenges of the 21st century. Once again, others have been working on our behalf and the International Commission on Education for the Twenty-First Century (UNESCO, 1996), recognizing that 'there exists today a global arena in which, whether we like it or not, the destiny of every individual is to some extent played out', has proposed four pillars as the foundations for such an education: learning to know, learning to do, learning to be and learning to live together. In giving greater emphasis to the last of these, the chair of the commission, Jacques Delors, drew particular attention to the importance of: 'developing an understanding of others and their history, traditions and spiritual values and, on this basis, creating a new spirit which, guided by recognition of our growing interdependence and a common analysis of the risks and challenges of the future, would induce people to implement common projects or to manage the inevitable conflicts in an intelligent and peaceful way'.

Establishing a language for international education

So, having proposed a set of shared values and suggested a shared structure around which to build an international education, we are in a better
position to construct its language. To breathe meaning into those ambitious words and phrases that make up its vocabulary we need a syntax,
and that is provided by formal programmes such as those offered by the
IBO. Ian Hill (Chapter 2) has suggested how the concept of 'world citizenship' can be constructed logically through planned experiences at
three different levels: knowledge, skills and attitudes, while Helen
Drennen (Chapter 5) has illustrated a similar approach to cultural understanding. Martin Skelton (Chapter 4) has proposed four aspects of an
international curriculum and insists that international-mindedness
should be carefully taught, not left to be caught. We know how to select,
how to order and how to sequence our material: we have a syntax of
international education.

But this is not enough. If our language is to convey its intended
meaning with conviction and clarity, we need a grammar that describes
its whole system and structure, and it is with a description of that system
that many of the chapters of this book have been concerned. At the heart
lies the teacher: the initial training, appointment and professional development of an 'international teacher'. Mary Hayden (Chapter 9) has
examined the initial, induction and continuing phases of support for
teachers involved in international education and has suggested how each
might be improved. If national governments are to be helped and
encouraged to develop more internationally-minded teachers, then this
is surely an area where the international school community should speak
with a clearer voice. What is their own experience and what can they
recommend as their best practice?

Another key component of the system is the governance of schools. As
David Wilkinson (Chapter 14) has explained, the board of a school that
intends to become more internationally-minded takes upon itself 'a
commitment to a wider concept, which makes both practical and philosophical demands'. In this respect, national schools have a certain
advantage over their international counterparts because they do not
suffer from the debilitating turnover of staff, students and parents that
characterize international schools and which complicate the practical
tasks of school boards, often rendering the boards themselves danger-
ously unstable. They have another advantage, too, because the very
absence of the term 'international' in the school's title and history makes
the school board think hard about why and how it expects the school to
become internationally-minded. In being thereby forced to confront the

philosophy of international education, the national school may arrive at a more convincing interpretation than many international schools where the title itself has never been fully explored.

The board of any school, national or international, must represent the school's stakeholders and some of the most influential of these will be part of the school's local community. Thompson (1998) has stressed the significance, in the minds of teachers and students, of the interaction between the international school and its surrounding community but a number of contributors to this book have drawn attention to the inherent problems that this entails. Keith Allen (Chapter 10), echoing Matthew Arnold's watery image of isolation, uses the powerful metaphor of the isolated 'atoll' while Brian Garton (Chapter 11) insists that it is 'the relationships of each school with the wider community of contacts... that will affect the truly international status of each school', drawing a parallel with the ongoing national/international tension within the United Nations. James Cambridge (Chapter 12) asks how the employment policies of many international schools, which discriminate against locally hired teachers, can be reconciled with the values of an international education.

Once again, the successful national school may have an advantage, being already an integral part of its local community so that its international-mindedness will grow from, and take account of, the local environment. The language of international education will therefore acquire a number of different dialects. But this is already apparent. The IB state school in Virginia, United States, writes: 'We see the connection we have with the larger world in the individual struggles and triumphs that small communities like ours have in places as diverse as Moldova or Britain or Mexico', while the IB private school in Amman, Jordan, has a different perspective: 'In order to maintain its international position... we have to accept that not to become a player in the global village is to commit economic suicide. In effect, all graduates have to be qualified internationally to serve their patriotic interests', and the IB school that educates orphans in Ghana is confident that this will: 'help the students to develop a sense of social responsibility and a commitment to Africa's development'.

Future options

'In the future', writes Richard McDonald (Chapter 15) 'it may become increasingly absurd to talk about "international" schools... we are heading in all likelihood towards a future where global issues are an inescapable part of all educative process'.

And as we look into that future, three different paths seem to open up for international education (Walker, 2000). It could seek to offer a globally branded product that is available alongside the globally branded soft drinks, clothes and motor cars, all around the world. This would indeed be a truly international system of education with internationally monitored standards: familiar, safe and reliable in Beijing, Boston and Buenos Aires. But it is hard to imagine how educators in China, Massachusetts and Argentina would perceive it as other than an unwelcome threat to their national identity, and at a time of increasing emphasis on cultural distinctions, such international conformity is unlikely to appeal.

The second option would be to leave international education where it started and, it might be argued, where it really belongs: in the international school. There we expect to find a rich cultural mix of students, idealistic teachers and students and parents who are motivated by the practical support it gives to globally mobile families. But this would be too narrow a vision and would restrict the experience to a small minority of privileged students, many of whom are already too isolated from the reality of the real world outside.

The third option recognizes the relevance of international education to the development of all young people around the world, who are being told to 'think globally but act locally', but have little idea what this means. International education has the power to transform national education and Terry Haywood (Chapter 13) surely speaks on behalf of all the contributors to this book when he writes: 'if the term "international education" is to have any value beyond the parochial, then its definition must be an inclusive one. It must also be one which all schools that describe themselves in such terms should be able to identify'.

The lessons from the League of Nations, meeting in Geneva in 1921, are still relevant today. No one can impose a template of international education; no one can police a system of international education. But instead, the growing number of organizations in this field, represented in the chapters of this book, can continue to work together to develop and share a language of international education so that others can be encouraged to learn it, to adapt it to their cultural environment, and then to speak it back to us.

References

Arnold, M (1864) *A French Eton or Middle Class Education and the State*, Macmillan and Co, London

Arnold, M (1877) *To Marguerite – continued*, Lyric Poems, Macmillan and Co, London

Blaney, J J (1991) The International Schools System, in *International Schools and International Education*, eds P L Jonietz and D Harris, Kogan Page, London

The Courier (2001) *Can we educate for world peace?*, UNESCO Courier December, Paris

International Bureau of Education (1999) *A culture of peace*, Innovation No 100, September, IBE, Geneva

Mattern, W G (1991) Random ruminations on the curriculum, in *International Schools and International Education*, eds P L Jonietz and D Harris, Kogan Page, London

Organization for Economic Cooperation and Development (2002), [Online] http://www.oecd.org

Peel, R M (1998) International education comes of age, *International Schools Journal*, **XVII** (2), pp 12–17

Rossello, P (1944) *Forerunners of the International Bureau of Education*, Evans Brothers, London

Thomas, P (1995) International Education System pilot project, *IB World*, 9, p 7

Thompson, J J (1998) *Towards a model for international education*, in *International Education: principles and practice*, eds M C Hayden and J J Thompson, Kogan Page, London

UNESCO (1974) *Recommendations on Education for International Understanding*, UNESCO Paris

UNESCO (1996) *Learning: the treasure within*, UNESCO Paris

UNESCO (2000) *Education for All No 39*, UNESCO Paris

United Nations (1998) *Universal Declaration of Human Rights*, UN Office of Public Information, Geneva

Walker, G R (2000) International education: connecting the national to the global, in *International Schools and International Education*, eds M C Hayden and J J Thompson, Kogan Page, London

World Bank Group (1999) *Education Sector Strategy*, The World Bank, Washington DC

Index

Made in the USA
Coppell, TX
14 October 2022